Suzanna Leigh

Volume I A Memoir

Paradise, Suzanna Style

Copyright © Suzanna Leigh 2000

The right of Suzanna Leigh to be identified as the author
of this work has been asserted by her in accordance
with the Copyright, Designs and Patterns Act 1988.

It has not been the intention of the author to reproduce any part
of any book that she might have read - or be in any way derogatory
to anybody in any way. All of her thoughts are purely observational
and personal.

All illustrations are reproduced here in the spirit of publicity, and whilst
every effort has been made to trace the copyright owners, the author
and publishers apologise for any omissions and will undertake to make
any appropriate changes in future editions of this book if necessary.

First published in Great Britain by
Pen Press Publishers Ltd.
39-41 North Road
Islington, London N7 9DP

ISBN: 1 900796 99 6

All rights reserved. No part of this publication may be
reproduced, stored in or introduced into a retrieval system, or
transmitted, in any form or by means (electronic, mechanical,
photocopying, recording or otherwise) without prior written
permission of the publisher. This book is sold subject to the
condition that it shall not by way of trade or otherwise, be lent,
re-sold, hired out, or otherwise circulated without the publisher's
prior consent in any form of binding or cover other than that in
which it is published and without a similar condition including
this condition being imposed on the subsequent purchaser.

9 8 7 6 5 4 3 2 1

A CIP catalogue record for this book is available from
the British Library

Typeset by Kick Design, International House,
20 St Mary's Road, London W5 5ES

3D Modelling on cover by Mike Hoenes of Emajin Graphics
Email: mike@emajin3d.co.uk

Printed and bound in Great Britain by
Antony Rowe Ltd, Chippenham, Wilts.

I thank God for giving me
the strength to do what had to be done.

And to my Guardian Angel Daniel,
for never leaving my side

§

For my daughter Natalia-Charlotte Leigh,
whom I love so much.
Thank you.

Part I:

RETURN TO SENDER

Chapter 1:   The King and I

Chapter 2:   Crying in the Chapel

Chapter 3:   Vivien Leigh's Protègè

Chapter 4:   The Sex Trap

Chapter 5:   Arabian Nights

Chapter 6:   An étoile is Born

Chapter 7:   Roamin' with Polanski

Chapter 8:   Hal Wallis Presents...

Chapter 9:   Heartache

Chapter 10:   Hollywood!

Chapter 11:   The Paramount Girl

Chapter 12:   Aloha, Richard Harris

Chapter 13:   Elvis's Little Sister

Chapter 14:   The Mean McQueen

Chapter 15:   Exile on Sunset

Part 1

Return to Sender . . .

2001

Chapter 1

The King and I

"Imagination is the highest kite one can fly."

Lauren Bacall, *American actress*

ELVIS walked into my trailer at Paramount Pictures. This was the last day of *Paradise - Hawaiian Style*, the feature film we had been making for the past three months, and his limo was waiting outside with the engine running. We couldn't possibly prolong the shoot any longer - the film was already several weeks over schedule - but we would soon be back in front of the cameras together.

The thought of parting for four months until we started work on our next movie, *Easy Come, Easy Go*, was depressing, even more so because of a prediction I had been given just two days earlier. Natalie Wood had taken me to see her clairvoyant, Dr Mary Young, who had informed me that I would soon leave America and that Elvis and I would never see each other ever again.

It was a nonsensical prediction: I was about to set up home in Beverly Hills under a seven-year contract with the independent producer Hal Wallis. Elvis, who was also under contract to Hal, had expressly requested me as his leading lady in *Easy Come, Easy Go*, something he told me he had never done before. This was to be a newly contracted film between Hal and the Colonel, so that Elvis and I could work together again. The film was to be written specifically for me.

Working together was the only way Elvis and I could see each other without creating too much gossip. Well, almost. We were already having trouble with the Colonel on one side and Hal on the other.

The Colonel, Elvis's rotund and devious manager Colonel Tom

Parker, was opposed to our friendship - aggressively so, seeing it as a threat to his power over the King. He had recently planted a totally fabricated and most unpleasant "interview" with me about Elvis in a magazine in the hope of turning him against me.

Hal, however, was very excited about the publicity that a romance between two of his stars would engender. He had been pressuring me to co-operate with the Paramount press office, who were keen to suggest to the public that Elvis and I had been doing more than just making a movie for the past twelve weeks.

I had steadfastly refused to exploit my friendship with the man: it was far too precious to me to allow others to intrude, especially Hollywood press agents. Yet Elvis and I were not lovers. For all the physical attraction between us, we had kept our relationship on a platonic level: he the brother I wished I'd had; me the little sister he'd always longed for.

During the last three months Elvis and I had opened up to each other in a way that would forever link us by invisible threads and, for that reason, I decided it would be foolish to allow a stranger's warning to spoil this moment. Elvis took my hands and kissed them.

His blue, blue eyes looked deeply into mine and I knew he was reading my thoughts, something he could do almost at will from the day we met. I saw, too, he didn't want to believe what was going through my mind. His face clouded, then suddenly he clasped me to him and kissed me.

Incredibly, this was only the second time we had kissed. We had no smooching scenes in the film, but one day in the stills gallery we were goofing around one moment and the next he was kissing me. He said at that time: "This won't do your career any harm, baby." The bulbs flashed and within days a photograph of "The Kiss" was run in newspapers throughout the world. Strange that a candid picture of two people kissing could create such enormous interest, but whatever Elvis did was big news.

This was different, though, and just for a tiny moment I hesitated before letting myself be swept into his arms. His kisses held an intensity that melted my very being. I slipped my arms around his neck and our bodies entwined. This was all madness, but we didn't stop. A person could go to the gallows with such a kiss lingering on their lips and know that life had been good.

A rap on my trailer door and the moment was broken. I had a press conference in an hour's time and my hairdresser was here.

"Just a moment," I called out.

We slowly parted, gazing into each other's eyes to capture this day in our memories.

"See you in February, baby," he smiled, and with that he was gone.

I slumped down into my chair and looked at my reflection, framed by glowing bulbs in the huge mirror.

"Well, kiddo, you've done it. Every wish, every dream, they've all come true. Now what?"

Here I was, just turned twenty. I had a string of films to my credit, my own television series in France, a long-term contract with one of America's most important producers, my face on the cover of Paris Match and a clutch of fan magazines. And I had just finished making my second Hollywood movie, starring opposite the biggest name in the world.

An hour or so later I had pulled myself together and was standing in front of twenty or so journalists at the press conference. I was the Paramount Girl-of-the-Moment and no opportunity for publicity was missed. Behind me on the screen flashed clips of *Boeing-Boeing*, the comedy I'd made with Tony Curtis and Jerry Lewis.

"Ladies and gentlemen, Miss Suzanna Leigh," beamed the press rep.

"What's next, Suzanna?" asked the first reporter.

I stared at him blankly. What *was* next? I had truly achieved all of my ambitions, ambitions which I had thought totally unattainable only a few years before. As a star-struck London teenager, my wildest dreams were all about going to Hollywood and starring with Elvis, and the chances of that happening had seemed as remote as flying to the moon.

"Suzanna... Suzie... what's next for you?"

"I'm putting my name down for the first passage to the moon," I replied off the top of my head.

"After Elvis, It's The Moon For Me, says English Star", read the headlines. If only I'd known...

I was born at Cavisham, Berkshire, on July 26, 1945, right at the end of World War II in Europe. My father, Edward Smith, was an English Protestant and my mother, Mary Agnes O'Donnell, an Irish Catholic. None of their parents attended the wedding, an ominous sign of things to come.

I was a very healthy baby and, at eight pounds, quite unusually heavy for those days. My family had two homes at that time, a flat at No. 128 Mount Street, Mayfair, and a large country farmhouse at Cavisham, which my father bought at the beginning of the war. His theory was: "If there's going to be a war, at least this family's not going to starve." He stocked the farm with chickens, pigs and cows, as if the family were about to be marooned on a desert island. My father, of course, did not have the faintest clue about how to run a farm and, when all the labourers were called up to fight, he was totally flummoxed.

To face the task of slaughtering a pig or a chicken, Daddy would have to get drunk on black-market whisky. My parents, like the two hopeless townies they were, had given all the livestock names and, when my father did manage to kill a pig, he happened to pick Joey, who was my mother's particular favourite, and there were such floods of tears that no one could eat even a mouthful.

Although I always think of myself as an only child, I do in fact have a brother, Eric, who is ten years older than me. It's always been a cause of great sadness to me that Eric and I have never been close. He was a stranger to me throughout my childhood and remains so to this day. The age gap seemed insurmountable, but it was also clear that Eric did not like the idea of having a little sister. He was always away at boarding school and, on the few occasions our paths did cross as children, we had nothing to say to each other and, to be honest, didn't like one another.

The war had brought my father a great disappointment. His dream was to join the Royal Air Force and he had bought this particular farm because it was located close to Reading airfield, where he hoped to be based. When he volunteered for active service, however, he failed his medical due to a heart condition. It was the kind of thing that would be sorted out these days with a quick and simple heart bypass. Back then, however, all that was on offer were some little white pills and they didn't seem to do much good. Daddy hated to be stuck at home while his friends went to war. Many of them took off from Reading, never to return. Daddy did his bit for the war effort by throwing big parties - well, somebody had to for those who, in his opinion, were lucky enough to be enlisted.

My parents best friend was the famous band leader Jack Hylton, whose sister, Dolly Elsie, was a well-known singer and my mother's best friend since their school days. Daringly for the time, Dolly lived openly with the composer Hugh Charles, Uncle Hughie to me, who wrote *There'll Always Be An England* and many of Vera Lynn's wartime hits.

Jack Hylton arranged entertainment for the troops, so it was simple for Daddy to borrow his band to play at his parties. The Crazy Gang were also regular visitors. Before the war, Jack Hylton, Bud Flanagan and my father were often seen at the races together. Daddy was one of that rarest of breeds, a successful gambler. His nickname was "Lucky Eddie". I believe that he and Sir Victor Sassoon were co-owners of the Derby winner Never Say Die.

Rumour had it that my parents were canny manipulators of the black market, so many servicemen left for the war in high spirits, having had a very good send-off at one of my parents' parties. My mother was also a manipulator in her relationships with other people. Her name changed from Mary to Marie or Maria, depending on who she was speaking to, but she hid the fact from everyone that she was a former shop-girl who had married the boss's son.

Daddy's mother was one of those extraordinary English women who owned factories, the houses in which the factory workers lived and even some of the shops in which they spent their wages. Apparently, she had been married five times and it was said that she not only bought the car that won the Monte Carlo Rally, but the winning driver as well.

Mummy's parents bred trotting horses in Ireland, but moved to Aintree, Lancashire, in the early 1900s and my grandfather opened a gym in Liverpool and set himself up as a boxing promoter. My mother, a clever young woman with a forceful personality (and a great pair of legs) was born in Liverpool and left home as a teenager to go into business on her own. She opened a little hat shop in Reading, which impressed my grandmother sufficiently to offer her a job as sales girl in one of her dress shops.

"Marie" was extremely popular with the customers and she was promoted to manager at the age of twenty, which is when she met my father, a dashing young heir who drove a Jaguar. Grandmother, however, was scandalised when they announced their engagement. She refused to give them her blessing and was not the least bit surprised when the marriage turned into a sham.

Even before I was born, my parents began to lead almost separate lives. Daddy would be in London while Mummy would be in the country, or *vice versa*. Divorce was almost unheard of in those days and, as my mother was a Catholic, it was entirely out of the question. They still had to be seen in public together on occasion, of course, if only to keep up appearances.

When my mother found she was pregnant with me, she was furious. As for Daddy, she said he got her pregnant on purpose just to spoil her chances. She had just opened a new business. I know now that she resented me from the moment I was conceived.

My father adored me, but my mother was a distant being in my young life. She took no interest in me or anything to do with me; she had only ever wanted one child, her son - so much so, that, even when she died, she left everything to him and nothing to me.

I'm sure my early childhood must have been fairly normal, if only because I can remember so little of it. I recall a loving father, a nanny whom I adored, horses, people laughing and smiling, and lots of back-slapping. Being around a gambler has always been a bit glamourous and Daddy had established a reputation as a man who could not lose. He also had a penchant for sports cars and they all had to be the same colour: racing green. Before the war, he would race around the Silverstone track, just for fun. And all the time his heart, like a time-bomb, was silently ticking away.

My father died in the winter of 1951 when I was six-and-a-half and he was forty-two. It was I who found him dead and it was then that my life changed as dramatically as any could. We were living in a flat in Albion Gate, Hyde Park, just Daddy, Nanny and me. He must have felt the attack coming on because he got up in the middle of the night and went into the kitchen to warm some milk in a pan. The pain must have increased, because he left the pan without lighting the gas (for years I couldn't stand the smell of gas) and went into the sitting room, where his pills were kept in a small side table.

He collapsed on to the floor, with his arm outstretched towards the table, and that's how I found him the next morning as I was running through to his room, where we always started the day with cuddles and kisses. I remember everything about the next few hours as if they happened yesterday.

I remember trying to wake him and screaming, "Doctor, doctor" into the white telephone. Nanny came running out of her room to see what the pandemonium was about. No one knew where my mother was, although it turned out that she was at the Ritz. The doctor arrived and, after looking at my Daddy, promptly gave Nanny a tranquilising shot.

It must have been so long since I'd seen my mother that, when she eventually arrived, the doctor almost had to re-introduce us. I was so traumatised by Daddy's death that I developed "shock asthma" and was gasping for breath, but the attack miraculously passed after a few minutes. Nanny was sacked that afternoon and my toys were given to the poor. Looking back, I'm almost certain that my father was having an affair with Nanny and I certainly hope so because I loved them both.

The "shock asthma" came back when I moved in with my mother and I spent some time in and out of the Great Ormond Street Hospital for Children. She would drop me off and say, "It'll only upset me if I stay; I'm no good in hospitals. Be brave - you're in the best place", and with that she was gone. Once out of hospital, I was packed off to boarding school, which, looking back, seems very unusual to me as I wasn't yet seven years old.

Luckily, Aunt Sally, my mother's sister, rescued me after a couple of weeks, saying, "Your father would turn in his grave if he knew she'd put you in there." Aunt Sally took me to live with her in Brighton, where she had a flat above her antique shop and hairdressing salon.

Now this was fun! Aunt Sally had never married, so she wasn't too *au fait* with what small children should, or should not, be doing and very soon I was running wild and enjoying the attention of her friends and customers alike.

It was very hot that summer of 1952 and the beach and the penny arcade on the pier were the places for me. Another fun thing was to collect stray, and sometimes not-so-stray, dogs and cats.

I would put my pets in separate rooms and play house with them. Sometimes these reluctant animals would vent their frustration by clawing my arms, legs and face, and my aunt would cover the scratches with iodine, not the most attractive of substances. It got to the point where their owners would drop by Aunt Sally's flat on their way home to ask if the "scarred woman of Borneo" (why Borneo I never knew) had their beloved pet.

From what I have gathered, my mother had got mixed up financially with a nightclub called The Orchid Room at this time and her lawyer had run off with the money. This one lapse aside, Mummy was a pretty shrewd businesswoman and before long she had opened a tea-dancing place on the seafront at Brighton.

As Mummy was now living in Brighton, it seemed only sensible for me to move into the large flat she had bought in Brunswick Square. There was a Great Dane called Bruce on the scene, too, and the two of us were always hungry. I think because she never had much to do with child rearing on a day-to-day basis, Mummy would forget that Bruce and I needed to be fed, and daily. We must have looked a funny pair, walking along the beach in search of holiday-makers who wanted to pet him and offer me a sandwich or an ice-cream. I was a latch-key kid, only without the key.

We would wander around all day, sometimes going to the tea-room. Nobody would exactly shoo us away - after all, I was the boss's daughter - but with a slobbering Great Dane taking swipes at the cream buns on the trolleys as they passed and me with no shoes and a scruffy face, we were gently pushed out the door.

Hunger was such a big thing with me that I resorted to looking for food in other people's homes. I was sweet and chatty to one old retired couple and they invited me in. They left me alone in the dining room with a bowl of peaches for a few minutes and I was so famished that I took a bite out of every peach, then carefully rearranged them to hide the marks.

Mummy saw me coming out of their house and, when we got home, she interrogated me. Secrecy, apparently, was of the utmost importance and, when I admitted I'd been talking to some of the neighbours, she said: "I'm going to have to teach you a lesson."

She beat me black-and-blue on the buttocks with the fireside coal shovel, but first she kept me waiting for a day-and-a-half, wondering what was going to happen to me.

As she well knew, the mental torture was far worse than the physical pain.

Chapter 2

Crying in the Chapel

"We are the hero of our own story."

Mary McCarthy, *American writer*

WHEN I was about seven, I suppose it became apparent, even to my mother, that I really ought to have been in school. And so off I was packed as a weekly boarder at a private girls' convent, Our Lady of Sion, in Chepstow Villas, Kensington.

On Fridays, Mummy would come to fetch me for the weekend, but only at the eleventh hour; the nuns would be going to bed when she appeared and there would be me, staring out of the dorm window, waiting for her. She'd have me back as soon as it was decently possible, too; Sunday night was the latest that the girls could return, but I would always be back straight after Sunday lunch.

"Tell me that you love me, Mummy," I would say, pulling at her skirt. "Tell me that you love me."

"You're here, aren't you? You're not in a home."

This was not what I needed to hear.

The Jesuits say, "Give me a child until he is seven and I will show you the man". I may have had only six years with my father, but those six years had made me. Deep inside of me was an indestructible seed of confidence that he had planted; I had been the very centre of his universe. For him, the sun shone out of me.

My mother could tell me again and again how stupid I was, how useless; the nuns could stand me in the corner with the dunce's cap on my head, or beat me for staring out of the classroom window, or for my appaling spelling (dyslexia hadn't been given a name back then). They could do what they liked. I'm not saying it didn't hurt: after all, I was only a little girl. There was, however, a place inside of me that was warm and strong because the most important person in my life, my father, had loved me.

The school chapel was my safe place. They had told me that my father was in heaven, so perhaps the chapel was the logical place to feel close to him. I would sit gazing at the man on the cross. I could relate to him, a man, living as I was now, in a world of women. And I could relate to his suffering because I knew I was suffering, too. In the chapel, where no one could get at me, I began to feel that it wouldn't always be like this; that one day I would leave this dreary life and be taken to a place of beauty and delight, a place where I would be loved.

That place in my dreams was Hollywood and the life of an actress. I knew then, with absolute certainty, that I was going to be a film star.

We girls used to make little crystal sets and listen to radio programs in bed under the covers. There was *Educating Archie* and *The Goon Show*, and later a complete change in broadcasting arrived in the form of Tony Hancock. He was quite brilliant and totally different from anything that had gone before. We would also tune into Radio Luxembourg, which played Pat Boone, Guy Mitchell and the like.

But then, a couple of years later, came Elvis and rock 'n' roll and we were all electrified.

My bible at this time was *The Girls' Annual*. I carried it around with me everywhere because it contained the story of Vivien Leigh, the fairy tale of her life and how she went to Hollywood to make *Gone With The Wind*. When I sat in the chapel, positively visualising the life that I knew would be mine, it was her story that was my blueprint. I would run it over and over in my mind, the story of my own success and stardom and it worked like a charm. Perhaps it was a matter of survival.

But now, when my mother dropped me off on Sundays and said, "You'd better hope nothing happens to me this week", I would no longer be in a state of terror, thinking that if something happened to her then it really would be "the home". Now I had my dreams, my future to hold on to; I was going to be okay, better than okay, a star, no matter what happened to her. And when the nuns would throw my dyslexic essays into the bin and groan, "My dear girl, what will become of you? Some poor wretched man will have to marry you," I would reply without a care, "But it doesn't matter, Sister. When I'm older, I'll be a film star and then I'll have a secretary to do all of this stuff."

When I was nine, I felt a stabbing pain in my side and, after I had complained for days, Mummy took me to a doctor, who X-rayed me and, finding nothing wrong, put it down to "growing pains". The pain was getting worse, but Mummy said, "You heard what the doctor said: there's nothing wrong with you." I had contracted peritonitis and was rushed to hospital for an operation. Just after I had the pre-med, I turned green and my appendix burst. I spent weeks recovering in a nursing home run by nuns. Mummy used to visit me, never failing to remind me what a trauma it was for her to have to come within fifty paces of anything resembling a hospital.

When I caught whooping cough, the sisters were terribly brusque and would have me out of bed at every opportunity. Let me tell you, forced exercise with a body-racking cough is no way to recover from stitches. After some time of this torture, Mummy came to take me home, but she was not rescuing me out of any sudden act of mercy, not a chance. No, she had had a brain-wave: she'd finally found a use for her hopeless daughter - as a housekeeper.

At this point in her life, my mother was very busy racing around Belgravia purchasing houses, doing them up and selling off the leases at great profit, and she was finding it difficult to make time to care for Eric. Having completed his education, he was now working in a bank. A friend of my mother's was something at the National Westminster and it was arranged for Eric to work there to find out if he was suited to the banking profession.

After a couple of years, Eric would decide that he hated the job and my mother would buy him a partnership in an estate agents in Beauchamp Place, Knightsbridge. But right now he was trying his wings at the bank and living in a little mews house in Paddington. As she was living at Ebury Mews, Belgravia, there was no one to look after him.

The interrogator's tools are kindness alternated with cruelty: give with one hand and take away with the other, making sure that it hurts. My mother cajoled me into keeping house for Eric by employing both these tools. First, she told me that it would only be for a short while. Every day or so, she would say that she would be back next week and the living arrangements would be changed. At the same time, she told me that it wasn't as if I was giving up any friends: I didn't really have any; she was my only real friend. To prove the point, she said I could go to a party I'd been invited to that weekend.

She dressed me in an odd assortment of clothes: my first communion dress, except with a new pink sash, and an unflattering ermine jacket. It was not just these odd clothes that made me feel like a complete outsider: I felt even more wretched because I didn't know how to play the games the other children were playing. So into the bathroom I went and there I stayed, crying, until she came to collect me.

This made me sufficiently insecure to be almost relieved to stay at home. To sweeten the pill, she bought me a little black poodle. I called him Monty after a particularly heroic black poodle that I'd seen in one of the movies my aunt had sneaked me into in Brighton when I was seven. This clever dog had managed to save Sally Anne Howes from an acid bath or some such dreadful fate and that was the kind of dog I needed. I trained him for hours to do tricks.

Monty kept me company. I was alone most of the day, shopping, cooking, making up a fire, boiling sheets and putting them through a mangle, which would leave me with a permanently damaged back. And all the time my brother never said a word to me. Nothing. So one day I went on strike: no breakfast, no fire. Still he said nothing, but he must have phoned Mother because she came over to the house.

"What's all this about, then? Your brother told me that there was no lunch for him and no clean shirt."

I told her I would do nothing else for him unless he spoke to me. I remember that this was the first time I'd seen her laugh, at least at something I'd said.

"Well, I'll say something for you, you're not as stupid as you seem. Still waters do run deep. I'll have a word with him. What exactly do you want him to say to you?"

"Nothing special, just 'Good morning', things like that."

"I'll tell him, then".

I later found out that they always went out to dinner and a movie on Thursday nights, but even after she'd spoken to him Eric could only bring himself to say "Good morning" in a sarcastic fashion. And because I wouldn't bow down to her son, I was going to experience another display of my mother's cruelty. She told me a few days after this event that she was putting Monty into kennels, using as an excuse that he was costing too much to feed.

There was no financial logic to this since kennels cost a great deal more than dog food. It was simply a punishment for speaking out. I'd had Monty for only six months; she kept him in kennels for ten.

I still remember the day she took him away. I stood with him in my arms, feeling my little heart breaking, sobbing and looking at the sky. I made a promise to Jesus that I would never forget that day.

Far from bringing me to heel, breaking me and turning me into a blindly obedient servant, this episode turned whatever love I might have had for my mother into dislike and any trust to mistrust (although for years

I kept the door open in hope). It would colour my future, at times giving me incredible strength and, at other times, inflicting terrible pain. More importantly, that afternoon effectively killed all my chances of regaining a normal childhood.

After years of being alone, I cried tears so hot they could have melted a glacier - tears for friends unknown, for formal education and childhood itself, but mostly for a loving parent. And all because I had asked to be treated as a person rather than a slave.

One day a larger-than-life character appeared in our little mews, shouting, "I'm back! I'm home!' in a wonderful, rich voice. He was an actor, tanned from filming *Alexander The Great* in Spain. His name was Peter Wyngarde. I came to make friends with his girlfriend, Dorinda, on a search for a cat, and I would knock on his door, offering to pick up his clothes from the cleaners when I was passing that way. I would do errands for him just for the pleasure of listening to his voice.

I was thrilled when Peter got a part in a production of *Duel Of Angels* in the West End. The star was Vivien Leigh. Two years later I saw him on television in a production of *A Tale Of Two Cities*; his performance has never been bettered. Peter and I became friends years later, but I never reminded him about my childhood crush.

Every day my mother would give me a pound to do the shopping, quite a lot of money in those days, but Eric always got the best and off I would traipse to Cooper's in the Edgware Road. Even the girl behind the counter began to wonder what on earth I was doing there and why I wasn't in school. I suppose the fact that I had been in fee-paying schools made it easier for me to slip through the academic net.

The next stop would be The Rosary, a Catholic church in Paddington. One day the priest asked me how it was that I was such a regular church goer, and during school hours, too. I explained to him that I had to stay home to take care of my brother.

"Ah, I see," said the priest, with great concern. "And how old are you?"

"Nine."

"And how old is your little brother?"

"He's nineteen."

The priest offered to speak to my mother, but I suggested that he send round the police instead. For me, although I didn't recognise it as such at the time, I had instinctively shown that Victim didn't have to be my middle name.

The police were round within the week.

Chapter 3

Vivien Leigh's Protégé

"It is by spending one's self that one becomes rich."

Sarah Bernhardt, *English actress*

I WAS going back to school and, as my mother had written me off as a complete academic no-hoper, it was no skin off her nose what kind of school I attended. I chose the Arts Educational School and started there at the age of ten.

It was perfect. It was wonderful. The most famous "old girl" was Julie Andrews (a fact we were never allowed to forget). I began to study dance, but it soon became clear that I was going to be too tall to be a ballerina. I made friends. Best of all, I studied drama.

The following summer my mother decided to take me on holiday with a good friend of hers, Rosemary Manzi. We stayed at a hotel in Monte Carlo before going along the coast to Menton. It was incredibly beautiful and picturesque, the only down point being the stones on the beach - too much like Brighton for me. But the trip had given me a glimpse of the glamourous side of life in another country.

The same thing happened when I was twelve and Mummy took Eric, myself and our aunts and uncles to St Moritz for a few weeks to celebrate Eric's twenty-first birthday. Money was clearly no object when it came to Eric, his mother and my mother being two different people who just happened to be wearing the same outfit.

While we were in St Moritz, I took the opportunity to learn to ski and found that I was rather good at it. Whizzing down the nursery slopes gave me a sense of incredible freedom and, once more, I added an exciting new image to my dream.

I moved in with my mother on a permanent basis in 1956 when she bought Nos. 46 & 47 Cadogan Place, Belgravia, two Regency houses turned into apartments. There was black-and-white marble and oak-paneling in the entrance hall, a wrought-iron elevator and a resident porter and his wife. Some fairly distinguished tenants moved into that block, including the Mavroleons, the Greek shipping people, Sam Wanamaker, the American film maker, and aristocratic Lady Rennick. Mummy also built two mews houses at the back of the property in Cadogan Lane, including a sweet little place at No. 42 called The Cottage.

While I was at Arts Educational I met Roy Montgomery. He was married to my acting coach, Helen Goss, or Helen Gossip as she was known. Roy acted as agent for the big stars whenever they came to England, the likes of Sophia Loren, while Helen was acting coach to the stars on many British-made movies. These two people made up the core of what now seems to have been some kind of dream team. I also had Maude Spector, the most important casting director of the time, on my side, while Jack Hylton, who hosted *The Royal Variety Show*, was always introducing me to the people who mattered in show business. But it was Roy who took on my dreams as if they were his own.

Roy and I would sit in his kitchen at Draycott Avenue, Chelsea, plotting and planning, filling up sheet after sheet of paper with how it was going to be.

"Tell me again," I would prompt him, "when we go to Hollywood..."

"Just another gin and tonic, darling," he would say and we'd go through it again, one more time: what would happen when the limo rolled up to take me to the set or the premiere. These were practice runs so that, when I turned up for my first photo session with Cornel Lucas, the stars' photographer, I would know how to pose and how to smile like a seasoned professional.

Roy taught me how to walk, with just the right amount of wiggle, and, very important, how to keep my legs as straight as possible, so that I wouldn't get saggy knees later on. I worked out to keep up my muscle tone and all the time I was perfecting my expressions and experimenting with my make-up.

Roy was always around, from the time I was twelve, checking my progress and pushing me in the right direction. For us, my imminent stardom was totally real, a *fait accompli*.

One evening we were passing Marble Arch and saw a huge crowd outside the Odeon, milling around Kirk Douglas, who was appearing at a premiere. At first, we started to move towards the throng, but then we looked at one another and, with one voice, said, "Quick. He mustn't see us."

If I ever met him when I was a star, he might remember me asking him for his autograph. It may seem insane, but that's how we were thinking.

Nevertheless, it was a preposterous idea; I mean, how many English girls had actually made it all the way to Hollywood? Vivien Leigh, Jean Simmons, Joan Collins, who else?

Jack Hylton used to take my mother and me to La Caprice, a restaurant next door to the Ritz, a very "in" place to be seen by people in show business. You came in through the revolving doors and were guided by the maître d' to a seat at the bar. All the high, red leather chairs had a star on the back and the name of a major personality written in gold. If one of the stars came in and someone was sitting on their chair, the maître d' would move them along and sit the star down. If I forgot his or her name, I just had to take a peep at the back of the chair.

I would sit very quietly, eating my lunch and watching all the famous faces. As the first British band leader to take his band to America, Jack knew all the names: Bob Hope, Danny Kaye, the Crazy Gang. He introduced me to my first-ever black family, Nat King Cole and his beautiful wife. They were both charming. At the end of the lunch, Jack asked me if I had had a good time.

"Oh yes!"

I leaned forward and whispered in his ear.

"But you mustn't take him to the Victoria Palace."

This was one of the theatres that Jack owned and where the Black and White Minstrels were playing eight shows a week to packed houses.

"Why is that then, lass?" he answered seriously in his strong Lancastrian accent.

"There'll be trouble, you know," I said, nodding my head solemnly. "They all have to wear make-up and he doesn't. I promise you, Uncle Jack, there'll be trouble."

Jack gave me a big hug.

"You could be right, lass. It's not a show I'll take him to. Now, when are we going to get you on at the *foll-de-rolls* in Blackpool?"

I hated the idea of the *foll-de-rolls*, or any other kind of variety show; I knew it just wasn't me.

"Oh no!" I said firmly. "I'm going to be a film star and go to Hollywood."

"Right," he said. "Come on, then, there's Burt Lancaster over there and he's the biggest star they've got at the moment. He'll get you meeting a few of them."

I got to meet some really important people through Jack Hylton and

I met even more when David Jacobs took over the lunching tradition at La Caprice. David was a sort of Godfather to me and the great thing about having lunch with him was that he was an eccentric: for one thing, he was the only man I knew who wore make-up. He was also a highly successful lawyer, specialising in show-business clients. He represented many of the top pop groups and always seemed to be sorting out drug problems for one or other of them.

One lunchtime he was late because he'd been called out in the early hours by Mick Jagger. The police had raided Keith Richards' house to look for drugs and it seems they had found Marianne Faithfull, Mick's girlfriend, in a somewhat tricky position. There was a lot of talk of chandeliers and chocolates and, for years afterwards, there were Mars Bar jokes.

I was fascinated by big rock bands and how they lived and, later, I went to a lot of their parties, but their way of life held no appeal for me. Stars living in the glare of publicity were in constant fear of being caught with drugs and a conviction meant being banned from working in the United States. The drug culture had brought many careers to an abrupt end and that wasn't going to happen to me.

It was not uncommon for the pupils of Arts Educational to take time off from school to work on some of the films that were being made at that time. Francesca Annis, who was one of my best friends, dyed her hair blonde and disappeared for a while to be one of Elizabeth Taylor's handmaidens in Cleopatra. We were all green with envy.

I was twelve when I got my first taste of the film world. I got a tiny part in *Tom Thumb*, an American musical, starring Russ Tamblyn, Jessie Matthews, Peter Sellers and Terry-Thomas. I still have my salary cheque for two guineas; I didn't have a bank account to put it in.

Although I was little more than a glorified extra, the experience was wonderful. Some kids get bored sitting around on film sets, but not me. We children were supposed to be standing in a corner, watching Russ Tamblyn doing his stuff. As the camera panned around, it would catch little more than a glimpse of us. At that moment, I did a little pirouette, making sure that my head was back in camera view just as it rested on my face.

Everyone wanted to help me, except my family; everyone took my dreams seriously. Perhaps the fact that so many of my adult friends approved of my fantasies had something to do with my conviction regarding my name. I hated my name. I always had.

My mother used to say smugly: "That's something you can't blame me for. Your name was your father's choice, not mine." And it was true. For weeks after my birth, my father had been dithering between one name and another, some of them very beautiful, until one day Jack Hylton told him on the way to the races: "You've got to register her birth. If you don't do it now, you'll be breaking the law."

My father had rushed to register me and, in the hurry, picked the worst possible name, Sandra Eileen Anne Smith, to be exact - I mean, *please!* And it wasn't just the fact that giving someone the initials S. S. was slightly clumsy in 1945.

I chose my own name at the age of seven. Suzanna, spelled the way I heard it, was lovely. Leigh, after Vivien Leigh, my heroine and my father's friend; the combination was perfect: Suzanna Leigh had arrived.

I stopped answering to Sandra. I was so determined about this that people stopped treating it as a childish whim and began to take me seriously. Nobody questioned it at Arts Educational, where it was accepted that an actress would change her name. I was known there as Suzanna and Jack Hylton would introduce me as Suzanna to his friends. Roy thought it was a smart move, cashing in on Vivien Leigh. As he said, no one remembered Archibald Leach, Diana Fluck or Bernie Schwarz. But Cary Grant, Diana Dors and Tony Curtis were household names.

One day I walked around to Vivien Leigh's big house in Eaton Square to ask for her help.

"Yes?" the butler inquired, staring down at me.

"I have something rather important to discuss with Miss Leigh."

"Is she expecting you?"

"No. But my name is Suzanna Leigh and I really must speak with her."

Somewhere in the house Vivien must have heard my voice and been intrigued. The butler was signaled to let me in.

"You wished to speak with me?"

She was beautiful, poised and elegant. I explained to her who I was and she remembered my father.

"In fact," I said, "you might have been my Godmother."

"That's possible. I'm Godmother to so many little girls I can't possibly remember them all."

"Well, the thing is, I'd like to use your name, if you don't mind."

She smiled wistfully.

"I know a girl called Suzanna Leigh. I could have helped her a little more. Perhaps I can help you. What exactly is it that you'd like to do?"

"I'm going to be a film star."

"A film star! Well, this does sound interesting. I must just fix myself a drink."

She left me for a minute and returned with a glass in her hand.

"Right. And how old are you exactly?"

"Well, actually, I always lie about my age."

"But of course you do, darling, don't we all? But aren't you just a little young to be worrying about all that?"

"Well, the thing is, I have to tell people that I'm a little bit older than I am. For work purposes, you understand? Actually, I'm going to be thirteen very soon."

"I see. And you're going to be an actress?"

"Oh yes".

I told her all the plans that Roy and I had made and how I was going to Hollywood, but I was going to do some films here first.

"Funnily enough, I knew exactly what I wanted to do when I was eleven," she said, taking a sip of her drink.

"Oh yes! I know all about everything that happened to you."

And I told her about *The Girls' Annual* that I had carried around for so long and how I knew her life story off by heart.

"Well! This really is a lovely story," she said, smiling slightly. "And what are you doing now? Do you have any help, any pieces that you can do for auditions?"

"Well, Helen Goss is my drama coach. And I've learned a piece from *Sabrina Fair*."

"That's good, one of my favourites."

"And Maude Spector is helping me, too."

"That's fine. Well - you certainly are more interesting than most of my God children. Would you like to come over to go through your piece a couple of times and perhaps choose some more?"

Private lessons with Vivien Leigh? Who could turn that down? It was only years later that I discovered that the other Suzanna Leigh she had talked about was her own daughter from whom she had become estranged.

A week after my first visit to Eaton Square I was back again, performing my piece from *Sabrina Fair* for Vivien Leigh.

"Very good," she said when I finished.

I was holding the book of the play in my hands as though reading from it and she asked me to read some more.

"I'm sorry," I said, "I have a real problem reading straight out."

"Oh, that's all right," she said nonchalantly. "I don't read, either. Always learn your lines so that you never have to think about them when you're in front of the director. Memorise everything and never show your weaknesses. Make love to the camera and, if the camera loves you back, it will always pick you out, even if you're only an extra."

It was at Arts Educational that I learned that, even if my home life was grim, things could have been a great deal worse. One of my friends was a Hungarian girl called Heide, who had escaped during the Hungarian Revolution in 1956. She didn't talk about it much, but I gathered that both her parents were dead. The Communist guards had opened fire and she had been pulled from under a pile of bodies and smuggled to the West.

I left Arts Educational in my fourteenth year. "No man wants a clever wife," my mother declared. "I left school at fourteen and didn't do too badly." If she could have married me off then, she would have, but luckily there was a law against it.

Just before my thirteenth birthday, and without my knowledge, my mother had entered me in a competition in the Evening Standard to pick the prettiest girl in London. The first prize was a sitting for Annigoni, famous for his portrait of the Queen. Although I had come second, this seemed to convince Mummy that I was no longer in need of education; I had all I needed as far as she was concerned.

I was in an academic no-man's-land, with only a reading list from my friend the Jesuit priest to improve my mind. For the moment, my mother had no plans for me.

But I did.

Chapter 4

The Sex Trap

"One is not born a woman, one becomes one."

Simone de Beauvior, *French writer*

THERE was no one to structure my days, so I had to do it for myself. I was up and out in the morning and only came home to sleep. The intervening hours were spent cramming my mind with as much knowledge as I could gather about my chosen craft. Like most fourteen-year-olds, I had puppy fat, but I wasn't about to wait until I grew out of it. I wanted those Jean Simmons cheek-bones and I wanted them NOW!

Mary Wood was a beauty therapist to the stars, so three times a week I would go for facials and gaze at the famous faces on the wall, listening to stories Mary would tell as she applied her magic creams. She told me about a client of hers, Thelma "Toodles" Furness, who had been the girlfriend of Edward, Prince of Wales. Toodles had gone on a trip to India, telling the Prince, "Don't worry, darling, I won't be away long and I've told my lovely little American friend to take care of you." The "lovely little American" turned out to be Wallis Simpson.

Roy would take me to the Victoria & Albert museum to give me a little cultural education. I went to the movies almost every day, sometimes twice a day; a great way for me to learn. I studied the stars' performances with a sharply critical eye. Jack Hylton's office also arranged house seats for me at every play and musical in London; I only had to call up a theatre and mention his name and I would have my own box. My favourite play was *Irma La Douce*, the Les Miz of its day.

The Dorchester Hotel on Park Lane had a health-and-beauty club and for £1 you could wander from the sauna to the steam room to the cool room, or, for another pound, a masseuse would rub you down with a Turkish glove, hose you off with something that resembled a water cannon, then give you a massage, ending with a cold plunge. Take my word, cold really meant cold. The pool went so deep into the ground that a thin skin of ice would form on the surface of the water.

Most days at the baths I would chat with two of the original Gaiety Girls. One of them still did the cold plunge, too. I used to love hearing about the old days and they would bring photographs of themselves to show me. All the Gaiety Girls had been incredibly beautiful, of course, and many of them ended up marrying into the aristocracy.

They also loved to hear about me and my plans and they seemed to approve of how I was going about it. Their one piece of advice was: "Treat the body as a temple, darling, and tend to it every day."

I was still fourteen when I met Alan Sievewright, a man who was to have a huge influence on my career and my mind. He was a top fashion designer in London, a member of all the grand ball committees, and terrific fun. He designed dresses for Shirley Bassey and Marlene Dietrich. He took me to the ballet to meet Margot Fonteyn and to the opera to hear Maria Callas in *Tosca* (first night and closing night). He gave my sketchy education real cultural depth.

I think Alan was the only person whom my mother and I agreed upon and she became a devoted supporter of both him and his talent. She even encouraged him to call her "Mummy".

My next film was *Oscar Wilde*, produced by Roy's best friend, David Middlemas, and starring Robert Morley, Ralph Richardson and Dennis Price. I had only one day's shooting, but spent many more than that on the set, soaking up all the information I could. I also had two non-acting jobs, my first at Louis and Rosemary Manzi's seafood restaurant off Leicester Square. I stayed behind the scenes, putting the butter pats in dishes.

My next job came through Arlene Blundell, my mother's ex-business partner. She re-opened their shop in Mount Street and came over to visit us in Cadogan Place. Arlene had known my father well and told me he had been good-looking and great fun and that he had had the luck of the Devil. "You're so like him," she said, "much more so than your brother."

She asked me what I was doing with my life and then told me that her house model was unwell - would I like to take her place for a while? Would I! For a few weeks I was the house model at this very glamourous Mayfair boutique. One particular perk was that Arlene and I would fly to Jersey to visit one of her clients for a private show and fittings. We took a little six-seater plane and I revelled in the excitement of it.

When I was fifteen, I met Lionel Bart, the composer who had founded British youth culture in the Fifties. He had formed the rock group Tommy Steele and the Cavemen in 1953, taking the name from a dive they used to play, the Cave down Waterloo Road. Lionel also discovered Cliff Richard and wrote his quintessential hit, *Living Doll*, as well as all of the songs for the musical *Fings Ain't Wot They Used t'Be*. Later, he suggested to Pete Townshend and Keith Moon that they should name their band The Who.

The Sixties opened with everybody humming the melodies from *Oliver!*, Lionel's musical twist on Dickens that had Tin Pan Alley begging for more. Lionel had spent two years working on the lyrics, book and score and, starring Ron Moody as Fagin, *Oliver!* had just opened at the New Theatre in St Martin's Lane. Lionel took a shine to me and we often had a cup of coffee and a chat. He was known as Lionel "Never Lost for a Line" Bart. In my eyes, he was stardust and charisma, with a halo of glitter.

He had been born Lionel Begleiter in the East End and the popular myth was that he had named himself after St Bartholomew's Hospital, affectionately known as Bart's, but this wasn't the case at all. Lionel had trained as a commercial artist at St Martin's School of Art and had formed a silk-screen printing works with a friend, John Gorman. "Our company was called G and B Art," he said, "and an office boy thought our names were Mr Gand and Mr Bart - that's the real reason I called myself Bart."

One morning Roy called me to tell me that I was to meet a young Australian actor, Tony Palmer, and that we would be rehearsing a scene for a movie called *Bomb In The High Street*, directed by Terence Fisher. The plot of the film concerned a gang of criminals who dress up as bomb disposal experts to evacuate a small town in order to rob the bank. I play the daughter of a factory owner who runs away with one of his workers (Tony Palmer) and we are caught in the empty town, unaware of the bomb scare. The cast included Ronald Howard, son of Leslie Howard of *Gone With The Wind* fame, and Peter Gilmore, later of *The Onedin Line* series on television.

I was incredibly excited. It was my first main role in a feature film and I was only fifteen.

Most of the shooting was on location in a typical English village. The film company took over the village inn and ran the make-up and wardrobe departments out of its rooms. I was in twin-set and pearls like a young Doris Day and Tony wore a duffel coat. I spent most of the day in curlers; they had to be put back in after each shot because my hair was too heavy to hold a curl and heated rollers hadn't been invented.

We finished on location and came back to London to complete filming at Shepperton Studios. It was a wonderful place, though sadly we were the only film in production and it was eerily empty apart from our little crew. I had my very own dressing room, decorated in those particularly Fifties shades of yucky green and cream, with a pallid pink bathroom. Diana Dors had been the last occupant. I had a white telephone and called Roy twice a day. He told me who to look up and what departments to visit and to keep my eyes and ears open.

We were there for only three days when everything went horribly wrong. I arrived one morning to find that the gates at Shepperton were locked and there was a sign saying, "Closed Until Further Notice". At first, all I could think of was my best winter coat, locked inside with all the bits and pieces I had brought to make my dressing room more homely. It was a miserable scene. Feeling very let down, I went back to Roy's flat in Draycott Avenue.

But, of course, the locked gates meant something far more serious than the loss of my coat. Shepperton Studios had closed and that day marked the beginning of the end for the great British studios. They told us, and kept telling us, that the studio would re-open and filming would re-start in two weeks. But it was two years before Rank bought up the film and we all went back to finish *Bomb In The High Street*, now re-named *Time To Kill*. With the time lapse, I exit one scene as a very young girl and re-enter as quite the young sophisticate.

It was about this time in my career that a certain issue inevitably appeared: sex. I was young and naive and, although I had heard rumours of actresses sleeping their way to the top, I had no clue as to just how endemic sexual favours and sexual abuse were in the business, almost the adhesive that stuck it all together.

For young hopefuls, the road to fame was like a mine field. Producers and directors wanted, no, actually *expected*, a girl to sleep with them, yet they would not give the time of day to someone who was known to sleep around. It was a Catch 22 situation for all young actresses and I, for one, didn't consider myself canny enough to negotiate it. I had heard about one extremely talented actress who completely destroyed her career by sleeping with the wrong people; she came to be known as "Second Unit Sal".

In Hollywood, the most famous advocate of this system was Harry Cohn, the thuggish head of Columbia, of whom it was said that he practically had a clause in the contracts of every one of his actresses (in invisible ink, of course) obliging them to have sex with him whenever he required their services.

It was common knowledge that one of his favourite stars had been a hooker. She was an exceptionally beautiful young woman and had been promised an interview with Cohn by one of her clients, a small-fry agent. Cohn couldn't find the right actress for a new movie he was producing and declared: "I'm going to make the next girl who walks into this office a star."

In came the hooker and got herself a serious promotion; not the kind of thing they put in press releases.

My first experience of the casting couch happened while I was still fifteen. Roy called me about a new Otto Preminger movie, *Exodus*, starring Paul Newman and Eva Marie Saint. There was a good part for a young girl, a freedom fighter on an Israeli *kibbutz*. He thought I would be ideal.

A meeting was arranged between me and Mr Preminger for six o'clock one evening at his office on the corner of South Audley and South Streets, Mayfair. I sat in a hallway as, one by one, the writers went home, then the secretaries, then the assistants. Finally, I went into his office and sat down opposite Mr P; just him, me and his massive desk. He was big, with a heavy paunch and a large nose; not a very attractive man.

There was no indication that anything was amiss and I chatted away. I was thinking, "This is going very well", when all of a sudden this enormous man launched himself across the desk and lunged at me. I was quick on my feet and managed to side-step him, leaving the famous director to land smack on his rather large nose.

"You stupid little bitch!"

His guttural voice was even more nasal than ever. One hand was covering his rapidly swelling nose and he was yelling, "You'll never work for me. Never!"

Terrified, I ran out of the room.

Early in 1961 Helen Goss was on location in Ireland as Kim Novak's drama coach in Somerset Maugham's *Of Human Bondage*. Roy felt it would be a good move for me to go over and spend a weekend meeting some useful people. So off we went. I had a lovely time; everyone was sweet to me, the little *ingenue* trying to get into the business.

Laurence Harvey was the leading man and he was slightly peculiar. He would eat dinner, then go and make himself sick to avoid putting on weight. For nourishment, he would actually drink blood. I'd never encountered that level of eccentricity before or, for that matter, since. Kim Novak was very reclusive, spending most of the day in her room, so I didn't get much of a chance to talk to her.

I was in my room on the second night of our stay when there was a knock on the door and I opened it to find Jack Headley, one of the actors, with blood streaming from what appeared to be a pretty deep cut in his finger.

"Suzanna, I don't suppose you happen to have a plaster somewhere around, do you?"

"Oh! That looks nasty! Let me clean it up - I'm sure I've got a plaster. I'll have a look."

Jack came in and I held his finger under the tap and I cleaned it up pretty well, rustling up a plaster among my travel things. We had a chat and off he went into the night. The next morning at breakfast no one would speak to me. Everyone avoided my gaze and not even Roy could find out what the problem was. I had become *persona non grata* and I didn't even know why. We packed our bags and came home under a cloud.

It was not until years later that we found out what had gone wrong. Roy bumped into someone who had worked on *Of Human Bondage* who mentioned "The Bet".

"What bet?"

"Jack bet us all he'd be able to get Suzanna into the sack. He really cleaned up."

Jack had spent half an hour in my room and then gone down to the bar to collect his winnings from the boys. The cut? Self-inflicted. I've bumped into him since I learned the truth and been sorely tempted to knock his teeth out.

I remember one English actress confessing her movie-making policy to me: first she'd sleep with the producer to ensure the part, then with the director to make sure she was directed well, then with the director of photography to make sure she looked good. Goodness knows when she found time to make the film. I'm no angel, but I have to face the fact that I probably lost some great parts by not playing that game.

After *Time To Kill*, Roy and I decided that I should only go for substantial movie roles. In the meantime, I certainly didn't want to be making a name for myself as an extra, nor did I want to become known as a child actor; so few successfully made the transition to adult work. I wanted to remain a secret entity while I did some acting that no one who mattered would actually see.

Ironically, it was through my brother Eric that an opportunity arose. Eric was a member of the Challenor Catholic Club in Sloane Street, which ran a rather good dramatic society. I managed to coerce him into taking me along for an audition. I had to lie about my age again, but I got myself an audition and a leading role in their play, *Our Town*, by Thornton Wilder.

The advantage, as Roy and I saw it, was that I could use my real name,

Sandra Smith, to cover my tracks and no one would be the wiser. I threw myself into rehearsals, practiced my American accent and the performance went off very well. However, it wasn't like being on a film set; it wasn't the movies.

I started going out at night and Mummy took me to my first nightclub, the 400 in Leicester Square. She bought my dress from Mary Leigh's, an up-market, second-hand shop in South Moulton Street, the last resting place of models' dresses from the top couturier houses. I was in a Givenchy at half the price when we arrived at the 400. No one questioned my age; I was with my mother and, anyway, in those days there was no such thing as a teenager. You were a child and then you were an adult, with nothing in-between.

Actually, the 400 Club turned out to be a bit of a drag; it wasn't very trendy and the patrons were rather too old for me. However, I soon found that a much younger, faster set were practically living on my front doorstep. Mother had bought 79 Cadogan Place, the last privately owned house in the street, and Eric and I had moved in with her, all three of us occupying separate floors.

A neighbour of ours, Knut Robson, invited me to a cocktail party in his home and it was there that I met the group I was to run with for quite a while. I met Jeremy Walker of the Johnnie Walker Black Label whisky family and Nick Freeman of Davidoff cigars. Almost as soon as I walked through the door I found myself being chatted up by Blair Heskith, who became my bank manager at Hill Samuel twenty years later.

Blair invited me to a party that he and Jeremy were throwing at their flat in Cadogan Square a week later. When I stepped out of their elevator, I could hear Ray Charles singing over a lively buzz of conversation. They also played blue-beat imports from the West Indies and it all seemed terribly bohemian. I usually drank wine and, in those days, no one drank wine except with dinner, so I asked for a gin and tonic and spent most of the party pouring endless refills into the plant pots. Although everyone took me for eighteen at least, I was still sixteen and I felt more out of my depth among these glamourous twenty-year-olds than I ever had with Jack Hylton's friends.

After the party, we all piled into cabs and went on to the Blue Angel, a trendy club, nothing at all like the 400. We sat at small tables, listening to the great black jazz singer Hutch, who was rumoured to be the secret lover of Lord Mountbatten's wife, Edwina.

The racing season starts with the Cheltenham Gold Cup and I was invited along by Blair and the gang. Despite Daddy's passion for racing, it was the first time I had ever been to a meeting. I don't know if picking a winner runs in the blood or whether it's just a matter of luck, but that day I certainly was on a roll. I won all six races, then hit the jackpot from a slot machine in a pub on the way back to London.

Someone suggested that we go to a new gambling club, the Pair of Shoes; I wasn't sure if I would pass for twenty-one, the minimum age required by law, but I was admitted without any trouble. I'm sure the owner, Eric Steiner, wished I'd been turned away at the door because I left with my bag bulging with cash. Daddy would have been proud of me for winning, but I was going to need more than luck very soon because it was at this point that Mummy decided to marry me off.

I was walking Monty in Belgrave Square one summer's day in 1961 when Tony Leeds, an American, stopped to admire him. We got talking and became friends. Tony's mother was a New York society hostess and Mummy was delighted when she invited us to New York for Thanksgiving.

I was gazing out of the window of our hotel, the St Moritz, overlooking Central Park, when I noticed that people on Fifth Avenue were stopping and staring at something. Then I spotted the Everly Brothers, Don and Phil, walking down the street. They were very big pop stars at the time - remember *Cathy's Clown*? - and I watched them closely, while my mother rambled on in the background.

"Listen, Suzanna, if Tony asks you to marry him, do something sensible for a change and say 'Yes'. He can give you a good life. And your mother - (she always referred to herself in the third person when she was about to make me feel guilty) - wouldn't mind a few trips over here before she dies. God knows, she deserves it."

I couldn't understand why she was pushing me on to Tony - he was Jewish and my mother had always been rabidly anti-Semitic. Could it have had anything to do with his money?

"Tony is very sweet, but I'm not in love with him," I said quietly. "Besides, you always said you couldn't stand me even dating a Jew."

"Don't get smart with me, young lady, they can make very good husbands."

I continued to stare at the Everly Brothers, who were now stepping into a beautiful, long, black limo.

"Love isn't everything," she went on. "Anyway, you can learn to love him in time. Marriage isn't about love. It's about looking after your husband, cooking and keeping house and having children. The trouble with you is, you think that you're clever. Men don't like clever women. They want someone to keep house."

Any qualms I'd ever had about being an actress flew right out of that window and sat on top of that limo with the Everly Brothers.

"Mother! I'm not getting married, at least until I'm thirty, and that's that! You can't force me to. Now let's just let the matter drop."

As far as she was concerned, I was useless at everything and no amount of evidence to the contrary would convince her otherwise. My only hope in her eyes was marriage. When she realised I would not marry Tony, she came up with another little trick. She made me sign a contract stating that I would have to pay her some vast sum of money if I did get married before the age of thirty.

Despite her craziness, I couldn't afford to antagonise my mother. I was still under-age and I needed her to sign my contracts. I also needed her permission to change my name by deed poll to Suzanna Leigh.

Looking back at some of the strokes she pulled, I find it hard to believe they actually happened. To frighten me, she carried out an oft-repeated threat. She had told me she had the power to put me in an institution and one day she locked me in my bedroom in Cadogan Place and called a doctor to have me certified insane. She had told me in advance what she was planning to do and, once again, the waiting for it to happen was agonising.

There was a knock on the door and I found myself sitting in my room opposite an elderly psychiatrist. He chatted with me briefly and then left, closing the door quietly behind him. I listened as he spoke to my mother on the stairs.

"The only thing that I can suggest to you, madam, is that you seek medical help. You are obviously not in your right mind. There's nothing wrong with that child and you'll be searching long and hard before you find a doctor who'll sign anything saying that there is. Good day."

It seems incredible, but this is how things were then, I promise you. Even though I lived in a grand Belgravia house, the nastiness inside that house was as horrible as any in the most deprived slum.

Chapter 5

Arabian Nights

"Life is what happens to you when you're making other plans."

Betty Talmadge, *American meatbroker*

MY life wasn't all a nightmare, however. Alan Sieveright took me to Countess Rosse's fabulous summer ball. The Countess was Princess Margaret's mother-in-law and lived at Osterley Park, which was almost a palace on the outskirts of London. There was a massive display of fireworks in the garden and all of the guests were sitting on the steps, looking up at the night sky. I was jumping up and down with excitement and sat down on the foot of the person behind me. I heard a low moan and, turning around, found myself looking into the pained face of the Queen Mother.

"Oh Ma'am! Was that your foot? I'm so sorry!"

"Oh, don't worry, my dear. It's nothing, really, just rather a shock..."

I felt absolutely dreadful. I rushed off to find the Queen Mother a cushion. Throughout the evening, I kept glancing at her foot and, to my horror, saw that her shoe had split and seemed to be bulging rather unhealthily. I searched out one of her ladies-in-waiting and whispered the state of affairs to her, trying not to point at Her Majesty's toes. The lady-in-waiting whispered something in Her Majesty's ear.

The Queen Mother beckoned me over.

"What is your name?"

"Suzanna Leigh, Ma'am."

"Well, please don't worry yourself, my dear, my foot really doesn't hurt. I'm sure it will be perfectly fine."

"It doesn't look fine, Ma'am. It doesn't look fine at all."

She assured me that all was well, but I was not convinced and everyone remarked that the Queen Mother left unusually early that night.

At a cocktail party, I met Joel Lerner, who became my boyfriend for a while and a very good friend for years to come. Joel's grandfather, Lord Marks, had started the penny market stall which became Marks & Spencer, while his stepfather, Gerry Marco, was a charming and slightly notorious playboy; my mother remembered him in The Orchid Room with various wealthy women. He was great fun, full of stories about the stars of the Golden Age of Hollywood, particularly Errol Flynn, with whom he had roamed the world for a year or two.

Joel's mother was a racing fanatic who used to give pre-meet parties, with champagne, smoked salmon and mountains of strawberries and cream. Joel squired me around the whirl of cocktail parties, dinners and dances that made up my social life and, at one of these, I met Princess Nezha, youngest and favourite sister of King Hassan II of Morocco, who had come to power the previous year. Nezha was extremely chic and had been a huge hit with the press a few months earlier when she accompanied the King to America as a guest of the Kennedys.

Lala Nezha, as we all called her (Lala being the Arabic word for princess), invited me to spend a few weeks' holiday at her palace in Rabat. I would also attend a special celebration in Casablanca for the King. We travelled by Air Maroc, the plane having to wait because Nezha was running late. When we landed in Tangiers, an amazing commotion greeted our arrival. The area had been cordoned off and people were rushing around, bowing, walking backwards and kissing the Princess's hands and feet.

We spent three days in Tangiers before driving to Nezha's pink palace in Rabat. As we approached, I could smell the spicy aromas of the dishes that the royal chefs had been preparing for days in anticipation of her arrival. I grew to love the rosy marble walls and floors of the palace and the spectacular mosaics that lined the inner courtyard, where there was a swimming pool and cool, sparkling fountains. Every one of the royal palaces had its own cinema and, as the Princess couldn't go out the way she did in London, she had her own nightclub.

Lala made it clear to the court officials that I was to be treated with the greatest respect. I was given a Cadillac for the duration of my stay and had my own servant, a Berber girl whose hands were intricately decorated with henna. She was as loyal to me as if her life had been dedicated to my well-being. She slept in the corner of my room, on the floor, just in case I needed anything during the night. We stayed in bed until two o'clock in the afternoon; nothing could happen until Princess Nezha awoke and no one was permitted to waken her. To rouse a royal personage from their sleep would take seconds off their life, so the saying went, and the servants remained curled up on the floor until she stirred.

After a late lunch, we were driven down to the beach and carried into the water by servants so that our feet would not be burned on the scorching sands. Lala Nezha's brother, the Crown Prince, Moulay Abdullah, was a great water skier and he would jump from the back of the jetty and skim behind the speedboat on his bare feet!

We were always surrounded by a squad of armed guards and, at night, a sentry was posted outside my bedroom door. He marched up and down the corridor all night and the noise kept me awake. I mentioned this to the Princess, *en passant*, and the next night he put some sort of covering over his boots to muffle the sound.

One day at the beach there was an enormous commotion among the soldiers. They were tracing their way over the dunes, systematically bayoneting the sand. A would-be assassin had made an attempt on the King's life the previous night and it was suspected that he had buried himself in the sand, breathing through a hollow reed. Eventually, there was a terrible scream; the soldiers had found their man.

Serge, Count de la Marshe, a friend from London, came for lunch one day. We could hear him through the window, calling from the courtyard below, "*La Princesse! La Princesse*", in his terribly correct Prussian way, waving a cigar. Lala thought he was too pompous for words and decided to play a trick on him. She had a massive Alsatian and at the word "Attack!" from the Princess, the dog went bounding down the steps, baying for blood.

Serge was terrified; moving faster than I've ever seen any man move, he leaped on to the roof of the car that had brought him to the palace.

"Get him off me!" he was yelling at the top of his voice.

We laughed. The Princess had a rather wicked sense of humour and I realised that this connected deep down with my own because we had both experienced the crueler side of life.

The King, a small, austere man, arrived flanked by armed guards - and this was just a family visit. He had heard about the guard-dog incident and was furious with his sister for her frivolity. She told me he had instructed her to attend a feast to be held in her honour by a Bedouin sheik at his camp deep in the desert. There was a distinct possibility that the sheik would offer himself to the King as her husband, a definite sign that her playing days were drawing to a close.

I was invited to go with her disguised as a lady-in-waiting and we were driven into the desert, with the sand flying in clouds around the Cadillacs, until we reached a vast tented city lit by flaming torches. As a sign of the high esteem in which he held Lala Nezha, the sheik had arranged an evening of exotic entertainment, starting with a race between pure-bred Arab stallions, while their riders brandished sabers, and continuing over dinner with an exhibition of knife-throwing and some incredibly erotic dancing. The whole atmosphere was medieval and there was such a massive undercurrent of violence that, being *incognito*, I spent the evening walking on egg-shells.

As Lala's friend, I was given the privilege of attending the great celebration in Casablanca in honour of the King. Dressed in traditional Moroccan garments, I was taken to the top of a watchtower by one of the guards and permitted to look at the ceremony through an arrow slit. The hills surrounding the tower were clothed in the white robes of men, and only men, and they seemed to move as one, their voices raised in a single, shrill cry that echoed around the hills.

Smoothly, like a wave rippling in the shimmering sun, a gap appeared in the crowd and King Hassan appeared in a traditional white gown, riding a white horse. Walking behind him on foot (and clad in an immaculate blue suit by Worth) came the only woman, Princess Nezha. The only time I had ever seen anything like these scenes was when Sam Spiegel invited the Moroccan Royal Family to a private showing of *Lawrence of Arabia*, but that was a movie and this was the real thing.

That night, I was formally presented to the King, whom I had already met casually, as far as it could ever be casual in his presence. I bowed and walked backwards, as though I had been doing it all my life. I returned to London with some wonderful memories of Morocco, but the fabled pink palaces of Hollywood were still a mirage on the far horizon.

I finished *Time To Kill*, the re-named *Bomb In The High Street*, and made a few appearances in TV shows, girl-in-the-typing-pool sort of thing, and, more impressively, as the lead girl in an episode of *The Saint* with Roger Moore.

Then Roy and I decided it would be worthwhile for me to spend some further time at drama school. We knew I couldn't go for the full three years because of the importance of youth in my career; as Roy said, a woman's shelf life on screen was drastically shorter than that of a man. Even at seventeen, I was worrying about wasting time and being over the hill. On the other hand, I was still a little young to start drama school.

Nevertheless, using a combination of deviousness and charm to avoid producing my birth certificate, Roy and I managed to convince the head of the Webber-Douglas School, a formidable man called Rochester, not only to accept me as a pupil, but also to allow me to attend for only one year.

Roy felt that, as I already knew the basics, all I needed was a potted version of the course and, somehow, Rochester had the confidence in me to consent.

I was in.

I felt at home immediately. After the past few years of educating myself with no support, the rigors of drama school were a pleasure. And after school there was my hectic social life. Joel Lerner or his friend Andy Braunsberg would arrive in a car to pick me up from Webber-Douglas in Kensington and off we would go to a party.

At the end of my first term, my mother asked me how I was getting on there. And I made a stupid mistake.

"I'm loving it," I said. "It's so much fun. I'm really fitting in and I'm learning so much."

The next day she wrote to tell them that I would not be coming back for the following term. I should have said that I hated it; that they were beating me because I couldn't read; something like that. Then she would have made me stay.

Roy used all his powers of persuasion to convince her to let me move into one of her empty flats in Cadogan Place. It had three bedrooms and stripped wood floors and a very smart address. I started throwing little dinner parties of my own. All my friends were impressed.

"You're so *cool*, S.L!" they said, the ultimate compliment in 1963.

I started seeing Ian Heath after I met him at his twenty-first birthday party at the Carlton Tower. Ian was a romantic at heart, a trait he inherited from his parents. His mother, Joan, was an American, pretty, rich and with a great love of life; mostly, though, her love was for Sir Barrie, Ian's war-hero father. The Heaths had a town house in Mayfair and a country estate, but their favourite abode was The Prospect, a Queen Anne house at Cowes on the Isle of Wight.

This was the base for Sir Barrie's great hobby, sailing; he was Vice Commodore of the Royal Yacht Club and the times I stayed there Prince Philip and his sailing companion, Uffa Fox, a superb raconteur, popped in almost daily.

Ian Heath was witty, a sharp dresser and had a nickname for everyone. We all picked up his little catch phrases, such as "throwing a moody" or "going spare", and we had to decide whether someone had "aristocratic ankles" or not. He called me a "Hot Flush".

Ian was PR for Heinz and his best friend, Nigel Dempster, was PR for Lord Kimberley. Nigel's ambition was to be a newspaper columnist and, through Ian, he met Sir Max Aitken, the press baron, who had a half-share in The Prospect. Later that year Nigel started work on the William Hickey page on the Daily Express and went on to run his own diary on the Daily Mail; then, as now, one of the cleverest journalists in Britain.

Sometimes Nige brought along his girlfriend, the Hon. Roxana Lampson, or Bunty. She was the daughter of Lady Killearn, a beautiful Italian who was noted for pinching her daughter's boyfriends. Bunty was one of the trendiest young women in London and had hired the Rolling Stones for their first-ever society gig when they performed at her coming-out dance for just £20.

Our friend Count Paul Orstich, (Ostrich, of course) had brought Vicki Hodge, known aptly as "Tricky Vicki", into our gang. She was always the opportunist, as Prince Andrew found to his cost during a trip to Barbados a little later on. Vicki had just started to work as a photographic model and she was the first girl I had ever seen draw a black line all around her eyes.

Then there was Colin "The Creamer" Slater, a good-looking blond, whose stepfather, Lord Rootes, the millionaire car manufacturer, gave him a Sunbeam Alpine for his twenty-first birthday.

Ian Heath became the first great love of my life and, no matter what happened to me over the next four years, he was always there for me. We were a formidable gang and all of us had good careers on the go - this was the Sixties and you had to have a Ph.D. in stupidity not to have some sort of job.

My connection with Jack Hylton paid dividends when he staged the musical *Camelot*. All my friends were desperate to see the smash-hit show and I proudly took possession of my complementary box every night until all of them had seen it. I was also back in my old daytime routine of facials and movies when I wasn't working and I'd called Roy twice a day.

And then one morning:

"Darling, this could be just what we've been looking for. A friend of mine, Vivian Cox, is co-producing a TV series with Danny Angel. You know, he did *Reach For The Sky*. It's going to be shot in France for something called Pay-TV."

"What's Pay-TV?"

"There's a box on top of the TV set and you put money in when you want to watch a special show; something like that. The series is called *Trois étoiles - Three Stars*. The first star is the country, the second is the car - an MG - and the third star is the girl. It's a kind of cooking-travelogue-glamour thing."

The concept was that the girl would drive around the French

countryside in the MG, stopping at an *auberge*, where she would get into conversation with the patron about her extraordinary resemblance to the original mistress of a nearby chateau. Through this connection, or something similar, we would discover the history of a famous French dish.

"The great thing," said Roy, "is that we can use it as a launching pad for Hollywood because we've no time to waste on Rep."

"Aren't I a bit young to be carrying my own series?"

"Details, darling, details. And it will be just the thing to get you your Equity Card."

I couldn't get a full union card without a full-time job and I couldn't get a full-time job without the card, so this was the perfect opportunity. I would live in France for a year, spending much of the time in Paris of all places. I'd been reading every book that Ernest Hemingway had ever written, some twice over, as well as Balzac and Colette. French sophistication and French culture were irresistible. I wanted to sit alone in a Left Bank café, like Jean Rees in *Good Morning, Midnight* and live in a small hotel, as she had done in *Goodbye, Mr McKenzie*. I had also read Nancy Mitford's *The Sun King*, so I was dying to visit Versailles.

Then there was my favourite raconteur, playwright, story-teller, human being *extraordinaire*: the wonderful Oscar Wilde. I would be able to seek out Oscar's last resting place, room 16 at L'Hotel, and find out just what that wallpaper was like!

It would be bliss: Sacre Coeur, Notre Dame, Napoleon's Tomb, galleries, museums, Madame Curie's house and, a bit further afield, the Cannes Film Festival.

I just had to get this job!

Chapter 6

An étoile is Born

"I think that wherever your journey takes you, there are new gods waiting there, with divine patience - and laughter."

Suzanne Watkins, *American writer*

ROY and I had lunch before our meeting with Vivian Cox and Danny Angel to discuss *Trois étoiles*. We chose Manzi's because I loved their scampi and chips and the manager, Luigi, Louis Manzi's son, hardly ever let us pay.

"Filming starts in September," said Roy. "How is your French?"

"I can just about order dinner."

"We'll have to work on that."

We made our way excitedly to Danny Angel's office in the West End, where we were also going to meet the prospective director, Maurice Regume. His job wasn't in the bag, either.

"I think you should answer in French if Maurice asks you anything," Roy suggested. "If he asks you whether you speak French..."

"I'll say, '*Mais oui?*'" I answered hopefully.

"Exactly. I've got a little sentence here for you."

He passed me a piece of paper on which he'd scribbled: *"Oui! Bien sur! Je parle Francais. C'est necessaire pour vous parlez lentement par c'est que je m'apprend Francais maintenant pour le travaille a la cinema."*

I had memorised this by the time we reached Danny Angel's office, where Vivian Cox, a nice-looking, slightly round man of about fifty, was waiting in reception. He told me the series was to be made for France, Britain and Canada, quite an impressive audience. Suddenly, a rather attractive, obviously French man of about forty walked into the room.

"Suzanna Legg? Maurice Regume."

To the French, my name comes across in print as "Legg" and he had obviously only seen it written down.

We shook hands firmly.

"Leigh," I smiled.

He rattled off something in French and I was completely lost in a few seconds. After a moment's silence, he said: "*Parlez-vous Francais?*"

"*Non. Un peu.*"

Not what he was hoping to hear because he obviously did not speak a word of English.

"*Ah, non. Pas bien.*"

We smiled at each other.

"*Oui, mais je m'apprend maintenant,*" I said.

I needed this job really badly and, reading him quite well, I could see he needed it, too. I had to think of something. When Vivien Cox went in to see Danny Angel, I told Maurice in my bad French to say "Yes" or "No" to whatever Danny asked him, trying to give the words intelligent inflexions. When we sat at Danny's desk, I would sit next to Maurice and if the question required a "Yes", I'd tap him on the foot once, two taps for "No".

"*Ca marche!*" he said.

We went into the meeting with Danny.

"Will the episode in St Tropez cost us a fortune?"

Two taps.

"Nooo. No!"

"You've had a word with Suzanna, I suppose. Will her French be good enough?"

One tap.

"Yes. *Bien sur.* Yes!"

By the end of the meeting, I felt distinctly pale. Danny came round from behind the desk and I was surprised to see he was in a wheelchair: a war hero, he had been invalided out of the British Army in 1944. We all shook hands and I went home, exhausted. It all seemed to have gone well, but I couldn't be sure.

That night Roy called me.

"You've got the part, Suzanna. It's all going ahead!"

I would have to use my own clothes and jewellery, but that was no problem; maybe I could use some of my mother's: I had noticed a lot of jewellery around the house lately.

Yvonne Sassoon, ex-wife of my father's racing friend, Sir Victor, had been dropping in more often than usual. She and my mother had always been friends and, during the Suez crisis, they had spent a lot of time discussing where they should live in the event of war. It was the only time I had seen my mother interested in politics.

But now Yvonne needed money and so she was selling her collection of fabulous jewellery, piece by piece, to my mother. As some of the best pieces had already been pawned, she even sold her the pawn tickets.

Back in 1951, Yvonne had been awarded a record divorce settlement, but Sir Victor had told her on the steps of the court, "You'll never get a penny out of me and you'll never see me again." With that, he disappeared, never to be seen this side of the Equator again. Yvonne had spent a fortune on detectives in unsuccessful attempts to track him down and she was never on top of her life after that. The wine merchant had become her closest friend.

Yvonne's jewels were to be given an early airing in public because Eric was getting married. The bride, Sylvia Robinson, was an ink heiress and, as her parents were paying for the wedding itself, Mummy took it upon herself to give the couple something that would out-do them. She presented them with a house, completely furnished, in Belgrave Mews South.

Eric and Sylvia were married at the Oratory in Brompton Road, with me as bridesmaid. After the ceremony, my mother hired a boat leaving from Cadogan Pier for a party on the Thames. It was a beautiful, sunny day and the water was calm as glass. I had been allowed to invite some of my friends and, with champagne and a rock group, it was a good way to repay some of the hospitality I had received.

Before I packed my bags for France, I shot an episode of *The Sentimental Agent* with Carlos Thompson, working again with John Paddy Carstairs, who had directed my episode of *The Saint*. Carlos was a star in Germany, but was not known to the same extent in England, although he was married to the famous actress, Lili Palmer.

I was playing the female lead in this episode and I have to admit I was not as diligent as I could have been in following Vivien Leigh's advice about learning my lines. I knew them when I was at home, but once on set... WHOOPS! Fluffing lines is always an embarrassing situation, particularly when you are young. I learned my lesson, though: since then I've always made sure that I know practically the whole script backwards as well as forwards, so they can change anything and I won't be thrown off my stride.

The night before I left for Paris I went to the Oratory and thanked God for all the amazing things that were happening to me. Somehow, despite the obstacles that could have held me back, I was on my way.

Vivian was at Orly in a blue MG-B to meet me when the plane

touched down. We drove out of Paris towards the Loire Valley, where we were to stay the night in a small village and meet up with the film crew to do background shots. Autumn was beginning, but it was warm and we had the roof down.

I was expected to map-read for Vivian, a skill that the Jesuits had failed to instill in me, and he became progressively short-tempered over my inability to point us in the correct direction. We got to see a great deal of the beautiful river, but we were both pretty crotchety by the time we reached our destination. We sat on long benches with the film crew, just like at school, eating impossibly rich food, drinking wine and laughing. It set the mood for the whole series.

Henri, the lighting cameraman, was a Communist, the first I'd ever met, as Communists were a little thin on the ground in Chelsea society. He was nothing like the gun-toting thugs that Heide had described to me at Arts Educational, so maybe they weren't all monsters.

The first days of shooting were easy, just driving along country lanes to and from various chateaux. I didn't get to see one close up until the third day when we were to shoot at Chateau Chambard. I shall never forget the sight of driving towards this massive palace: the sun was dazzling, peeping between the chimneys, all 365 of them, Vivian told me, one for each day of the year. Moliere used to premiere his plays there for Louis XIV.

Next came the Chateau of Chenonceaux, which was owned at one time by one of my favourite women in French history, Diane de Poitiers, who had been the mistress of King Henri II. She must have been an extraordinary woman because, on his death bed, the King advised his son to take her as his mistress as well because of her unsurpassed wisdom and the Prince took his advice. This chateau became my favourite, mainly for the water that encircled it, but also for its nickname: the Castle of Six Women, which referred to Diane de Poitiers and five other women associated with its history.

Each episode in the *Trois étoiles* series would take ten days to shoot. At first, I though this was a generous amount of time, but the hours were eaten up because each scene had to be shot for French, French-Canadian and English versions, which entailed driving from place to place three times, an exhausting process. It was important that I felt comfortable in my role and I did; my character was a happy English girl, who, like me, was curious to find out more about this beautiful country, its art and history. Each story about the origins of a recipe was true, or at least part of a legend that had been passed down within families from generation to generation.

We spent one evening in a vast vineyard in the Burgundy region.

The wine grower, quite a young man, took us around his gargantuan cellar in a train! The cellar had a small section behind bars which contained bottles of Napoleon brandy; not the brand name, but bottles actually taken from Napoleon's own cellar.

The vintner took us to see his grandfather, a genuine wine buff. We took along five bottles of the local wine, chosen from over fifty years of the vineyard's history. We blindfolded the old man and he took a little sip of each wine. Not only did he recognise every vintage, but he had a story about the year in which the grapes had been pressed. "Ah! That was the year it rained so hard the grapes were bruised," he would exclaim, even though the time he was speaking about was forty years ago.

We also visited a snail farm, where the snails were given wine (marinated from the inside out, as it were) two days before sacrificing their lives to the Gallic palate; not a bad way to go if you were a snail. Watching these inebriated creatures weaving their way up the walls, bumping into each other and tangling up their antennae, was very funny, if slightly sad.

Many well-known French actors appeared in the series, some of whom I was thrilled to recognise from their movies. One episode featured Louis Renault, who had been in *Casablanca*. I was not incredibly well paid, but money came low on my list of priorities; France was like a cultural open university to me.

In one episode, I was working opposite a very charming man. We were supposed to run through our lines, but after lunch he was nowhere to be seen. I decided to seek him out in his room, so I went up and, after knocking on the door, made the mistake of walking straight in. Well, let's just say I left - shaken. I bumped into Vivian on the stairs.

"What's up?"

"There's something pretty nasty going on in there with a duck and it's not getting flying lessons."

"Oh well, my dear, each to their own. It's just lucky for the *patron* we're not in Wales."

Whenever I had a free weekend, I flew back to London, although I was supposed to stay in France to be fresh for the next episode. I would buy huge bottles of duty-free scent, Le Deux, By Givenchy and Miss Dior being my favourites. Dousing myself in French perfume was my idea of absolute luxury. I also bought myself Louis Vuitton luggage and the occasional Hermes scarf. I would return to France with newly released Beatles records; it was 1963 and the Beatles were huge and all the clubs borrowed my records.

Ian came over to visit me and took me to some expensive restaurants, places I could not afford to go myself. I spent Christmas between the two countries. Life was good.

Maurice had been flirting with me for months. I don't think he was particularly serious, but he was French, and a man, and it was unthinkable that he should not make some effort to chat me up. I liked him and his stories and he also taught me how to play the drums. When we went down to St. Tropez, our continuity girl fell ill and had to leave us. This gave me the opportunity to do something for Maurice. I found a replacement, very pretty and single, and introduced them.

He liked her so much he married her.

Back on location, however, we were all beginning to flag. There seemed to be no rules in France governing the number of hours you could legally work in one day. When I wasn't actually filming, I was travelling and I rarely got to sleep for more than four hours at a time in a real bed. I would catch a nap at every opportunity, curling up in the car while we were driving from one place to another. Maurice would stop the car, saying, "Oh, this looks like a good place for a quick night shoot," and I would drag myself together.

When things got really tough, we all looked forward to the weeks we were due to spend in Paris and the promise of living in the City of Light kept up our morale. Maurice told me stories about the people he knew; about Greta Garbo, who, it was said, owned so much of Paris that the city had to issue a law to protect itself. I was promised dinners with fascinating people and then, of course, when we were set to do the episode in St. Tropez, Maurice casually informed me that he was a friend of Brigitte Bardot.

This was the year that the Hotel Byblos was in full swing and Tahiti Plage the beach on which to sunbathe and eat grilled corn on the cob - or maize, as it was called - with a distinctive taste of charcoal. There were guitar-strumming musicians walking from restaurant to restaurant and gorgeous people everywhere. For the first time, I saw girls topless on the beach, but it took me another year to summon up the courage to take my top off. I loved the sun, and, luckily for me, my skin survived as well as it did because, for continuity reasons, I wasn't allowed to get too tanned.

Before Brigitte Bardot made *And God Created Woman* for Roger Vadim, St. Tropez had been a sleepy old fishing village a safe distance along the coast from Cannes, Nice and Monte Carlo, but now the young smart set, the *jeunesse dorée*, had made it *their* place in the sun.

Maurice spent ages trying to get Brigitte to walk through one of our scenes and I really don't remember whether he succeeded or not. I know she was sweet enough to let us shoot footage at her house, La Madrigal. Then we'd go back to the gleaming little port, where Vadim's blue-gray Ferrari would rest its nose on the bar at Le Gorille.

Heady stuff for a teenager.

It was in Paris that I realised it was possible to lead a double life without losing my identity. I was seduced by the *avant-garde* scene of Montmartre, yet I dressed to kill for lunch at Maxim's. At night, I'd go from a bohemian dinner on the Left Bank to a party in Avenue Foch, where it was possible, as I discovered, to bump into a cheetah cooling itself in the bath.

I spent my first few nights in a small, shabby hotel in Place Emile Gondeau, which had witnessed the beginning of the art world as I knew it. Picasso, Modigliani and Jean Gris had all taken rooms in that street at one time or another. In the Latin Quarter, I hung around Rue du Cardinal Lemoine, where Hemingway had lived in the Twenties when he was "broke but happy".

People approached me and willingly took time to answer my questions about him. They told me he would take detours to avoid the torture of the bakeries. He could not have chosen a worse place to live: the area was suffused with the aroma of warm croissants! How I would love to have been at one of Gertrude Stein and Alice B. Toklas's parties, hanging out with Ernest, Pablo, Matisse and Sherwood Anderson.

I also stayed at L'Hotel, where Oscar Wilde had written *The Ballad of Reading Gaol*, and where he had uttered the immortal phrase, "I can't stand this wallpaper. One of us will have to go." The place where he had died was still shabby, but had the most beautiful, wrought-iron *élévateur*, a time machine back to the *Belle époque*. As for the wallpaper, I regret to say that the room had been redecorated some years before I got there.

I was in Paris the day that Edith Piaf, the Little Sparrow, died. It was a day of national mourning, theatres and cafés closed their doors and the streets were thronged with people simply showing their respect. We didn't work that day, either.

Along with my love affairs with French food and wine, I also found out the meaning of "*cinque a sept*". These were the hours that many Parisian husbands and wives spent with their respective lovers and swore blind that the tradition kept their marriages together. It was impossible to make an arrangement to see anyone during those two hours, so I used the time to learn my lines.

I noticed how differently women were looked upon by French men: all women were prized and, if you happened to be pretty, you were adored; it was not something to be hidden away. Ballet teaches you how to walk well and in Paris men admire a woman who can walk well, even if her face is not attractive.

One lunchtime I was standing in line at a Paris studio commissary when one of my favourite stars, Alain Delon, turned round in front of me and asked me how I liked France. I was so stunned that Alain Delon was talking to me that I picked up a slice of chocolate *gâteau*, oblivious to the fact that it was not on a plate. I didn't even look at it until he walked away. Then I found that the chocolate was dripping through my hand on to the floor, much to everyone's amusement.

A bigger thrill was in store when Maurice arranged for me to meet Louis Malle, one of the great directors of the French New Wave. We had lunch at his house and, even though he and Maurice rattled away in French, it was great just being there.

As I sat in the cafés in Saint Germain des Prés, I began to listen to the conversations of the people around me. It was a bewildering, politicised time; President Kennedy had been shot in Dallas, Texas, only a short time earlier, the civil war in Algeria was a huge issue and Marlene Dietrich had become a Communist. She saw it as the only way to give everyone a fair chance and equal rights.

The cafés were abuzz with talk of government corruption, of revolution and of contempt for De Gaulle; heated dispute mingled with the whiff of cognac and Gauloises among the existentialists at the Deux Magots and the Café de Flore. I was fascinated that people of my age didn't sit around gossiping about sex and clothes, but talked about running their country.

I felt as though I was well on my way to achieving my ambition of being truly grown-up by the time I left France.

The theme for the 1964 Opera Ball was historical figures and I went as Louis XV's mistress, Madame du Barry, whom I had played only a few weeks earlier in *Trois étoiles*. The previous year I had gone to the ball as Juliet and had not been the only one.

This time, however, Alan and I had been making plans since the end of 1963 and my entrance was going to be a little more memorable. He designed a theatrical masterpiece for me, embroidered with lace and hand-sewn with sequins. It cost more than £1,500.

As the night of the ball drew near, Rosa Hepner, my publicist, sent out a press release. I'd always believed in the power of the press - we'd just seen the newspapers pull down the Macmillan Government over the Profumo Affair - and now it was time for them to spotlight me. The photographers came to see my *pièce de résistance*, a sedan chair in which I was carried through the streets of London. It was the first time for a century-and-a-half that anyone had travelled this way.

The next day pretty well every newspaper in England and many overseas carried a picture of me sitting in the chair as Madame du Barry.

With luck, I thought, some important producer might see that photograph and remember me.

Chapter 7

Roamin' with Polanski

"He was the cock who thought the sun had risen to hear him crow."

George Eliot, *English writer*

RAYMOND, or rather Roman, Polanski was moving to London to live with Gene Gutowski, a Polish producer who was married to Judy Wilson, a friend of mine. Polanski had defected from Communist Poland and was fast becoming the most celebrated *émigré* in the film business. I was as keen as anyone to make his acquaintance.

Gene and Roman had a great rapport, partly as a result of their similar backgrounds: they were both survivors from the Krakôw ghetto. Gene told us that Roman, being very small, had been able to squeeze through cracks in the ghetto walls to get food and, as children do, had turned these expeditions into a dangerous game of hide-and-seek with the German guards. Roman's life was saved by his father, who paid for him to live with a Catholic family outside the ghetto and, as a result, he evaded the Nazi death squads that rounded up Jews, including his parents, for extermination in Auschwitz.

Gene had met up with Roman in 1963 at the New York Film Festival, where Roman's first feature film, *Knife In The Water*, was being screened. The following year the film was nominated by the American Academy of Motion Pictures Arts and Sciences for an Oscar in the Best Foreign Film category. While waiting to go to Los Angeles for the awards ceremony, Polanski was living in Paris and, in early 1964, Gene rang him and convinced him that he should move to London. London was the "happening" place, he said, and the British film industry would snap him up. Roman did not need a great deal of persuading: he was broke and, as well as offering board and lodging, Gene even paid his air fare.

We drove out to Heathrow to form a welcome committee. Although Polanski was thirty years of age, my first impression was of a tiny, tousle-haired boy swimming inside a vastly oversized coat: a snapshot of the bereft, post-war child refugee. It was hard to believe that such a waif could have made *Knife In The Water*, which I considered a very grown-up film.

It didn't take very long, however, for me to discover that, diminutive though he might be, Roman Polanski was a rather frightening character. He was extremely egotistical and took offense easily; it was common for him to fly into rages if he thought he was being slighted or obstructed. It was assumed in our set that his personality must have been damaged by his wartime experiences, but I had no idea whether that was true or not because he never spoke about the war; he regarded his past as irrelevant to his career and, therefore, unimportant.

Somewhere in his psyche, however, he harboured a lust for revenge, not against the Nazis who had murdered his family, but against women. The main target of his anger was his ex-wife, the Polish actress Basia Kwiatkowska, who had run off with a German actor and left him poverty-stricken while he was struggling to complete *Knife In The Water*. Scores of young women ultimately paid a high price for Basia's betrayal.

I was still doing post-production work on *Trois étoiles* in Paris and, whenever I flew to London, I would meet Polanski at Gene's apartment or at the Ad Lib, the most exclusive disco in the West End. Surrounded by an entourage of gorgeous young girls and impressionable male hangers-on, he always greeted me with the same line: "Ah, Suzanna - the first beautiful girl I met in London!"

One thing that amazed me was that on his arrival he hadn't been able to speak the language at all, yet within weeks his English was good enough to insult people with a string of vivid Anglo-Saxon expletives. He was the centre of attention wherever he went and people were curious to know whether he was a genius or just a one-movie wonder.

Roman hadn't won the Oscar in Los Angeles - it went to Fellini, his idol - but even being nominated for an award by this august body had brought him international recognition. While his fascination for many people was based on his radical film-making ideas, it was also true that the Polanski Culture Club had strong undertones of sex and drugs.

I bumped into Roman again in Cannes that May. He was with Michael Klinger, whom I also knew fairly well. Michael was producing *The Pleasure Girls*, a film I was about to make with Klaus Kinski, Francesca Annis and Ian McShane. Roman himself was signing a deal with Klinger to make his first film in England, *Repulsion*, and I was very keen to land the part of Carol. I was beginning to be looked on as a cool Grace Kelly-type and the aspect of Carol's sexual repression appealed to me greatly.

I discussed the role with Polanski, and Klinger also raised my name with him. I was definitely in the running for the part, but there was a big - and, for me, insurmountable - problem: it was obvious that Polanski wanted to have sex with me. He didn't attempt to hide the fact that this was nothing to do with romance; it was strictly business. He told me he could never work with anyone he had not had sex with and the fact that his first leading lady in Poland had been his wife seemed to support this assertion.

I don't know whether this applied to males as well, but at least one actor who went to his office for a casting ended up as the victim of some bizarre sado-masochistic game. Over lunch, Polanski told me that he had just left the actor, whom he named, trussed up like a chicken, with a carrot stuck in a delicate part of his anatomy. What a charmer!

Halfway through the filming of *Repulsion* at Twickenham Studios, I went to dinner with Andy Braunsberg, Polanski and Catherine Deneuve, who had been cast as Carol. Catherine had been launched by her lover Roger Vadim as "the new Bardot" and was clearly not accustomed to the sort of crude abuse that Polanski dished out on the set every day. She sat in a corner, looking subdued. I took her to one side and asked her what was wrong and she told me that Roman had forbidden her to go to Paris for the weekend. She had just given birth to a son by Vadim and was missing her baby.

They weren't even shooting that weekend, so I asked him why he was treating her this way.

"Suzanna," he said in a voice heavy with sarcasm, "do not interfere with things you know nothing about. If Catherine doesn't get sex for the whole picture, she will be sexually frustrated enough to give me the performance I want - not that this is something you would understand, of course."

I looked down, my face burning.

"Now come on, Suzanna," said Polanski, "see if you can find me a pretty actress who will come and have fun - (he looked hard at me) - since you won't."

I hated being bullied in this way and, to make matters worse, Andy, who had been a good friend of mine, sided with Polanski. He was hankering to produce his movies (an ambition he later achieved) and refused to stand up for me.

"For God's sake, Suzanna, it's not much to ask," he hissed. "Please, call a few friends for Roman."

I'd never seen Andy like this before; in a few months, he'd changed from a nice, quiet guy into a hustler. It was 12.30 at night; who could I possibly ask who would go for this sort of thing? If I'd received a call like this, I'd tell whoever it was to take a hike. I thought for a moment, then called a number.

"Hello. I'm sorry to call so late. Could I speak to Jackie Bisset? Oh, hi! It's Suzanna Leigh. Look, I don't know if you'd be interested, but I'm in a restaurant with Roman Polanski and a few friends and I wondered if you'd like to come over. I'm not sure what exactly is on offer, but Roman said, 'Ask some pretty girls' and I thought of you."

I hoped she would not take offense.

Far from telling me to take a hike, she said: "Sure, thanks a lot for calling, Suzanna. Where are you? Do I need to get dressed up or will jeans do?"

"No, jeans are fine."

I left the restaurant shortly after Jackie arrived and I have no idea whether she succumbed to Polanski's advances that night, or on any other, but, it's perhaps indicative that she never worked for him. Either way, I've always had an enormous amount of respect for her as an artist.

I drove home to Belgravia feeling rather depressed about the incident in the restaurant and wondering how many other directors and the like would drop me because I was not prepared to sleep with them. It was distressing to think that a director like Polanski would abuse his power in order to pressure me into having sex.

I later saw the uncut version of *Repulsion* and was so sickened by the film's violent, psycho-sexual theme that I was relieved I hadn't got the part. Fortunately, film-goers were spared some of the most disgusting scenes, which were left on the cutting-room floor.

At home, I found a note on the table inviting me to lunch with a very good friend of mine, George Sidney, who was a far more accomplished director than Roman Polanski. He'd made *Pal Joey* and *Kiss Me Kate* and his most recent film was *Viva Las Vegas*, with Elvis Presley and Ann-Margret.

The other guests at lunch would include David Niven Jr, Belinda Wright, an actress, and Roderick Mann, an important show-business journalist. This cheered me up. I reminded myself that comedy was my *metier* and there would be plenty of films that were right for me, films that did not revel in the dark side of life.

Over lunch George talked about making *Viva Las Vegas*.

"Elvis is underestimated as an actor," he said. "He's a very intelligent young man. You'd like him Suzanna. It would be really good for you to make a film with him."

No one at the table, George included, knew that I was keeping a secret that fitted in perfectly with that scenario. One night a short time earlier all of my dreams had unexpectedly slotted into place.

Chapter 8

Hal Wallis Presents . . .

*"I've always believed that if you want something badly enough,
you should go all out for it, no matter what the odds."*

Rita Hayworth, *American actress*

WHILE I was in Paris in March 1964, I had read in the papers that the Hollywood producer Hal Wallis was about to sign an English actress, Samantha Eggar. I immediately rang Roy in London.

"But he can't! He hasn't met me yet!"

Oh, the conceit of youth!

"You have to get me an appointment with Hal Wallis. He has to see me!"

"I'll try, darling, but if I can't, he's staying in the Oliver Messel suite at the Dorchester. Why not gatecrash?"

"I'll be on a plane this afternoon."

"I'll try to let him know."

I went to see Maurice.

"Oh, cherie! Je suis malade! Je suis trop fatigue. Est-que c'est possible pour moi a dormir ce soir?"

"Ah, mon petit monstre!"

"Little Monster" was my nickname, coined by the film crew because I had thrown a moody one day and behaved like a real *petit monstre* - I remember it well - and the next thing I knew they were walking around with crocodile T-shirts bearing my photograph.

"Absolutment!" Maurice said. *"Dormez-bien!"*

I'd never asked for time off before. I shot to the airport, got on the first plane to London and jumped in a taxi to the Dorchester.

50

Knowing which suite Hal Wallis was staying in, I sneaked up to his floor utterly determined to make the most of this opportunity. I knocked on the door. As luck would have it, he was alone.

"Hello?"

The producer of *Casablanca* and *The Maltese Falcon* was somewhat disconcerted by my unannounced appearance.

"Mr Wallis! Here I am! The star you've been looking for."

Did I really say this? Yes, I'm afraid I did.

"What?"

"My name is Suzanna Leigh, I'm talented, I'm funny, I want to be a big star and I'm the girl you've been looking for!"

Just writing this makes me blush. The thought of doing anything like that nowadays is unthinkable - having said that, any top producer would have legions of people to bar the way.

"Come in, come in."

He had not seen anything like this for quite some time and, instead of calling Security, he invited me to sit down. He was a thick-set man of about sixty-five, but looking younger.

I breezed in and started chatting away, being as bubbly as I could. He asked me questions, studying me closely as I answered. Suddenly, his face lit up.

"You're the du Barry girl!" he exclaimed.

After that, I hardly felt nervous at all. This was the chance I'd been waiting for. In the middle of our conversation, the telephone rang. He picked it up, still looking at me, saying to whoever it was on the other end: "I've found her... no, not her... it's another one - (looking at me) - what's your name again?"

"Suzanna Leigh."

Just like that. I couldn't believe it.

The phone call had been from Hal's partner, Joe Hazen, and we talked contracts.

"Non-exclusive, of course," I said, only because I couldn't think of anything else to say. Wasn't that what everyone asked for in Hollywood? I didn't really know.

"Non-exclusive. Okay."

I was totally flabbergasted. Maybe he was tired of searching: he later told me he'd been looking for six months for someone to take over from Shirley MacLaine, whose contract was about to expire. I'd knocked on the door and that was it. It happened just like that.

"My sister Minna is in town," he said. Minna Wallis was famous as the she-dragon of Hollywood.

"We're all going out to dinner. You'll come, of course?"

"Oh, I'm so sorry. I'd love to, but I must fly back to Paris tonight. I'm working over there. I have my own TV series."

Here I was trying to impress this famous impresario, the man who had discovered Shirley MacLaine and Kirk Douglas, and didn't he have Elvis under contract, too? The moment the words were out of my mouth I could feel it wasn't such a clever line and I got up to leave.

The outer door opened and I heard Samantha Eggar's voice. She'd arrived with her agent to sign her contract, or so it seemed. I stared out of the window, thinking, "Ouch!", while Hal Wallis walked out to meet them and bluntly informed Samantha that he'd found someone else.

Hal and I said our goodbyes and I flew down to the hotel lobby to ring Roy and tell him the whole story.

"This is it! I mean, Hal Wallis! Oh, my God! I really think I'm going to faint. It's just so huge! Oh, Roy, is it possible to be this happy?"

I could almost hear Nanny's voice in my head, saying, "We mustn't get too exited, otherwise it will all end in tears."

"Look, stay calm," Roy advised. "I'll meet you in Les A. and we'll talk it over. I'll be there in a minute."

I walked down to Les Ambassadeurs, or should I say I floated; I danced, I sang, I laughed.

"Now, darling," said Roy over a G&T, "I don't want you to get too exited. After all, we haven't actually signed anything."

I ran through everything once more and reminded Roy that Wallis had told Joe Hazen that he'd found her, meaning me. And he'd told Samantha Eggar that he'd met the girl he was looking for, also meaning me. Only then was Roy caught up in the excitement. He ordered another G&T.

"Look, my darling, we'd better wait and see what kind of contract he offers; he's known to be mean. He'll want to know how much you got paid for the French Game (our little name for *Trois étoiles*). The trouble with starting on low money is that they try to keep you low as long as possible."

"I don't care if he pays me nothing, just picks up my hotel and car bills, as long as he gives me the contract. Why don't we do it that way?"

Roy said slowly: "Marilyn Monroe used to say that sort of thing when she started out. 'I'm not interested in money, I just want to be wonderful' - and wonderful she was; every man in the world dreamed of her at night, but none of them paid her rent. When she died, she left unpaid taxes totalling $900,000.

"Let me deal with the business side. Your mother will have to sign the contract anyway. Hopefully, there won't be a problem."

At the airport, Roy gave me a big hug and said: "You are so wonderful, darling. I'm proud to be your agent and friend."

I loved that man for being with me for all those years and I was going to make it up to him once we got to Hollywood. I arrived very late that night and slipped into my hotel room, but I could not sleep a wink. Two days later it was in the Parisian papers that I had signed to Hal Wallis.

"But how could he have seen you?" asked Maurice. "You have been here all the time."

"I guess he must have seen my photograph."

 Well, he did too...

I went back to work, knowing that my life was about to change dramatically, but nothing that wasn't in accordance with the immutable law of the Sixties: it was a time of change for just about everything connected with music, fashion, politics sexual attitudes and, of course, the movies. A revolution was sweeping the British film industry, spearheaded by director Lindsay Anderson and his "Free Cinema" slogan. As he later said: "I was to make people, ordinary people, not just top people, feel their dignity and importance."

Tony Richardson, director of John Osborne's eponymous kitchen-sink drama *Look Back In Anger*, explained: "The image speaks. No film can be too personal. Style means attitude; attitude means style." "Free Cinema" is a broad term, but in essence it meant that directors were given the freedom by the film companies to make intensely personal statements about subjects that were previously sacrosanct. This new license was first perceived in Karel Reisz's *We Are The Lambeth Boys*, a film riddled with class consciousness: so-called socially superior guys and girls go "slumming it" in lower-class jazz clubs. Now hadn't I done that a year or so earlier with Blair and Jeremy?

The cinema had been a place of dreams, where working-class people could briefly escape the drudgery of everyday life. Working-class voices, once heard only as stereotypes in films, were now raised in anger against the Establishment. The new social realism was being loudly proclaimed in Cockney and other regional accents, while the grandiose Lady-of-the-Manor and the stiff-upper-lipped Guards Officer were permissible only as caricatures.

Tony Richardson took the New Wave even further with *The Loneliness Of The Long Distance Runner* and then combined with Karel Reisz on *Saturday Night And Sunday Morning*. In France, François Truffaut (*Les Quatre Cent Coups*) and Jean-Luc Godard (*A Bout de Soufflé* - or *Breathless*) were making films of equal power, but with distinctively Gallic twists, while in Italy Federico Fellini unleashed his scathingly satirical exposé of modern Roman high society, *La Dolce Vita*.

Although I welcomed the changes, I'd already had it up to my teeth with kitchen sinks in childhood. My heroes were not Tom Courtenay or Albert Finney; it was mean-but-magnificent Steve McQueen for me - Hollywood's "Dream Machine" still sounded as good as ever to my ears. Besides, I liked the idea of the studio system, so much reviled by my peers as destroying originality and creativity. It promised me the chance to be part of a great family, which was how many stars had described being under contract to one or other of the big Hollywood studios.

It was ironic that, a little later that year, the pendulum of the Class Thing swung so far that it nearly knocked me over. I was doing a screen test for *Sands Of The Kalahari* in London and, just before we were due to start, I heard Cy Endfield, the writer of the film, and Stanley Baker, the lead actor, joking in that deadly serious way that makes you want to do anything but laugh. They were speaking to each other in exaggeratedly upper-class English accents.

"Here comes m'lady."

"Oh yes, Lady La-di-da."

"Should we bow, old boy?"

"Absolutely!"

I looked around, thinking they must be referring to somebody walking behind me. Then I realised it was me they were sending up, even though I did not speak in those cut-glass tones. Nigel Davenport, the actor I was testing with, told me not to be put off; I was as much a self-made person as any of them and they, as actors, should have known that things were not always as they seemed.

On one of my trips home my mother had told me that, if I was going to be a film star, I'd better start getting some of the things to go with it, so I bought a full-length mink coat, three jackets and a chinchilla wrap from her. I was also allowed to move into The Cottage, the mews house my mother had built at 42 Cadogan Lane. Alan made some beautiful evening dresses for me and, of course, I bought jewellery, including some of Yvonne's expensive pieces from my mother. It wasn't any wonder that the press thought I was an heiress.

I also bought an MG, silver and really gorgeous. The MG people gave me a special deal because one of their cars had starred in the French series. I paid them only ten per cent of the retail price, although, of course, the press didn't know that. When I was travelling, I hardly ever had to pay, either: a photograph of me smiling on the steps of an airline guaranteed me a free ticket. I was also recognised in restaurants and rarely presented with a bill. I was high as a kite on life and, at night, I got on my knees to tell Jesus what fun I'd had and how wonderful he was to let all these things happen to me.

In the autumn of 1964 I began shooting *The Pleasure Girls*, a portmanteau film about four girls sharing a house in Sixties London. It was cast by Irene Lambe, now a major casting director who says that I was the first person she ever cast in a picture - "And didn't she do well?" Harry Fine, whom I'd met when he was producing *The Sentimental Agent*, was producing the picture for Compton Films. He was a sweetheart and it was always nice to be asked back; you knew you must be doing something right. Gerry O'Hara, the director, had also written the script.

Having just spent months almost entirely with "the boys" on *Trois étoiles*, I got on much better with the production team than with the other actresses, Francesca Annis, Anneke Wills and Rosemary Nicols. I tried to warm to everyone, but I always felt as though I wasn't one of them. Perhaps it was due to the fact that many of my co-stars had had to waitress their way through drama school and the experience was still fresh in their minds. As I was picked up at the end of each day's shooting in an Austin Healey or Jaguar, it was the-rich-girl-slumming-it syndrome as far as they were concerned.

Compton Films also got me to do lots of publicity for the film because of my "new Grace Kelly" tag, which was great as tags go, but it did not help me to bond with the other actresses. My part is that of Dee Wells, a gold-digging bitch with a heart of gold who goes out with a gangster, Nico Drax, played by Klaus Kinski, the German actor who already specialised in tough-guy roles. While the other girls declare that they want to marry for love, Dee says she'll only marry for love and money.

The situation wasn't improved by a press release which confirmed my "privileged" status as a rich girl. "Brought up in an atmosphere of wealth and luxury," it gushed, "Suzanna admits that she is fortunate in being able to afford all the trimmings required by stardom. At nineteen, she already possesses those envied symbols of film success - the mink coat and the sports car."

If that rubbish hadn't already alienated them, it went on to quote me as saying: "People have always regarded me as a gold-digger, rather like the role I play in *The Pleasure Girls*. For some reason, blondes always suffer from this kind of reputation and the fact that I number several very wealthy young men among my friends doesn't help me very much, I'm afraid."

As Nigel Davenport had said, things were not always what they seemed.

There seems to be an unwritten law in the world of film-making that your worst scene, or at least the scene that you are going to find the trickiest, is always the first shot on the first day of filming. That's certainly how it happened in this picture. I had only just been introduced to Klaus of the "Strange Eyes" and there I was in a house in Earls Court, sitting on a plinth with nothing on but a bikini bottom, with a magazine strategically placed to cover my breasts.

Roy told me to play it as though I did this sort of thing every day and Harry very sweetly closed the set for me, so there were only the cameraman, Michael Reed, and a couple of crew members around. I'm not sure whether it was mandatory or not, but when a topless scene was shot in the early Sixties, the make-up artist would always stick Elastoplast over the "pink bits". I can't think of anything sillier than sitting there trying to act naturally with sticking plaster taped over your nipples.

I had been shooting for only three days when I got a call from Hal Wallis. He wanted me to do a screen test for my first picture for him, *Boeing-Boeing*, with Tony Curtis and Jerry Lewis. He told me that American Equity demanded that at least ten girls should be tested for the role.

"I'll call you in a few days to let you know more."

I put the phone down in a daze. I was going to be in a film with Tony Curtis. *Tony Curtis*! Tony was a huge star - a superstar. Half of the male population of England had been walking around with his slicked-back hairstyle a few years earlier. I stood there, day-dreaming about what I'd just heard.

The test was to take place in a month or so and, in the meantime, I was instructed to fly to Paris to meet Edith Head, chief designer of Paramount Pictures, a legendary Hollywood figure who was rumoured to use Oscar statuettes as door-stops. We were to look at designs and also have fittings for my costume for the location shooting, which would take place in - yes, you've guessed it - Paris! I was somewhere higher than Cloud Nine when I rang Alan Sievewright to tell him the good news. He was very excited for me.

"Edith Head is one of the greats, darling," he said. "She can glamourise anyone. She's worked with Grace Kelly, Dorothy Lamour and Bette Davis. And she made Gloria Swanson's clothes for *Sunset Boulevard*. You are going to look wonderful."

Roy and I went to check out the stage version of *Boeing-Boeing*, which had been playing to packed houses in the West End for three years, with David Tomlinson in the lead. I was to play Vicky Hawkins, an English air hostess, and was delighted with the role: it would give me a real chance to sparkle as a comedienne.

Then I asked Harry Fine if I could slip out of the country for a few days to attend the wedding celebrations of Princess Nezha in Rabat.

The sheik's spectacular "variety show" in the desert had apparently failed to impress and she was marrying M. Ahmed Osman, a French diplomat. My invitation covered the whole of the wedding, an affair that extended over eight days, but, as I was in the middle of shooting, I had to explain to Lala Nezha that the producer would not let me have more than six days off. What Harry actually said was: "That's enough for anyone's wedding. I don't care who they are", but I didn't tell Nezha that.

At the pink palace, I bathed in goat's milk and, dressed in a shocking-pink Channel suit, mingled with heads of state and dignitaries from all over the globe. Lala's bridal dress was a white sari, with a veil draped around her face. On one of her hands was a diamond, allegedly from King Solomon's Mines, that was so big she couldn't bend her finger.

Seated on silk cushions on a raised, canopied platform, she looked every inch the beautiful eastern princess, though there was a sadness in her eyes. At least she had experienced more riotous fun in the previous few years than any of her predecessors had in a lifetime.

Back in London, Hal Wallis called to say that the French scenes of *Boeing-Boeing* had been postponed until early in the New Year, so the costume fittings would have to wait. He asked how things were going on *The Pleasure Girls*, a title he hated.

I laughed.

"Don't worry - it's not as bad as it sounds."

"Better not be - you're to be my bright new star."

He told me that Sally Nichols of Paramount would be doing most of the work on my contract, which I still had not seen. "You'll be half mine and half Paramount's," Hal said. "They're a good bunch to work with. The screen test for *Boeing-Boeing* will be directed by Lewis Gilbert. He's a fine English director and, as I haven't seen you on screen, I want you to look good. Keep well, little girl, and have a good holiday."

"Oh yes, Happy Christmas, Hal." I said and phoned Roy with the news.

On the day of the test I was taken to the studios and made up. There were about ten actresses, including some well-known faces, all excited because this was a Hollywood film. Usually, there seemed to be some catty girl who, just before I went into the interview, would say something like, "Good luck - shame about the legs, though", or some similar line to put me off. As I was always rather proud of my legs, I spent a lot of time at interviews, or screen tests, crossing and uncrossing them. But this was different.

Lewis Gilbert was the director of *Carve Her Name With Pride* (Roy's favourite film) and *The Good Die Young* (mine), as well as *Reach For The Sky*, the film that Danny Angel had produced.

As we began the test, Lewis said: "Well, let's see what you've got. You're the one, I believe."

"Hopefully," I replied.

Lewis Gilbert was a lovely man to work with, kind and interested in putting my best points across. We spent a while talking about how he wanted to shoot the scene and then we shot it: one take and one for the gate. Hal phoned to say how pleased and delighted he was with the test and told me I had all the signs of a star. Beautiful, too, he said.

"I don't think so," I laughed.

"Oh, you're one of those girls who don't think they're pretty. Well, don't worry, Hollywood has a whole lot like you. You'll be in good company."

At nineteen, I had never really thought of myself as being particularly pretty; rather fat-faced, I thought. In fact, I was a little under eight stone, but because the screen puts on ten pounds I always watched what I ate. Having said that, I could dance all night and lose six pounds, so dieting was fun. I loved everything about my life at that time.

On December 11, 1964, I took Roy to Paris to have fun for a few days and we had dinner with his friend Georges Simenon, author of *The Blue Room* and creator of Inspector Maigret. We had a fabulous and funny evening telling stories - I told the one about Maurice putting a Coca-Cola bottle down his pants, then asking me for a dance - was I impressed! - and about a wealthy playboy from Caracas who, as we were introduced, started to eat his champagne glass.

Georges told us that he wrote all his books in about eighteen days while shut away on his own in the mountains of Switzerland, with all his notes scribbled down on hundreds of tiny bits of paper.

It was a marvellous night and, when the conversation inevitably turned to my plans, I told Roy that I thanked God for him.

"Without you, I think the floodgates of hell would fall down on me."

"That, darling, is a mixed metaphor."

He laughed.

We flew back to London, having exhausted the shops. Roy rang me the following morning, but I asked him to call back later because I was still sleepy.

"Of course, darling," he said, as understanding as ever. "I'll phone back at lunch-time."

From top left: My Grandmother and Daddy in her garden - early 20's, Daddy as a little boy, my mother standing by one of my fathers cars, that he loved so much - 1920's, "The Lodge" my parents country house in Caversham, Daddy sorting out a dispute between 'Joey' the pig and one of the dogs - late 30's, Daddy, my brother and I - that swimsuit was made of wool - on holiday. 1948

Left: Bruce, the Great Dane - he of the cream cake scandal - and my Mother on the sea front at Brighton. Not far from her flat at Brunswick Square which she sold to Gladys Cooper. - 1953

Right: My doll and I. - 1954

Apparently this photograph of me hung in a 'photographer' shop window, in Reading, with the words - This is what you fought for boys - as a greeting to the solders coming back from prison of war camps in the Far East. - 1947

Left: Pretending to be a film star dark glasses and 'the look' on the steps of the Casino in Monaco. - 1957

Right: My Mother and Aunt Sally at the night club 'The Orchid Room' that she had a stake in. - 1953

Here I am dreaming of those bright lights. My first studio shots, - 1957/8

Who's the winner on the left? Yes, you've guessed Michael Winner - he'd been asked to move out of shot three times. Left to right: My Brother Eric, Uncle Jack, my mother, me and Jack Hylton's sister Dolly Hylton. - 1959

My Godmother, Vivien Leigh, on the set of "GONE WITH THE WIND". Viviens help and encouragement meant so much to me at the beginning of my career. - 1939

Below, photographs from Cornel Lucas's studio in Flood Street. Very 'grown up' I tried for the part of 'LOLITA', but was told I was to young. - 1959

With Helen Goss - my drama coach - in Terrance Rattengan's "OSCAR WILDE". If you even breathed you missed me. - 1959

The premiere of "EXODUS" and unaware of the skirmish between Otto Preminger and myself. Bill Bernside a writer friend of my Mothers, attempts to introduce us to each other. - 1961

My first staring role in "BOMB IN THE HIGH STREET" opposite Ronald Howard, son of Leslie - of "GONE WITH THE WIND" fame. It isn't purely coincidental that I have the Jean Simmons look, lots of work went into those cheek bones. - 1961

Left: Great excitement. My photograph on the wall of the illustrious Elstree, which was then one of the two great British Studios. - 1963

Below: Roger Moore star of "THE SAINT" who turned out to be even nicer than I'd hoped. - 1963

Top: MY FRENCH YEARS
The famous Maurice Regimay-director extraordinaire - what can I say, the man has style. - 1963

Middle: C'est mois in my M.G. in front of one of the many vineyards which featured so much in my French T.V.Series. - 1963/4

Right: Vivian Cox our producer of "TROIS -ETOILE" In his best gastronomic style, with my agent Roy, in the background, preparing himself to go into battle on my behalf.

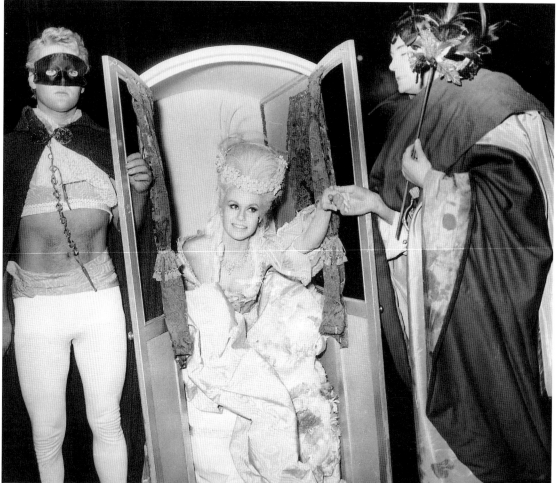

*I was the first person carried though the streets of London, since the 1700's.
Alain Sevewright opening the door of the sidan chair.*

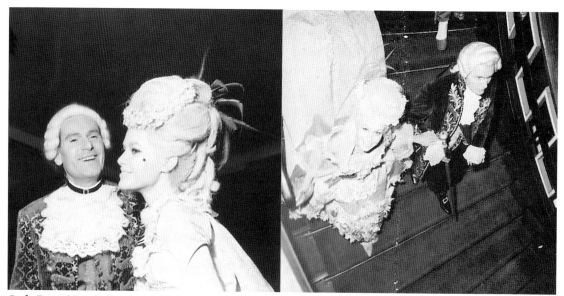

*Left: David Jacobs-lawyer and the best friend a girl can have - greeting me when I arrived
at the Grosvenor House Hotel in Park Lane. Right: Ian Heath on my arm.*

Movies and real life often merge into each other.

The first days shooting on a film are always a tricky, and this sure was.

"THE PLEASURE GIRLS" left to right: Francesa Annis - we were at school together - Ian McShane and next to me Klaus Kinski my gangster boyfriend in the film. - 1964

Left: Me at my most Regal in the dining room of my mothers house at 79 Cadogan Place. This room became the focal point of international stars, directors and writers, the likes of David Niven, George Sydney and David Hemmings. - 1963/4

Above: A Charity Ball in the Dorchesrter Hotel: Front, Left to Right. Joel Lerner, myself and Andrew Braunsberg. Rear, Left to Right: Anthony Blond, Vicky Hodge, Gilbert Lloyd and Sally Hodge. - 1963/4

Two beginners; In the springtime of our careers-Patrick Lichfield cousin to the Queen - he went on to become one of Englands finest photographers. - 1963

Busily packing in my London house, getting ready. The press made a lot of me going.

At last I'm off to Hollywood to make my first movie. - 1965

This was in a lot of European magazines, very french. - 1965

The only way Paramount could make me stand out a little more was for the nightdress to be an Edith Head special. I could have gone out to dinner in that nightdress. Also, with with me, Cristerna Smithner - in the middle - and Danny Saval with Three Smart Girls. Studio photo. - 1965

The main publicity shot of the picture that had all of us together.

Hal Wallis the intimidatingly powerful producer - interestingly enough Elvis held the power in their relationship - known as 'The Star Maker', on the set of Paradise Hawaiian Style, or 'Uncle Hal' to me -"I've been called a lot of things but never that."- was the producer that both Elvis and I were under contract to. - 1965

Insert: Elvis and I - the medallion I'm wearing he loved so much, he recreated the motif on one of his stage suits.

MY HOLLYWOOD DREAM HAD BECOME A REALITY.

Elvis and I are wearing our own clothes for this shot.

Elvis taking the punch full on the chin from Red, one of his 'boys', and he didn't hold back. As you can see from my face.

Left: Although I never did wear this in the film they used it a lot on front of house stuff. - 1966
Below: James Shigeta and I - remember him in FLOWER DRUM SONG - we worked well together, and got on. - 1965

Chapter 9

Heartache

"In youth we learn, in age we understand."

Marie Eschenback, *Australian writer*

AT 12.20pm on December 15, 1964, Roy Montgomery suffered a heart attack and died. He was found lying on his *chaise longue* at Draycott Avenue, telephone in hand.

"I wonder who he'd been about to call?" my mother mused.

I felt like a child who had been running happily along a beach and had crashed into a sheet of glass. I didn't see it, there was no warning, it came from nowhere. For weeks, I was confused, unsure, in shock.

Using the phone was easily the worst part because Roy and I had spoken to each other almost every day for years. For many months, I would automatically dial his number before I remembered that he was dead and then the raw pain would start. I couldn't cry for a long time, either; it was all just too much.

I went to see Roy laid out in the funeral parlor in Brompton Road. I knew he had drunk a lot, but thinking about it now the smoking must have contributed to his heart attack. He looked so much younger than his fifty years. I held his hand and promised him that all the things I would do in Hollywood he would do as well because he would be there in my heart.

My mother held the wake, which was very nice of her, and many people came. Helen cried nearly all that day - I felt so sorry for her that I bought her a puppy, a miniature apricot poodle. Roy had told me over the years how much they had both loved Coco, their coffee-coloured, standard poodle, so I thought Helen would love something live around the house, but I was mistaken.

A few weeks later, when I went to visit her late one evening, I heard a rustling noise from the dustbins just before I rang her bell. I investigated and there was the puppy. I took her home and named her Kimsham, which means "Little One" in Russian. I told her she was only there until I found a nice home for her, but she was still with me seven years later.

I missed Roy dreadfully. He had been my mentor, my agent and a buffer against my mother. I'd always put a lot of her weirdness down to the menopause and my Aunt Sally confirmed that my mother had given birth to me on the cusp of the change. Whatever the reason, she medicated herself daily with Krug champagne and ended each evening with a couple of "yellow perils" - Nembutal sleeping tablets.

I rejuvenated myself by going down to a health farm, which was, and still is, my idea of bliss, then headed for some skiing in St Moritz. Almost immediately, I bumped into Andy Braunsberg, who had abandoned the banking aspirations of his lovely German-Jewish parents and thrown in his lot with Roman Polanski, a move that could only end in disaster.

Andy invited me to a small dinner party with Brigitte Bardot and her new husband, the German playboy Gunther Sachs, who were spending their honeymoon just outside St Moritz in an alpine chalet the size of a Bavarian hunting lodge. We gathered in a vast, oak-paneled drawing room, complete with candelabras and minstrel's gallery, while live Bambis frolicked on the snow-covered lawn.

Only one thing was missing: Brigitte Bardot.

An hour passed.

We chatted with Gunther Sachs over champagne, but Brigitte remained aloof and unseen upstairs. After two hours we adjourned to the dining room and ate the first course.

Still no Brigitte.

An hour later word passed around that she was making her entrance. We all trooped back into the drawing room and there, in the twinkling lights of a huge Christmas tree, was Brigitte, descending the grand staircase one elegant step at time. She was wearing a long black dress, slit at the sides, with cascades of golden hair tumbling on to her shoulders. Here was the quintessential superstar in person, the personification of The Look that had captivated women everywhere.

She was instantly forgiven for being three hours late for dinner.

I reminded her of our meeting in St Tropez, but made the mistake of speaking in English. I was dismissed with a toss of those golden curls and a sneer of those famous French lips. To speak English in Ms Bardot's presence was the ultimate faux pas. I spent the rest of the evening stumbling along in French.

When I got back to London, my mother summoned me over to her house to talk about my contract with Hal Wallis and Paramount Pictures. On the way to Cadogan Place, I was a mass of jelly. She held all the cards - I was still only nineteen and I didn't know what deal Roy and she had arranged, or if she had changed it since his death. David Jacobs, my lawyer, was away, so I couldn't get any legal advice. Very few people were aware of my odd relationship with my mother. My friends never saw her dark side and thought she was marvellous. I was ashamed and embarrassed and thought it must be all my fault.

I handed her some presents I had bought in Switzerland and gave her a big hug, hoping as always that she'd respond the way I wanted. Surprisingly, she did; she put her arm through mine as we walked through to the kitchen.

"Well, I saw Sally at Paramount and thrashed out the deal for you," she said.

"Oh, thank you, Mummy!"

"It was hard work and touch-and-go at one point as to whether they wanted you at all. You can't expect your mother to do all that for nothing."

"No, of course not," I mumbled.

She handed me a contract. At first, I thought it was the one between me and Paramount, but slowly I realised that it was between her and me, appointing her as my manager, for which she would take sixty percent of my earnings.

I looked up.

"I'll have to take this home," I said. "It's a lot to think about."

"What's there to think about? I'm your mother, aren't I? Just sign it and then you can get going - I'm sure you've got a party to go to."

It didn't take a mathematician to work out that if I gave her sixty per cent, paid another ten per cent to an agent (and I'd soon be needing one), paid my press agent and the tax man, I would walk away with five per cent if I was lucky.

"I want to give you something, Mummy," I said, "but I can't sign this."

A big row ensued and I stormed out, praying that she'd already signed the contract with Paramount. I cried all the way back to The Cottage.

The small amount of money she could earn from me was nothing compared with what she already had in huge property investments. Why couldn't she just love me and be a real mother? I needed someone I could love and have fun with, or just trust. I cried even more thinking about Roy, but, looking back, it was the first time I had ever defied my mother.

Through the years, our relationship got steadily worse, but after that night she never mentioned the contract again. She did, however, ask me to pay her back all the money I had cost her since I was born. This I did over a period of years, even though some of the bills she handed me were ludicrous.

She wasted a lot of her time dreaming up ways of making my life difficult. Once, I was at a really big premiere - very royal, lots of fans - and, when I came out of the theatre, she was behind the barricades, dressed as a tramp and calling out my name. She had even blacked out a tooth or two to make her disguise more realistic. Shaking like a leaf, I jumped into the studio's Rolls-Royce and was driven away.

With hindsight, that episode might sound amusing, but at the time it was a nightmare. It was no good suggesting she saw a psychiatrist because she thought she was completely sane and, anyway, her money gave her an immunity that wasn't available to lesser mortals.

She topped that attempt to ridicule me by sending the drug squad around to my home with a search warrant. They found no drugs and apologised for the intrusion, saying they had to follow up tip-offs. I asked them if the informant had been from a woman with a Northern accent.

"Yes, do you know her?"

That was my mother, all right.

I would have found the mother-daughter situation even more intolerable if I hadn't been going back to Paris to work. In early February 1965 I met up with Tony Curtis, Jerry Lewis and Christiane Schmidtner at London airport. Dany Saval, the fourth member of the cast of *Boeing-Boeing*, was already in Paris and we were flying there to start shooting the location scenes of my first Hollywood movie.

Tony Curtis was with his latest wife, the young German actress Christine Kaufmann, who was dressed like a school-girl right down to white, knee-length socks. Once we were airborne, I was chatting with Christiane Schmidtner about the film she had just made in the States, *Ship Of Fools* (sadly, Vivien Leigh's last film), when Tony Curtis came over to speak to us.

"Listen, kiddos," he said. "We'll be landing soon, so this is the way it's going to be: I get off first, then you count to thirty and follow. Okay?"

I didn't understand what he was talking about, so I must have looked a bit vague.

"There'll be a lot of fans out there for me," he explained. "So I get off first and you follow. Right?"

"Oh, right," I said. "Sorry - of course there's bound to be."

Tony Curtis going to Paris to make a film; sure there'd be fans.

Jerry Lewis, who was sitting behind us, smiled at me and I smiled back. I knew that he was truly adored by the French and I wondered if he knew it. They looked upon him as a genius of comedy, the American Jacques Tati. We landed and, as planned, Tony got off the plane first. Then we all counted in unison... 29... 30...

"Let's go," we said and, laughing, started down the stairs.

Suddenly, people were rushing forward from the loosely arranged barriers, yelling excitedly. But Tony Curtis was already at the terminal and the crowds were running towards US! Now I could hear that they were shouting, "JERRY LEWIS, JERRY LEWIS", and, as *Trois étoiles* had just opened in France, there were a few calls of "Suzanna Leigh".

I have no idea whether this incident soured things between Tony and Jerry, but I do know that, off camera, they disliked each other as much as they do in the film. There were huge arguments about who should receive top billing in the credits, a problem which was resolved by printing their names on a rotating disc so that neither name could be said to be on top of the other.

My suite at the Ritz was everything I had imagined: three grand, old-fashioned rooms with Louis Quinze furniture, oil paintings and tapestries on the walls, huge displays of fresh flowers every day and, best of all, a pink-marbled bathroom. It had taken Hemingway twenty years to move across the Seine to the Ritz, but I'd made it in one year.

As soon as I had unpacked, I went to see "make-up" and "wardrobe" and "hairdressing" and "body make-up". My character, Vicky Hawkins, needed only two outfits for the Paris shoot, although I'm sure real air hostesses didn't have hand-made silk shirts and suits made-to-measure by Edith Head. My hair was cut just above my shoulders and bleached very light blond, with lots of hairspray everywhere. The make-up was Sixties Hollywood style - no heavy mascara or white lipstick.

We shot many scenes at Paris airport, where I was often mistaken for a real stewardess. Usually, I confessed that I was an actress making a movie, but on one occasion I sent an extremely obnoxious woman in totally the wrong direction in search of her flight.

Boeing-Boeing is a classic French bedroom farce set in Paris and updated to the jet age. Bernard Lawrence (Tony Curtis) is an American foreign correspondent who is engaged to three air hostesses, Jacqueline Grieux (Dany Saval) of Air France, Lise Bruner (Christine Schmidtner) of Lufthansa, and Vicky Hawkins of British United. He keeps his complicated love life on track with the help of a wall chart, a book of airline schedules, a wrist watch with an alarm that times each of his assignations, and a thoroughly exhausted housekeeper, Bertha (Thelma Ritter), who juggles photographs, lingerie and favourite foods - *soufflé* for Jacqueline, wurst and sauerkraut for Lise, and fried kidneys for Vicky - according to whichever girl is in residence in his plush apartment.

Bernard's carefully planned deception of "one up, one down, one pending" falls to pieces when new superjets are introduced by the airlines, enabling his *fiancées* to cut hours off their flight times and return to his apartment at inconvenient moments. To assist the unraveling process, a rival journalist, Robert Reed (Jerry Lewis), turns up unexpectedly to stay with Bernard and meets all three *fiancées* in one 24-hour period. Robert marvels at the audacity of such "geometrical poetry"; in fact, he likes it so much that he plans to usurp the whole operation when Bernard is posted back to America.

I learned very early on that Tony and Jerry didn't always stick to the script and I enjoyed their improvisations, having worked similarly on *Trois étoiles*. If they thought of a funnier line, they'd do it. Both in their own way made me feel very good about myself and I started suggesting new lines. The script had been written by an American, Edward Anhalt, from the original French play by Marc Camoletti, and I injected a few more English-sounding phrases. Hal Wallis later told me to make the part "as English as tea and cucumber sandwiches".

One night there was an awful accident during a frantic taxi chase involving Tony Curtis and Dany Saval and one of the young crew members, who had only just got married, was crushed by a car and had to be shipped back to America. Even more distressing to me was that I received a phone call telling me that Jack Hylton had died. I couldn't get to his funeral, another source of sadness.

Ian Heath came over and we had a wonderful weekend together at the Ritz, which was strictly against studio rules and was certain to be reported to Hal Wallis. I wasn't sure how he would take it, so, thinking I might as well be hanged for a sheep as a lamb, I ordered caviar and champagne and charged it to my suite. As predicted, Hal did notice my extravagance and never let me forget it.

The remaining scenes of *Boeing-Boeing* were to be shot in Los Angeles, so my first trip to Hollywood was just a few days away. I don't think I slept much during that time. I returned to London and arranged with my Aunt Sally to look after my two poodles, Monty and Kimsham. The night before I left for the United States Hal rang me to say that he had booked me into the Chateau Marmont on Sunset Boulevard. As something of an authority on chateaux, I wondered how it would compare with the real thing, but I kept that thought to myself.

"I put you into the apartment that Garbo had for years," Hal said.

Garbo! I loved the sound of that.

"Hemoine Baddeley and Peter Finch are staying there at the moment. I'm sure you'll enjoy meeting them."

"Thanks for being so sweet to me, Hal."

"Well, I know you're missing Roy and I want you to be happy. We are bringing Helen over to stay for a while and I've booked her into an apartment near you. A happy worker is a good worker and I want you to stay with us. David Jacobs is giving a welcome party for you when you arrive."

I didn't sleep a wink that night.

Chapter 10

Hollywood!

"I'm not interested in money - I just want to be wonderful."

Marilyn Monroe, *American actress*

AT eight o'clock the following morning the press turned up at The Cottage in Cadogan Lane to photograph my departure for Hollywood. While I finished packing upstairs, the Paramount publicist, Jack Upfold, poured drinks for the photographers and, when I walked down the stairs, the flashbulbs exploded. There hadn't been an English girl signed to a major Hollywood studio for some time and they all wished me well.

After a couple of drinks, however, each photographer decided he wanted an exclusive picture for his newspaper. They photographed me packing and then unpacking, in a mink coat, out of a mink coat, in a hat, then bare-headed and, finally, getting into the chauffeur-driven car. At Heathrow, there were even more photographers to record my final wave before I got on the plane.

Theoretically, it took sixteen hours to fly to Los Angeles via New York, but after a long delay at Kennedy we were in transit for a lot longer than that. Helen Goss sat next to me the whole way, chattering non-stop about the Hollywood stars she had worked with and spilling the beans about their little secrets. Goss by name, Gossip by nature.

When I checked in at the Chateau Marmont, there were quite a few messages from Hal. He'd filled the enormous suite with welcoming notes, flowers and bowls of fruit. I rang him immediately and he sounded concerned.

"You'd better not be late on the set like this," he growled. "I've had people backwards and forwards to that airport."

"I'm terribly sorry, but the plane was delayed in New York."

His tone softened.

"Have you got everything? I've had your fridge stocked and if you want anything at all just phone the office. I want you to take a few days off to get acclimatised, but I'm sending a press release to the trade papers, announcing your arrival. Now you rest and we'll speak in a day or two."

I thanked him and hung up.

David Jacob's party was at the Bistro, which guaranteed a good turnout, including Jack Warner, Kirk Douglas, Zsa Zsa Gabor, Christopher Plummer and Peter Finch. I shook Kirk Douglas's hand, just as I had dreamed of doing when I was a star-struck child.

"I just saw you in *Spartacus* on the telly," I said.

Kirk did a double take.

"The telly? What's the telly?"

"Oh, TV - television."

"The telly, the telly - I love it!"

I was introduced to Richard Gully, whom David had appointed as my publicist. Richard was English and grandson of Sir William Grey, governor-general of Bengal and later Jamaica - "no title and not enough money, you know the sort of thing", he drawled - and I knew we'd get on famously. I needed someone in this town who knew the ropes and Richard had been Jack Warner's PR for years. He looked a bit like David Niven in Separate Tables, mustache and all, but younger and sharper. He was now working freelance and I warned him that I couldn't afford to pay him as yet.

"Oh, don't worry about that," he said. "You're going to be the hottest thing in town."

At our second meeting, he explained it was important for me to remember that the Hollywood pecking order was divided into three categories: an A-list, a B-list and a C-list.

"Never be seen dead with anyone on the C-list," he said, making it sound as though they were contagious.

The social scale wasn't the only problem I had to master: there was also the question of the Hollywood wolf, a beast that first manifested itself in the shape of Peter Finch, Vivien Leigh's old inamorata and my neighbour at Chateau Marmont.

Hermoine Baddeley, who had just made Mary Poppins with Julie Andrews, was staying in one of the bungalows and she invited me to a party. Among the guests were her friend, Lady Jane, an English aristocrat who had a stuffed cockatoo on her shoulder, and Peter Finch, who had a very large chip on his. The scowling Anglo-Australian actor was making *Flight Of The Phoenix*, an air-crash epic set in the desert, and the hot sun had clearly given him a raging thirst. I don't recall doing anything to attract his attention, but he kept fixing me with a beady eye over the rim of his glass.

The party was nothing like the saintly Mary Poppins and, when the other guests settled in for a some serious drinking, I returned to my suite. I was reporting to Paramount Studios in the morning and it was important that I got a good night's rest. I was fast asleep when suddenly there was a loud banging on my door and shouts of "Fire! Fire!"

I jumped out off bed, ran to the door and threw it open. In dashed Peter Finch, who launched himself at me, Preminger-style. He was very drunk and not very steady on his feet, so he wasn't that difficult to dispose of. I kneed him in the groin and whacked him on the jaw and he passed out on the floor.

As I did not want Peter Finch around the place in the morning, I got hold of his feet and dragged him out of the door and along the corridor, bumped his head down a short flight of stairs and deposited him in the hallway for someone else to find. When I saw him again, he made no mention of that night. Perhaps he'd forgotten all about it, but he must have had one hell of a headache.

For me, the Paramount arch was the most famous of all the landmarks in Hollywood. Hal Wallis had sent a car to drive me to the studio and, as we approached the gates, Gloria Swanson's immortal line from *Sunset Boulevard* came into my head: "I'm ready for my close-up, Mr de Mille."

The gatekeeper looked at me inquiringly.

"It's Miss Suzanna Leigh," the driver announced.

The studio man saluted and told a security guard to open the gates.

"Good morning, Miss Leigh," he said politely. "Mr Wallis is waiting for you on Sound Stage 5."

Smiling, I sank back into the seat and closed my eyes to let the moment wash over me. There would never be another that would hold so much magic. Anybody who has ever had their life-long dream come true in every detail will know just how I felt as the car swept through the gates into that vast studio complex.

The studio was even bigger than I had imagined, a city within a city, with rows of buildings holding producers, directors, acting classes, gyms, writers and everything else you needed to make movies. Hal greeted me at Stage 5, where he was conferring with some film crew, and then we walked up a flight of fire-escape stairs at the back of one of the buildings to the largest office I have ever been in.

The distance from the door to Hal's desk seemed about twenty yards and the desk itself was an enormous marble table, big enough to seat ten for dinner. There was nothing on it except a black phone, a pad and a gold pencil. The desk and the chair were on a dais, so anyone sitting in front of him was placed at an immediate disadvantage. Hal was the first of Hollywood's serious art collectors and from his desk he could gaze contentedly upon some of the masterpieces that he had quietly bought at European auction houses.

Hal sat there, exuding power. He was dressed in gray suit pants and shirt sleeves, his dark hair receding, but neatly parted, his face tanned walnut-brown from years of golf. Rumour had it that he would arrange film locations near golf-courses, having already set up the deal over a game of golf somewhere else.

Hal suggested that I should spend the day wandering around the studio and introducing myself to people. He told me who would be expecting me and where they were located. He handed me the keys to my dressing room and said he hoped I liked the furnishings that the actress Martha Hyer, who became his second wife, had helped to pick out. My on-set trailer would be ready when I needed it.

"I want you to like us," he said. "This will be you home for the next seven years."

"Oh, Mr Wallis, thank you. I just love everything already. You'll be proud of me - I won't be late, I'll know my lines, I'll learn everything you want me to."

"Hey, wait up," he pleaded. "That's for me to tell you later!"

Hal's voice had a lyrical quality when he was in this jolly mood, but I knew it could also be as hard and cold as winter in his native Chicago.

"I've got plans for you, young lady, which will mean a lot of hard work, day and night," he said. "But first, off you go, and be back at one o'clock and we'll have lunch in the commissary with my co-producer, Paul Nathan. You'll like him - he's a Francophile like you."

The outer office held his secretaries, who offered to do any typing I might need, while his PA offered me her number and said: "You just call any time if you need anything."

To get around the Paramount lot, Hal presented me with a little buggy with a pink-and-white fringed canopy. He also gave me a piece of paper with a few names and addresses, but I wanted to drive around and soak up the atmosphere before making any calls. Several people waved at me as I trundled past in my little buggy. Initially, I thought they had mistaken me for someone else, but after a while I smiled and waved back, realising they must have recognised me from the newspaper coverage.

This was so different from England. In England, if anyone recognised you, they would turn away and whisper to their friends as if you had the plague: "Don't look now, but that's so and so over there - no, don't look!"

There was so much to see that I decided to park my buggy and walk around. People in western costumes hurried past - of course! they made *Bonanza* and there were writers with scripts under their arms and messengers dashing about with coffee and mail.

I found the dressing-room block, which looked like a row of smart, semi-detached houses in suburbia, except that the front porches were raised, with a canopy leading to the street. Each front door bore a bronze name plaque.

I walked along, looking at the names: *Jerry Lewis, Tony Curtis, Frank Sinatra, Suzanna Leigh, Natalie Wood.* Sorry, let me read that again: I was between Frank Sinatra and Natalie Wood. I walked on. *Carroll Baker* - no, I had to go back.

Quickly, I opened my door and went into what looked like the living room of a beautiful English country house, with fresh roses in bowls and floral drapes and a day bed. An alcove led to my own personal make-up and hairdressing departments, with massive wardrobes, a wash basin, full-sized hair dryer and a dressing table with a mirror, ringed by lights, that ran the entire length of the wall. The bathroom was nice and pretty, the kitchen small but adequate. I opened the fridge and poured myself a glass of milk. I was toasting Roy when the phone rang.

"Suzanna Leigh? Welcome to the Paramount team. This is Wally Westmore. Would you like to come over to make-up for some tryouts?"

"Oh yes, please."

We arranged a time and I had hardly put the phone down when my doorbell rang and a happy-faced woman entered.

"Hello, Miss Leigh, I'm Janie, your dresser," she said in a sing-song voice.

"And Betty, body make-up," chirped another smiling happy face just behind her.

"Come in, please."

They rushed in, offering to tidy up, unpack for me and generally sort my things out. Nobody had told me to bring "things", but then I didn't really know anyone who had come to Hollywood. I was swept along on a magic carpet, with chattering, helpful women all around me.

"Mr Wallis told us you're a great reader. Would you like the chippie to put up a bookcase for you?"

On it went. They became "the girls" and I became Suzanna; they tried Suzie, but I told them very quickly I didn't like it.

"Oh, right! We'll remember."

I remembered I had to see Edith Head that afternoon. Oh God, yes, where was that note? By the time I'd gone over to Wally Westmore in make-up, had lunch with Hal and Paul Nathan - a great guy and future ally - and changed my appointment with Miss Head for the next day, I really felt as though I was part of a team.

No, more than that - after years of searching, I had found my home at last.

Chapter 11

The Paramount Girl

"To be successful, the first thing to do is fall in love with your work."

Sister Mary Lauretta, *Carmelite nun*

MY first day on the Paramount set was, of course, an important one for me. It started with a 4.30am wake-up call to my suite at the Chateau Marmont - well, three wake-up calls to be precise: one from reception and two more from the studio. I'd also set my little Asprey's alarm clock, just in case.

My driver took me to the studio and dropped me off at my dressing room, where Janie and Betty, my two dressers, were anxiously waiting. With a local radio station relaying the latest Hollywood gossip in the background, they swung into their well-practiced routine of preparing an actress for the stage.

My hair was washed and groomed, my nails painted and Bud Westmore, Wally's brother, started the long process of doing my make-up. At the last minute, I was dressed in my spotless air-hostess uniform and told not to sit down to avoid creases.

Flanked by my little entourage of helpers, I arrived at the sound stage just as they were opening the huge sliding doors as though in my honour. Taking care not to trip over the miles of cable that snaked across the floor, I headed on high heels towards the lights, the camera and the action.

Was I nervous?

Yes, but I hadn't come all this way to fall on my face.

Everything was bigger than Shepperton, Pinewood and Elstree added together, and hundreds of people were standing around, waiting for orders.

As usual, my first scene was a tricky one - the breakfast scene with Tony Curtis and Thelma Ritter. Not only did I have a lot of dialogue, but there was the added problem of having to eat kidneys throughout.

The director was John Rich, whose background was mostly in

television and, perhaps as a result, he seemed to prefer takes to rehearsals. In Hollywood, every take had to be perfect as regards make-up, hair, skirts and, in this case, new plates of piping hot kidneys prepared by a chef hired expressly for that purpose.

Thelma was only playing the maid, but let's not forget she had played some very memorable maids in her time and stolen a lot of scenes from very good actors, such as Paul Newman in *Hud*. I knew I would have my work cut out going eye-to-eye with two such masters of the camera as Thelma and Tony.

Vicky is having breakfast with Bernard in his apartment before dashing off to catch her flight and her line is, "Bernard, darling, do you think I've got time for some more kidneys?" Bernard checks his watch and Bertha produces another batch of kidneys from her frying pan.

A dozen takes and an equal number of kidneys later, I was feeling decidedly queasy.

"Hold it!" I pleaded. "I can't eat another single kidney."

John Rich jumped to his feet.

"Okay, kill the lights!"

Tony immediately walked off the set and Thelma joined her husband, who was always close at hand to support her, while the director, several writers, the prop man and one or two others huddled together for the great kidney conference. The chef was consulted and suggested that bananas covered in some sort of brown sauce might be substituted for the kidneys.

"What sort of sauce would you like?" he asked me.

"Chocolate?" I said, hopefully.

The chef dispatched one his people to Farmer's Market to get the necessary ingredients. Finally, a plateful of bananas, dyed brown and covered with rich chocolate sauce, was placed on the table and we shot the rest of the scene.

It had taken all morning and part of the afternoon, but I had learned a valuable lesson. Throwing little wobblies like that was not only expected, but encouraged: it was a sure sign to the crew that were working with a *bona fide* star. I had to be a perfectionist about my performance because perfectionism was actually built into the system and kept all those hundreds of people in work.

Once I got to know him, Tony Curtis was very easy to work with and I got into the habit of popping into his dressing room, which was almost next door to mine. His assistant, Joe Warren, had dressed the place like a home-from-home, very chic but masculine, with Tony's favourite photographs, books, records and tennis rackets on display. Outside was a racing green Roller, one of his huge collection of automobiles.

To make him even happier, his wife Christine popped in and out of his dressing room in her bobby-sox. She had met Tony when they were making the Cossack epic Taras Bulba with Yul Brynner. Tony told me that, between takes, "Yul the Skull" would stand imperiously on the set like the King of Siam, hold out one hand and click of his fingers. On this command, a gofer would place a lighted cigarette between his fingers and Yul, still staring straight ahead, would place the cigarette between his lips in one sweeping movement.

One day the gofer was a fraction slow and Tony grabbed the moment and placed his own lighted cigarette between Yul's fingers, but the wrong way round. Yul swept the lighted end of the cigarette into his mouth and sucked deeply. "You know," said Tony, "that guy was so tough he didn't even flinch."

One of the hints I picked up from Tony was to have all of my scripts bound in black leather, with the titles printed in gold. It looked sophisticated and certainly beat having them stacked under the coffee table.

The thing I respected about Tony most was that he wasn't always looking out for Number One - unlike Jerry Lewis. Jerry must have realised from our scenes in Paris that I wouldn't be a pushover for the individual close-ups which would be filmed in Hollywood and edited into those scenes. The director would choose the best shots and Jerry knew he'd have to fight me for every one or end up on the cutting-room floor.

I wish it wasn't true, but, while my close-ups were being shot, he stood to one side of the camera, pulling idiotic faces at me. In one close-up, I had to look serious - not easy when Jerry Lewis was doing his "Nutty Professor" routine to distract me. After a few takes like that, I walked off the set and phoned Hal Wallis from my trailer.

"Can I do my close-ups on my own?" I asked.

Hal didn't even ask why - he already knew about Jerry's antics from one of his spies on the set.

"Can you do that?" he asked.

I'd recently done close-ups with Klaus Kinski in London and assured him that I could cope without the other actor being present. Hal said he'd fix it for me. When I got back to the set, Jerry Lewis had disappeared and I did my close-ups playing to an "X" that had been taped next to the lens by the cameraman, Lucien Ballard.

Jerry's clowning covered up a very unpleasant streak in his personality. While the crew were setting up, he would ride around the stage on a push-bike, jumping off only at the last minute and running straight on the set for the take. The bike would freewheel across the stage until somebody grabbed it.

While we were shooting the scenes at Paramount, Jerry was invited to write the widely syndicated Hedda Hopper gossip column and he used humour to have a dig at Tony: "...by the time he gets his hair combed and his Brooks Bros 1910 spats on (this is not a period picture - he wears them all the time) you can put on a month or two.

"Oh, yes, we can't forget the health kick he's on... no more meat, no more regular food. Everything he eats must be boiled right there and then and examined by the county health officer. So when he asks for a lettuce sandwich, and won't work until he eats it, it's easy to go six days behind schedule."

Tony was a careful eater, and he did, of course, wear spats off set - just as Jerry Lewis always wore white socks, even with a dark gray suit; they were like his lucky charm.

I had been working in Hollywood for about three weeks when a woman knocked on the door of my dressing room and introduced herself as Paula Strasberg. I recognised the name as it was synonymous with the Method-acting school in New York that Marlon Brando had made famous. Paula, who had been Marilyn Monroe's friend, confidante and drama coach, said she had read in the trade papers that I was working with Tony Curtis and was tipped to go to the top. Perhaps she could be of some help to me? I was intrigued and asked her in.

She gave me a very quick sell on her abilities.

"Let me just give you this little gem to help you in your next scene," she chirruped. "You're working with two very tricky people here. When I was with Marilyn, we came across Tony in *Some Like It Hot*, so I know what he can be like. I'll just leave you with this and you think about it: every time you look at Jerry Lewis, you see Goofy, and Tony, well - he's Mickey Mouse, but *you* are Minnie Mouse and *you're* in charge."

With that, Paula was off - I never saw her again.

I couldn't wait to tell Tony what she'd said. He'd already told me that working with Marilyn Monroe had been a nightmare. He and Jack Lemmon, decked out in women's clothes, wigs and false nails, had to wait around on the set from six in the morning until Marilyn showed up. She was invariably late and they were understandably annoyed about it.

"Now it makes sense!" Tony said when I told him. "All that time she thought I was Mickey Mouse!"

One of the problems for Christiane, Dany and I was that we spent most of the film in our air-hostess uniforms, so there was very little opportunity to show any individual dress sense. Edith Head took this up as a personal challenge on my behalf.

"We've got to make you stand out from the other girls," she said, "and the nightdress scene is our only chance to do that."

For that scene, Dany was wearing a baby-doll nightdress and Christiane was in shortie pajamas. Edith made me a long silk jersey dress with slits down the side which, with the right accessories, could have been worn on the catwalk as an evening dress. With little ties hanging down from the slits, and worn with fluffy, high-heeled slippers, it just about passed as a night-dress. But I had to fight the front office to wear my hair up a la Bardot in that scene, rather than the very coifed "day look" that the others were wearing.

The most reassuring thing of all was that Hall Wallis was pleased with my work. He called me into his office to tell me what I had always dreamed of hearing - that he was going to make me a star. He said he would put me through the old studio system which had coached, cosseted and controlled many of the biggest names in the Hollywood pantheon.

"It hasn't been used for years, but it works," he said. "It's important that when we lend you out to another studio, no stupid director can faze you. It's how we worked in the old days, but nobody teaches actors anything anymore."

I mentioned my visit from Paula Strasberg and her offer of help.

"You don't need a drama coach," he growled. "You've got Helen already."

To impress upon me the importance of my mission, Hal told me that my contract was the result of a wager between him and his rival, Sam Spiegel. It seems that Sam had bet Hal a million dollars that he was too old to repeat his star-making success with Shirley MacLaine.

"When you walked into my suite in London, all the right bells went off in my head," he said.

Hal had a chart on his wall, mapping out my future: what I was going to do, with whom and where. He gave me some hints: never let a director do close-ups after four o'clock in the afternoon, no matter what excuse they gave - he would write that stipulation into my contract. He said it was important that a star knew her key lights, her best side, how to dress and how to sparkle.

I told him he sounded a little like Roy and nicknamed him "Uncle Hal". He said he'd been called a lot of things, but "Uncle" had never been one of them. He let me in on some of the films he had lined up for me -

Anne Of The Thousand Days would be a spectacular costume drama about Henry VIII's second wife, Anne Boleyn. I would be playing the King's third wife, Jane Seymour.

He also mentioned that he'd spoken to Howard Koch, the head of Paramount Pictures, about "a great little comedy" that would be "a good vehicle" for me, Barefoot In The Park. It turned out to be an enormous success, making international stars of Robert Redford and Jane Fonda and adding millions to the Paramount coffers.

But it wasn't all work. Admirers sent me masses of fresh flowers, with requests to meet me, and the phone was pretty busy with invitations to dinner parties and weekends "in the country", meaning the desert resort of Palm Springs.

The place I liked visiting most belonged to Ralph Stolkin, a billionaire and one-time studio head of R.K.O. I met Ralph at one of Richard Gully's parties and we would fly down to Palm Springs in his private plane. Ralph's house was a vast hacienda with three swimming pools, one of which cascaded over the far end, giving swimmers the illusion that they were swimming over the edge of a mountain.

It was while I was staying there one weekend that I first met my neighbour on the Paramount lot, Natalie Wood. She spent an inordinate amount of time reading the book of a film she wanted to make, but when she did eventually speak to me she was sweet and helpful.

Natalie advised me that, if I was really serious about winning a part, it was a good idea to arrive for the interview already dressed for it. She felt that few producers had any imagination and had to see what they were getting. She employed this trick at auditions for a film in which she wanted to play a Native American. At first they could see her only as a little white girl, but when she returned in chamois leather and moccasins, she was instantly hired.

Coincidentally, I met my first Native American that weekend, but, unlike the whooping stereotypes portrayed by Hollywood, he owned several oil wells and rode in a Cadillac convertible.

David Janssen, star of the hit TV series The Fugitive, was one of Ralph's neighbours and I adored going to his Sunday brunch parties, a Palm Springs ritual which attracted great company and provided some useful contacts. An actress at one of his brunches warned me that Frank Sinatra, my other next-door neighbour at Paramount, was to be avoided at all costs. Rumour had it that, if he fancied you and you spurned his advances, he could turn nasty - and he was a formidable enemy.

This actress told me that she couldn't get a job at any studio for almost three years after turning him down. After hearing this, I went to incredible lengths to avoid him - leaving my dressing room later than usual and returning early in the morning. I know that might sound silly, but at nineteen stories such as that easily panicked me. I needed experience, but not the kind that had made Francis Albert Sinatra notorious.

Back at Paramount, Hal took me to lunch and told me that Elvis owed him one more film before his contract expired. The picture was set in Hawaii and, he added, he'd make it a bit bigger, with me as the female lead. As he was saying this, he was spooning some relish on to his plate and the words were spoken so nonchalantly that they didn't sink in until later. At the first opportunity, I asked Hal what Elvis was like.

"He's a good kid, always on time, knows his lines and he can act, too."

I told him that *Love Me Tender* was my favourite Elvis film and that I'd dreamed of acting in a film with him ever since I'd seen it.

Hal looked serious.

"He has some strange people around him and you, young lady, must be careful who you meet up with. Still got that boyfriend in London? Yes? Good, that'll keep you out of trouble. Now off you go to your classes and remember: early to bed."

Even with Uncle Hal it wasn't all plain sailing. We had a run-in because I was late clocking in at the studio one morning. Driving along Sunset Boulevard, I witnessed a murder when a man standing at a bus stop was gunned down as we passed. I screamed at my driver to stop, but he was reluctant to do so.

We were on different wavelengths, him and me: where I came from, it wasn't a regular occurrence for people to be shot while waiting for a Number 73; over here, you acted as though you hadn't seen anything. The driver pulled up only because I insisted and we stayed with the victim until the police arrived. Just as they did, he died in my arms.

Despite Tony's repeated warnings to the contrary, I considered this a good enough reason for being a little late. When I arrived at the studio, however, an order to appear at Hal's office was awaiting me.

The outer office was silent.

There was no jolly greeting from Uncle Hal's secretary, just a curt nod towards his door. The walk from that door to his desk seemed twice as long as before and his desk was even bigger; nor was the man sitting behind it a sweet, benevolent uncle. Hal had turned into the heavy-handed producer that he was known to be and mercilessly read me the riot act. He said that he couldn't care less if a thousand men were killed in front of me - what was he supposed to do? Circulate flyers to the public, apologising that his star looked beat in this scene because she'd held a dying man's hand?

He glanced down at his notes and told me that I was four minutes late and that I was to be fined $1 per second - $240. He waved his hand in a dismissive gesture and, as if by magic, the door was opened by his secretary.

As with all good uncles, though, Hal was forgiving and a few days later a large bowl of flowers and a bottle of Miss Dior was delivered to my dressing room, accompanied by a note signed "Uncle Hal".

A number of people disagreed with this style of film production, but I wasn't one of them. Some years earlier Robert Taylor had said of his boss Louis B. Mayer: "As I knew him, he was kind, fatherly, understanding and protective. I wish today's youngsters had a studio and boss like I did."

I felt about Hal Wallis and Paramount in exactly the same way. No matter how loudly the Screen Actors Guild denounced the studio system for being elitist and patrician, I knew it was just right for me.

Somewhere in the archives at Paramount there is a dusty print of a film called *Paramount On Parade*, a revue featuring the talents of the stars who were under contract to the studio in 1930. The credits include (in strict alphabetical order): Jean Arthur, Clara Bow, Maurice Chevalier, Gary Cooper, Kay Francis, Frederic March, William Powell, Lillian Roth and Fay Wray.

I figured if it was good enough for them, it was good enough for me.

Mostly, my life was a roller-coaster ride through wonder-land. To get to the studio, I was up at five o'clock sharp every morning and, after work, I attended my classes.

Studying the process of lighting with Lucien Ballard, one of the best lighting cameramen in the business and ex-husband of Lana Turner, was exhausting. He would quiz me about the different types of lights - what they were called, which ones would flatter me most and which ones were best for close-ups. A 75 lens, or even a 50, would show a little of what I was wearing, but anything more, such as a 100, would have been bordering on the grotesque.

Lucien was a hard taskmaster and one who would think nothing of flicking his ever-present horsewhip across the back of my legs, particularly when I couldn't remember a lens.

Nellie Manley, head of the hairdressing department, was supposed to teach me about hair care. As a result, all of we blonde actresses sat in a row every Friday night, having our roots done out of the same dish! Carroll Baker always sat next to me and, as she was playing Jean Harlow at the time, my hair became progressively lighter!

Nellie's passion was watching baseball and she went to a ball game at every opportunity, often with another devotee, Doris Day.

I loved my fashion classes with Edith Head - the rumours had been correct: she did use her Oscars as doorstops. She was surprisingly small for someone with such a large reputation, with masses of pitch-black hair that seemed almost too large for her head; she wore most of it in a tight bun in the nape of her neck like a school mistress. Her complexion was very white, almost translucent, and she wore bright red lipstick and thick, black horn-rims. She talked in a low voice that was clearly used to being heard and obeyed; her aides were in awe of her and even the most garrulous of actresses fell silent in her presence.

Her studio was a bit like an architect's office, with art benches and large easels dotted around the place. Edith drew her intricate designs on huge sheets of paper that unfolded like the blueprints of major construction projects, which, of course, they were.

"I can see you're not new to wearing nice clothes," she said. "Let's see what sort of colours you like."

We discussed various styles and she taught me to be brave with lines, yet simple with material.

"The Grecian look suits you and you've got good legs, so we should show them whenever possible."

Edith loaned me the most wonderful dresses whenever I needed them for social occasions and she also gave me a beige mohair evening coat, lined in sable. I worked (at least that's what they called it!) all day, while my evenings were spent at small dinner parties, usually hosted by Kirk Douglas and his wife, Anne, or Liza Minnelli's father, Vincente Minnelli, and her stepmother, Denise. These two families were top of the A-list, very much the royalty of Hollywood. The B-list consisted mainly of TV stars and second leads, although David Janssen and Jill St. John had ascended into the A group.

I ran into trouble with this bizarre social scale when I bumped into Heide, my Hungarian school-friend from London, on the Paramount lot. She was working as an extra on a film and we chatted for a few minutes before dashing off to our respective sets. Within hours, Richard Gully was on the phone, telling me I had stepped out of line by speaking to one of the nobodies.

I couldn't believe what I was hearing - the whole of Hollywood was like a parody of the Court of St. James's and they even had spies reporting back to the chamberlain. This was brought home to me even more forcefully when Hedda Hopper and Louella Parsons began to mention my society connections in their columns. Hedda Hopper described me as

"Cinderella with a silver spoon" and added that "the England of country houses, Ascot and Cowes Week is her playground". Richard was obviously feeding them tidbits to enhance my image in the eyes of their readers. At the height of the Civil Rights movement, snobbery was alive and kicking in Hollywood.

Jerry Lewis proved to be another of the snobs, once bemoaning the fact that "they'll be letting extras on the golf-course soon." Even Uncle Hal wasn't free of the virus, calling me into his office to warn me against public shows of affection with "unknowns". He said that if I wanted to see people from my past, I was to do it behind closed doors, preferably those of my apartment at the Chateau Marmont.

Uncle Hal asked me why I never seemed to spend any money and I told him I didn't have any. It was then I discovered that my mother had lied to him, telling him that I had a large private income and that she didn't want me getting spoiled.

Naturally, Hal believed her and gave me only a basic expense allowance of £75 a week. From that day on, he doubled it to £150 per week and, as he paid my rent and car bills, that was fine. I was doing what I loved and I was twenty years old. In England, it hadn't been that long since Cliff Richard had made the front pages by earning £100 a week. Hal said that if there was still a problem, we could re-negotiate the contract when I turned twenty-one.

I was being courted by a number of rich men, mainly Hollywood playboys with an eye for a glamourous newcomer. I followed Hal's advice and they got nowhere.

Not all the predators were men, however. Jay Sebring, the coolest and kinkiest hairdresser in Tinsel Town, introduced me to a cabaret dancer in his salon. She was holding forth to the girls under the dryers about how her next trip to Vegas was going to be her last.

"It's millionaire time or bust," she said. "I don't care how old he is - in fact, the older he is the better because I'll be able to fuck him to death!"

We all laughed and gave it no more thought. A year or so later I was at a rather smart fund-raising dinner in Miami when who should I bump into but the one-time cabaret dancer, looking very chic and absolutely covered in jewellery.

"So where's the rich husband?" I mused to myself. "He must be here somewhere."

But there was no sign of him and, when we met in the loo, I asked her about him.

"I married the oldest man in Vegas the first week of my new

contract," she said. "He bought me out of the rest of the show."

That explanation still didn't answer my question as to his whereabouts, so she enlightened me: "We spent our honeymoon in a hotel in Vegas. I kept him locked in the bedroom and fucked him night and day for thirteen days. I couldn't believe that he managed to keep going for as long as he did, but then one day he had a heart attack and died. By this point, I could hardly walk."

"At least he died happy." I said.

She burst into a fit of laughter.

"You haven't heard the best bit. He was kind enough to leave me $13 million - a million for every day!"

Chapter 12

Aloha, Richard Harris

"Why not seize the pleasure at once? How often is happiness destroyed by preparation, foolish preparation?"

Jane Austen, *English writer*

I SHOULD have stayed in Hollywood once filming had wrapped on *Boeing-Boeing*. The studio rumour machine was pumping the trade papers with stories that I'd be teamed with Elvis Presley for my next film. But such speculation was premature - it was like Cinderella being tipped to marry Prince Charming weeks before the ball.

It was summer and, in the absence of any firm news, I decided to hit the South of France. Ian Heath was driving down to St Tropez with Colin "The Creamer" Slater, so after breaking my journey in England to see my two dogs, I joined them. We had been there for only a few days when I got a call from Paramount. They wanted me to fly back to America the very next day to begin work on a film titled *Hawaiian Paradise*. As predicted in the papers, my co-star would be Elvis Presley.

Hal wasn't terribly pleased with me because I should have remained in Los Angeles to meet Elvis, read the script and have my outfits designed by Edith Head. Instead, I had to get to Honolulu on the island of Oahu, where shooting was about to begin. Nevertheless, I allowed myself to become really excited for the first time because I was actually going to make a movie with Elvis - the very pinnacle of my dreams.

I returned to London to pack and to arrange for the dogs to stay with my Aunt Sally. This in itself was problematic as she was moving into one of my mother's flats and mother still hadn't forgiven me for taking Helen Goss, and not her, to Hollywood.

While I was sorting out these problems, the British press was going crazy - after all, this was the first time that Elvis's leading lady wouldn't be an American but an English actress. A number of journalist friends were genuinely pleased for me, so Heathrow became the venue for an impromptu cocktail party, with Fleet Street's finest toasting me on to the plane.

I flew directly to New York, where I had to change planes for Los Angeles, and thence to Honolulu. The publicity machine had been set in motion at both touch down points and I had to force myself awake to pose for photographs when all I wanted to do was curl up and sleep.

I was jetlagged and exhausted when I landed in Honolulu. As soon as I got off the plane, however, I was asked to do a quick day-for-night shot that was needed in the can that day. I hardly had time to unpack in my suite at the luxurious Ilikai Hotel at Waikiki Beach (the hotel that figures on the credits of *Hawaii Five-O*) before I was being whipped off to the location near Diamond Head.

Elvis was recording the film's soundtrack album in Los Angeles and his stand-in was doing the scene. He looked so much like the real Elvis that I wasn't surprised to learn that their resemblance was the result of plastic surgery. In this scene, I was supposed to be dropped off after a date with Elvis. It was just a long shot, but it took time and a few takes before the director, Michael "Mickey" Moore, was happy. As I'd had no time to recover from the gruelling nine thousand mile flight, he gave me the next day off.

It was only eleven in the morning, Hawaiian time, when I got back to the Ilikai, but my body clock was telling me it was nine in the evening. I ordered a daiquiri on the hotel terrace, planning to start work on the script and then go to bed. It was the voice I heard first, rich and resonant, with a beguiling hint of Gaelic mischief.

Oh my God, Richard Harris was sitting two tables away from me, holding court!

Like most aspiring actresses growing up in the Sixties, I was mad about the ruggedly handsome Irish actor. I had seen him dominating the stage at the Royal Court in *The Ginger Man* and loved him as the tough, rugby-playing star of *This Sporting Life*.

On the terrace of the Ilikai Hotel, however, he was in full make-up and wearing period costume of frock coat and buckled boots. He looked regal, a look that he would later make his own in the film version of *Camelot*. The film he was making here was James A. Michener's swashbuckling epic, *Hawaii*, in which he was playing opposite Julie Andrews.

I had read in *Variety* that the stars and crew had been here for months and that they were already well over budget and nowhere near on-schedule. It was inconceivable to me from my experiences at Paramount that events would be allowed to reach such a stage.

One of Richard's actor friends was at my elbow.

"Richard's desperate to meet you."

Acting as I thought a self-possessed British actress should in such circumstances, I went over to be introduced.

"I suppose you don't drink?" he said, a typical Richard Harris opening line.

"Sure I drink."

Right on cue, the daiquiri I had ordered arrived in front of me and, as if to prove a point, I downed it in one. There was a roar of approval from everyone at the all-male table. Richard asked me what I was doing here and how long I was staying. As soon as I mentioned I was making a film with Elvis, everyone started asking questions at the same time - what he was like and so forth. Richard wanted to meet him. I promised to tell them all about Elvis when I found out myself.

More drinks arrived.

As I was the only female present, I suppose I took this drinking thing as a sort of initiation into the gang. I know it sounds stupid now, but I didn't think about it at the time. The craziness really started when Richard decided to turn the session into a competition, with him drinking neat brandy to my glasses of wine. It was time for all those months of imbibing up and down the Loire Valley on *Trois étoiles* to pay off.

I sneaked into the hotel kitchen, where I devoured a loaf of bread - good blotting paper. When I came back, Richard was lining up the drinks and spectators gathered around taking bets, with Richard the odds-on favourite.

Everyone expected me to sink fast, but I'd eaten enough bread to soak up a gallon of wine, which was fortunate because, eight hours later, we were still going strong and half the hotel had bets on the outcome. Richard would finish a drink and the packed terrace would cheer. I'd put down a glass of wine and the cheers would be for me.

As the twelfth hour came and getting up became a fairly hazardous task, I was beginning to wonder if I could last much longer. Then, slowly and gracefully, Richard started to slip under the table. As he was disappearing from sight, he slurred: "I will not leave without inviting you to our party tonight."

With that, he was gone.

The cheers rang out for me, which I acknowledged as best I could. I had actually drunk the wild beastie under the table.

Getting up slowly with as much dignity as I could muster, I walked (without shoes, as I thought it safer) to the elevator. The palm trees were gently swaying, at least I thought they were. I pressed the button for my floor and the high-speed elevator took off like a rocket. The vineyard inside me sloshed around like a choppy sea as I clung to the rail with both hands to stop myself from sinking to the floor. Head spinning, I arrived at my suite and sank gratefully to my knees, groping around for the bed. Eventually, I found it and crawled in.

My next recollection was that the telephone was ringing and I was listening to Richard's voice in my ear.

"Where are you? The party will be over soon."

I hauled myself out of bed, showered, re-did my make-up, ate some fruit and took a few moments to marvel at the many bowls of flowers filling my suite, which had somehow escaped my notice. I made my way to the suite where the party was in full swing and was greeted by Richard like a long lost friend.

It was 5am.

We found a quiet spot away from the crowd and started talking. I was in awe of him as a prince of the screen and, as I usually did when talking to somebody I admired, I hung on his every word. He asked me where I had trained and I told him Webber-Douglas, adding that I had only stayed for about four months. He said he'd done the same at LAMDA, staying only six months.

Then we swapped stories: he told me of his love and respect for Joan Littlewood and her theatre at Stratford East in London and I told him about my dream of going to Hollywood and how I had forced the meeting with Hal Wallis at the Dorchester.

He laughed.

"That makes you bigger than anyone here."

He told me about the film he was making and the venom in his voice when Julie Andrews' name came up was awesome. His friend and drinking companion, Frank Harper, suggested lunch and I realised that seven hours had slipped by. We all marched off to the hotel terrace, with the boys ceremoniously carrying a large parasol to shield me from the strong sunlight. Even a little bit of sunburn would have placed me in deep trouble with the continuity girl. All the time, or so it seemed, Richard had a guitar player wandering behind us, playing romantic melodies like, "More than the greatest love the world has known."

Later that afternoon Richard took my hand and led me to the far end of the terrace.

"Let me show you the most beautiful sight on earth."

I have to say that, by that time, the magic of the setting and his Irish charm had me reeling, but nothing could have prepared me for my first Hawaiian sunset. The sky had become an artist's palette, incorporating all the colours that only God knows. How could I have missed this the night before?

"Dermot, let's have a party at the house tonight for the new member of the club," Richard shouted at one of the men in the group, who turned out to be his brother Dermot.

"What club?" I asked.

"It's the 65 Club - and bring your script."

I thought the club sounded like fun until he told me he'd formed it some years earlier because he believed the world was going to end in 1965.

Excuse me, but this was 1965!

Such an idea was too fatalistic for words, perhaps because I loved my life so much and never wanted it to end.

Dermot was dispatched to Richard's house to prepare for the party and I returned to my suite for a nap. There were lots of messages awaiting me. If only I could have phoned Roy; I missed his laughter, but most of all his guidance, which I badly needed. There was a message from Ian in London, hoping that I would make some nice friends soon. Another was from the assistant director, informing me that I wasn't needed for another few days and to go out and have fun.

It was still possible to tell Richard that I'd had enough, as I should have done, but I didn't. It all seemed a trifle dangerous and the danger was exciting. Besides, he was my new mentor. I was learning my job and I thought, as I was twenty, I could handle him.

The conceit of youth!

The party was held in a house that Richard had rented, a large ramshackle place near Diamond Head. He read me some of his own poetry and told me how he had learned to tell stories to himself when he suffered from TB as a child.

I told him about my lonely childhood and about the help I'd had received from a Jesuit priest who had encouraged me to read.

"Oh, the Jesuits never had any belief in me," he said. "It's Dylan Thomas who has it all between two covers."

Richard was obsessed with the Welsh poet and insisted that I take a copy of *Under Milk Wood*.

Richard read through the script of *Hawaiian Paradise* with me and intellectualised each of the parts. He played Rick Richards, Elvis's part, while I read my role of Judy Hudson.

"Tonight my life has changed and I am so happy," he shouted, wrapping his arms around me. "And it's you that's done it, girl. We will be *huge* together - you will star with me in *Heathcliffe*."

Apparently it had been his ambition ever since he had got started in the film industry to play Heathcliffe in a remake of *Wuthering Heights*, with Lindsay Anderson directing. He was so sure about it that it was impossible not to be swept along on the wave of his enthusiasm.

So ended my first day in Paradise.

Or was it my third?

In the morning, the warning bells in my head seemed a long way off. I knew Richard was married, but I didn't think of that as a problem. In the beginning, I swear, I just wanted to be "one of the boys" and have fun, but what started as an innocent adventure affected both our lives and almost ruined my career.

Richard pursued me relentlessly, even though he had to work at night and I was spending my days preparing to start work on *Paradise - Hawaiian Style*, as the film had now been renamed. I was kept busy all day, learning my lines, attending costume fittings and posing for publicity stills. But no matter where I was, a little note would turn up from Richard, saying: "Are you coming out to play?"

I answered that I was going to bed early these days and, anyway, I wasn't drinking anymore. Nothing deterred him. His sights were firmly fixed on me and, with the connivance of his friends, he kept up the pressure. If I said I had to learn my lines, he would offer to help, but I knew that would mean more boozing and declined as gracefully as possible.

"You don't have to do everything they say," he'd grumble down the phone. "Hal Wallis doesn't own you, you know."

I relented when Richard organised a party for me on one of the beaches. It was a lovely surprise and I was touched. Meantime, *Hawaii* dragged on and on. Richard was chronically bored and I had become a diversion for him. He had still got nowhere with me, but I was able to do *him* a big favour. I pointed out that, as his film had run over time, he was entitled to a new deal. Richard was delighted with the suggestion, spoke to the producers, the Mirisch Brothers, and made a vast amount of money as a result.

Then his wife, Elizabeth, arrived from London with his three young sons. He insisted that we go out in a threesome and he walked between Elizabeth and me, linking arms with both of us. Apparently, he told her that I was Frank Harper's girlfriend to allay any suspicions she might have had.

I tried to kid myself that everything would be fine, but, when he touched me that night, I knew that it wouldn't be.

Elizabeth went back. Or maybe she didn't and he just said she did. That night he made love to me at our hotel. It was the first time we had done anything other than kiss fleetingly.

I discovered that Richard was as well-endowed as he was eloquent and exploitative.

"You're only a child," he whispered, "and I didn't want to frighten you."

Looking at him standing there naked in the moonlight, I just laughed; after all, everything about him was larger than life.

So I went along with it - it was flattering to be chased by an older man, especially one whose talent I admired. After that first night, we'd meet either at the hotel or he would smuggle me into his house at Diamond Head. There was no sign of Elizabeth or his three sons, so perhaps they really had returned home.

With two major movies being shot in such a small area, Honolulu was crawling with newsmen. One night Richard left my suite late at night, only to return in a panic.

"The place is alive with reporters," he hissed.

Without another word, he shot out on to the balcony, hoisted himself over the side and clambered down to the next floor. He was willing to risk his neck to avoid a scandal and, although he succeeded in dodging the press on that occasion, a few nights later one reporter got a lot closer than he ever knew.

Richard and I were at a party in one of the suites when Richard got into an argument with the man and ended up hitting him. Frank Harper hustled the reporter out of the room and locked him in a cupboard while Richard and I made our getaway.

Understandably, our lovemaking was never very relaxed. Not only was there the threat of exposure in the press, but the mantle of Catholic guilt weighed heavily upon our shoulders. At least, I know it did on mine and I was finding the weight too heavy to support.

Then the King flew in.

Elvis booked into suite 2225 at the Ilikai and members of the Memphis Mafia took over the rest of the suites on his floor. We began filming together in Hanauma Bay on the eastern tip of Oahu. The rapport between Elvis and me was instantaneous and we disappeared from the set a couple of days later to talk in the privacy of his trailer. Word was put out to an inquisitive press that Elvis had "stomach cramps," although one reporter claimed he was "vacationing with an eager starlet who wanted to know him better".

The starlet was later described as "a nineteen-year-old blonde from Hollywood."

Close! I had just turned twenty.

As Richard was shooting at night and Elvis and I were shooting all day, I wasn't getting any sleep at all. I spent the whole twenty-four hours with one or other of them.

Inevitably, Elvis found out about Richard Harris and was not impressed; he was far from being a prude, but extramarital affairs were completely against his Southern principles.

My friendship with Elvis was still in its early stages, yet I started making comparisons between him and Richard. The first thing I realised was that Richard was not as much fun to be around as Elvis and, although he was only four years older, he seemed *much* older.

Richard could be a nightmare; not surprising, really, when his own life was like a film noir. He was the worst hypochondriac I have ever met. It would be nothing for him, if he was bored or felt ignored, to fling himself to the ground, screaming that he was having a heart attack. Naturally, I believed his every word at first and would rush to his side.

If he didn't get the response he wanted, he'd shout: "I'm fucked, for Christ's sake - can't you bloody see that!"

One night he cried in my arms, then kissed my tummy, saying I would give him the daughter he wanted so much. I didn't want to have a child yet - I was only one step above being a child myself. I knew in my heart that if ever I was fortunate enough to have a daughter, she would have my unconditional love and devotion, but, in this phase of my life, I wanted to live and that would mean letting Richard go.

Disentangling myself from him wasn't easy, however, and sometimes it was messy. One evening Elvis showed me some karate moves and then decided we were going to have dinner together. I already had a prior engagement to meet Richard and, when I told Elvis, he smashed a table with a karate chop, sending food crashing to the floor. This incident led to reports in the press that he was popping pills.

Realising that the bad publicity could hurt Elvis, the film and my career, I put my foot down. Richard asked me on to the set of Hawaii one night and guided me towards a director's chair marked "Mrs Richard Harris". Julie Andrews was there and I shrugged Richard's hand away.

"I don't think so," I said and walked off to a more discreet vantage point. I was glad to have witnessed the making of *Hawaii*, however, because the contrast between the two sets couldn't have been more marked.

By day, everything on the beach with Elvis was bright and shiny, with lots of strumming guitars, swaying palms, hula-hula skirts and Queenie Wahine's papaya. But at night Richard Harris strode the moon-lit sands, pouring port wine and brandy down his throat and muttering dire oaths. Everything to do with him was dark and satanic, even if it was all a bit Long John Silverish.

The breaking point came when Richard invited me to accompany him to another of the Hawaiian islands for a short holiday. Foolishly, I agreed to go with him. His strolling minstrel was serenading us at the airport when a photographer snapped our picture and a guy with a microphone asked me: "What's it like being married to Richard Harris?"

I was wearing a scarf over my hair and dark glasses, and he obviously thought I was Elizabeth Harris. The easiest thing was to go along with it and I found myself playing Richard's wife for a TV interview. But I was shattered. As soon as the interview was over, I went straight back to my hotel despite Richard's protests.

I decided to tell Elvis. He was furious. "First he gets you drunk, now you impersonate his wife. This man has no redeeming points."

"Well, he does have an awfully good singing voice."

"He can't sing," said Elvis, and that was that.

Elvis's Southern disapproval coupled with my Catholic guilt made my position untenable and I told Richard so. His response was to laugh, replying harshly: "If it was such a bloody good marriage, you don't think a little girl like you could mess it up, do you?"

Which put me in my place.

It also broke his spell over me and I plucked up the courage to tell Elvis that I wanted to end the affair but didn't know how.

"Leave it to me."

Within the hour I received a phone call from Hal Wallis in Los Angeles. I'm sure Elvis must have phoned him and told him everything.

Hal had no doubts about what had to happen.

"This affair with Harris has got to stop right now, or your image will be ruined."

I could feel the ice run through my veins. He told me pointedly that Hollywood break-ups had ruined careers bigger than mine.

"Are you really going to throw it away for Richard Harris? He's always drunk and fighting. Your association with him will destroy you. I'm coming over for a few days and I'll play golf while you read a script for a new Paramount movie that I want you in. After this picture, you can go away for a while."

He was right, of course. I told Richard it was over on the phone; the deception was too much for me.

"I don't want to go down that road," I said. "I'm sorry, I can't go on anymore."

He begged me to stay with him, that rich, resonant voice cracking with emotion. There were tears, but I was firm. Elvis was my protector now and I was no longer alone. He had even started calling me his "little sister". When I told him the affair was over, he smiled.

"That's good, baby," he said. "We'll never talk about it again."

And Elvis was as good as his word.

Chapter 13

Elvis's Little Sister

"God gives us our relatives - thank God we can choose our friends."

Ethel Watts Mumford, *American writer*

THE first day I met Elvis it was as though we both recognised each other, as people do if they're members of the same club. It was only a momentary thing, but it was undeniably there. The sun shone brightly behind him as I looked up into his face. He was standing with a cup of tea in his hand. He had assumed that, because I was English, I would drink tea, but tea always reminded me of the endless pots I'd had to make for my mother and I loathed the stuff.

I had been sitting on the set of *Paradise - Hawaiian Style*, perusing my script, when someone said: "Excuse me, ma'am, would you like a cup of tea?"

These were the first words Elvis spoke to me.

Without looking up, I replied: "No, thank you - I don't drink tea."

Then I glanced up with an automatic smile on my face, thinking the voice belonged to a runner, though the accent was so Southern that I really should have known. The first thing I saw was Elvis's profile, smiling at his friends, and a split second later his eyes met mine.

"Well, actually," I said, suddenly feeling very English, "I don't normally drink tea, but I'd love a cup."

Elvis handed the tea to me and sat down.

"We know someone in common," I said.

"Oh, really?"

"George Sidney."

Elvis told me he was a great fan of George's work and we were soon chatting away as though we'd known each other for ages. Elvis told me later that he was interested in me because I didn't try to push myself on him.

Then we went to work.

In *Paradise - Hawaiian Style*, Elvis plays Rick Richards, a head-strong pilot who returns to Hawaii in disgrace after being kicked out by his airline. Rick talks his friend, Danny Kohana (James Shigeta), into starting a helicopter charter business, Danrick Airways, even though he knows Rick's reputation for getting into trouble with girls. While trying to drum up business on the islands, Rick rekindles relationships with four girlfriends and Danny's worst fears start to come true. Then Judy Hudson, a cool blonde with a mid-Atlantic accent, flies in...

Predictably, the first scene I shot with Elvis turned out to be the most difficult. Judy lands her plane outside Danny's office at the airfield and Danny introduces her to Rick, who is auditioning numerous shapely applicants to work as a Girl Friday for Danrick Airways.

Rick: We met before - about two years ago on a surfboard.

Judy: Really?

Rick: Waikiki. You were wiped out - remember? I scooped you out of the soup.

Judy: "Oh yeah - I remember, you tried to give me mouth-to-mouth resuscitation!"

This last line may sound fairly easy, but even writing it now makes me smile because I simply couldn't get it right. Every time I tried to pronounce "resuscitation", I exploded into a fit of the dreaded giggles. Elvis didn't help matters by making jokes.

"Let's hear that again: re-what?"

Then Elvis got the giggles, too, when he has to say that he's going to call me "Friday" because "Judy reminds me of a clam-shucker I once knew."

He had the same trouble with "clam-shucker" as I had had with "resuscitation" and it turned into a comedy routine. I can't remember how many takes it took to get that scene in the can, but the finished print shows Elvis's shoulders shaking with laughter, so they clearly had to make the best of a bad job.

As I walked off the set towards my trailer, Elvis followed me. He said that if I wasn't doing anything special, he would like to talk to me about England. I said I'd love to tell him and was taken aback when he said, "Swinging, man" - an expression that had been all over London the previous year. I asked him where he had heard it and he explained that he had got to know some "very pretty" English showgirls in Las Vegas.

We went into Elvis's trailer with a few of the boys, Joe Esposito, Red West and Marty Lacker, but when Elvis gave a nod they melted away.

"You ever meet the Queen?"

"No, but I sat on her mother's foot once."

I told him about Countess Rosse's summer ball and how the butler had come over to me at the end of the evening and said, "Your chariot awaits, madam."

"Chariot?" said Elvis. "You had a chariot?"

"No, it was a smart car, but they call them chariots."

Elvis loved the sound of that and, from then on, he referred to his limo as his "chariot".

He was fascinated about the Royal Family's security - "all those guards in fur hats marching up and down outside the palace."

"Yes, but they don't have nearly as many as the King of Morocco."

I told him about my visits to Morocco as the guest of Lala Nezha and how the palace guard were armed with machine-guns. He asked if the King carried a gun.

I told him I didn't know, but that I didn't like guns and that the only thing I had ever shot was a hare.

"A hare is fast, baby."

"He was just unlucky - and I've never been able to shoot anything since."

"You have to have guns over here for protection."

"You could use peacocks, you know."

"Peacocks?"

"Sure, the royal families had peacocks roaming the grounds. They let out a piercing cry whenever they see a stranger."

Elvis laughed.

One of Mickey Moore's assistants tapped on the door of the trailer to say that we were wanted on the set for the next scene.

"I'd better go," I said.

"I'm not working today," Elvis told the man, "and neither is she."

Mickey had little or no control over Elvis while his movies continued to do a roaring trade at the box office. As no less an authority than Hal Wallis had once said: "A Presley picture is the only sure thing in show business."

I told Elvis that when we met I felt it wasn't for the first time and asked him if he felt the same way.

"Yep!"

"Do you believe in reincarnation?"

"I don't know if that's what it is, but I sure do believe in somethin'."

"I just know that we've been close before."

"In another life?"

"Possibly. There's certainly more to this than meets the eye."

"Say that again, baby."

"There's certainly more to this than meets the eye."

"Which eye, baby?"

"Don't call me baby."

"Sure thing, baby."

After that little exchange, Elvis and I looked at each other and laughed and I knew that we were going to be close to one another, but not as lovers. I loved his sense of humour and his ability to make me feel wanted just by talking to me the way he did. He wasn't at all surprised when I told him the next time we were alone that he was much more important to me than a boyfriend.

"Well, you're special," he said. "You're the sister I never had."

I was very proud of our relationship and, within a matter of days, it went to my head. I was looking out of the window of Elvis's trailer when I spotted an incredibly sexy-looking girl with long blonde hair, a bikini top and half skirt. Having just made a picture with two other blondes, I wasn't anxious to repeat the experience.

"I thought I was the only blonde in this picture."

"You are, baby."

"I don't think so. Who's that?"

Elvis joined me at the window.

"I don't know, but she'll be in a black wig tomorrow. How's that?"

"Cruel but necessary."

Those three words became a catch phrase of ours.

The blonde girl was Marianna Hill, who plays Lani, a cabaret singer and the pushiest of Elvis's on-screen girlfriends. Sure enough, when she turned up on the set she was wearing a black wig which completely altered her appearance. Being Elvis, he had taken it one step further: not only was she in a wig, but an ill-fitting wig at that.

"I can't understand why they can't make it fit ," Marianna complained. "In fact, I can't understand why I'm in a wig at all."

There were a few times when I asked Elvis to interfere in the film like this, even to its detriment. Like a spoiled child, I wanted to see how far I could go and he indulged my whims, saying: "Hal Wallis will make money out of this film whatever it looks like."

One scene in particular, in which Elvis sings a duet with Marianna, suffered from my precocious behaviour. This was the sexy bit of the film and I saw it as a threat to me - childish, I know, but it was as if my big brother was being taken away from me. I wanted his attention all the time; I didn't want to share him with anyone.

The scene was being shot in the Piki Niki, a mountain-top bar where Lani works as a singer. As the rehearsals went on and on, I complained to Elvis that I didn't like the way it was going. I was jealous.

When they were ready to shoot the scene, he picked me up and sat me next to the cameraman, Wallace Kelley, and, when he was supposed to be singing *Scratch My Back (Then I'll Scratch Yours)* to Marianna, he was actually looking at me. I was amazed that they kept this in the film because it completely destroyed the point of the scene.

Off-set, Elvis was very mean with his time and I took it as a great privilege that he spent so much of it with me. I started calling him "E.P.", which he liked. He still called me "Baby" to get a reaction, except I no longer reacted. Big brothers were allowed to tease little sisters.

Whenever I got moody, Elvis would sing: *"Oh, Suzanna, now don't you cry for me..."* which always snapped me out of it. The first time he did it, he sang the whole song in front of the crew on the set. Little things like that were great fun and made me feel accepted.

Elvis was one of the very few people who understood how hard it was for me to have any self-esteem because of my upbringing. He talked about his tough life as a boy growing up in poverty in Mississippi.

"I hate wearing jeans," he said. "They were the only thing we wore back then because they didn't wear out."

I told him that, although I had been brought up in big houses with lots of antiques, there was no love after my father died.

He said: "Yeah, I don't have any antiques at Graceland - all I ever saw as a kid was old furniture. We were dirt poor, but the one thing we weren't short of was love - Momma made sure of that."

I told him that his love for his mother, Gladys, and my love for my father would always bind us.

"She would have loved you, little sister."

I told him that he had been the most important part of my childhood dream about Hollywood and that, as well as making a movie with him, the fact that he was also my friend gave me a real sense of my own worth. I felt I belonged because he cared about me.

Elvis replied that I had been sent to him by God. He knew he had been put on earth for a purpose and he had prayed over the previous few months before our first meeting for guidance about the direction his life should be taking. He was looking for answers to many spiritual questions and, more than anything, he needed to exchange ideas with someone who thought the same way as he did.

One of the most important things, he later told me, was that I had spoken to him about my Guardian Angel. In the middle of the Sixties, talking about angels was not exactly hip, but when Elvis asked me a question I did just that.

"Tell me, baby, have you seen Him?" he asked.

"Well, it might not always have been Him, but I've seen faces and I've seen my Guardian Angel, Daniel. It was mostly when I looked at the sky, which I often did when I was alone and frightened at boarding school. He came for me out of the clouds. He was very tall, with the most beautiful wings. Of course, he may have only *seemed* tall because I was so small when I saw him."

"Baby, we are as one. I remember my Guardian Angel, too. He was there when I was born and he took Jesse with him."

After that, I told Elvis my innermost secrets, things that I had buried in the deepest part of my being because they hurt too much to remember. I told him how the nuns would ask us children when we went back to the convent on a Sunday night if we'd been to mass that morning.

Most times, I had to say I hadn't gone to church because my mother hadn't taken me. The nun in charge would rave on about how St Bernadette would walk three miles without shoes to go to church. My pleas that it wasn't my fault were neither listened to nor believed. I could have lied and said I'd gone to church, but that seemed a much worse sin. So the flat back of a hairbrush or a thin birch stick found its mark again week after week.

Elvis asked me why being hit most Sunday evenings for something like that hadn't put me off religion, or at least Catholicism. I told him that, on the contrary, it had bound my faith tighter to me, like a blanket in a storm. In the chapel, I'd ask Jesus to take away the pain and I would cry in front of the cross because of the pain he had gone through because of those nails.

"You're different from Priscilla," Elvis said. "You're the same age, but she's still a child."

"I don't want to be different."

Elvis laughed.

"I don't talk about any of this to 'Cilla. She'll take a while to believe that we're not making out."

Once, I was able to help Elvis carry off a difficult scene. He was with Julie Parrish in a helicopter with four unruly dogs, the idea being that he has to sing to calm them down. The dogs were howling and yapping, even biting, and Elvis was getting stressed about it. He hated singing to dogs because the Colonel had made him put on a tuxedo and sing to a basset hound on *The Steve Allen Show* when he was just starting to hit the big time.

This time, I sat next to the camera and helped him get through the scene as painlessly as possible. At one point, he smiles at me and shakes his head, and yet again they kept that moment in the film.

Sometimes Elvis would stop me in the middle of one of my stories and I could see from his face that he was upset by what I was describing. This happened when I told him about one of the nuns, Mother Luke, who had been more short-tempered than the rest.

The very mention of her name would be enough to frighten me and I'd have an asthma attack if I knew she was on duty in the dormitory. Mother Luke would react either by almost throttling me under the eiderdown or by sending me outside to stand in the hallway, that long, dark corridor of stained wood which seemed to take on a fearful aspect at night.

Elvis interrupted to say the good news was that he was here now and he would never let anyone hurt me again. I said that was great because Mother Luke had once put me in a large wicker laundry basket and put the stick through the straps holding the lid and promptly forgot about me for the rest of the night.

Elvis was appaled at the very thought of sending a child away from home for schooling. He thought that, as a Catholic, I might be narrow-minded in my views, but he discovered that I shared his need to find out more about other religions. We both believed that each religion had something pretty startling to offer.

I was unsure whether the God I knew was the same as the one worshiped under different names by believers in other religions. I loved the Koran from my trips to Morocco and I was into Egyptology.

This was music to the ears of a Memphian.

I had a bracelet of large Eastern gold coins which Ian Heath had bought me, one coin at a time, from a Mr Kuchinski in Knightsbridge. Elvis took a piece of paper and, referring to my bracelet, sketched a design for a thick, studded belt. I also wore a medallion around my neck on a chain and Elvis used this as the model for the motif on the back of his jumpsuit when he recorded the Hawaiian TV special.

Elvis was so wise about things that most of us took for granted and he had an inquiring mind. When I told him I'd just read *The Prophet* by Kahlil Gibran, he immediately had to have a copy. He asked me to tell him about every book I read, which I took as a great compliment and would go into as much detail he wanted. I was doing just this about the deposed King of Scotland when he interrupted. "Some of the guys around the King should have been Southern boys," he said. "It might have had a different ending."

The reason why Elvis and I were such avid readers was that we were both frustrated that we had never had a formal education. But although he was one of the most intelligent people I ever met (and he remembered *everything*), it suited him for people to think he wasn't too bright. He would hide his "grown-up" books from anyone who visited his trailer, even from some of the boys. He had a huge etymology dictionary to check the origins of words which he slipped out of sight one day when Marty Lacker came into the trailer.

I also found him reading a study of numerology, the mystical art of numbers. He said that he felt good with the numbers two, six and eight. "That's lucky," I said. "My birthday is on the 26th and The Cottage is No. 42 - added together they make six and multiplied they make eight."

Elvis said that the number one represented God. He said he was interested in Eastern teaching.

"Are you looking for Nirvana, then?"

"That's right, baby, we've got to cover all angles."

"Me, too."

I told him that, as Jesus was a Jew, I had once wondered why I was a Catholic and had taken lessons with a rabbi for a while. Elvis talked about converting to Judaism himself and later, when he played the Las Vegas Hilton, he wore a Star of David as well as a crucifix around his neck - "just covering all angles, baby."

One day I was in my trailer when I heard Elvis calling to me, but only in my head. I left the trailer and walked over to his and was about to knock when he opened the door.

"Did you hear me?"

" Yes!"

"Scary, huh?"

Elvis was interested in every aspect of the metaphysical and believed that his "mission" was connected to religion in some way. As he had been brought up on gospel and blues in Mississippi, I suggested he should spread the word through his songs.

"Maybe one day, baby, but right now I gotta kiss the girl or knock the guy out and then sing to 'em."

Gladys had taught Elvis the manners of a Southern gentleman and he called men "Sir" and women "Ma'am" as a matter of course, but he lived by some very rigid rules.

"It's a family thing, baby, from the time people were puttin' us down. Never let anyone tell you revenge is a bad thing. It's good karma. If anyone betrays you or puts you down, then cut them off like they no longer exist. The only reason you don't kill 'em is that there's a law against it - in most states, that is. And never let them back in, no matter how hard they beg. I live by that rule: it's cruel but necessary."

Soon after hearing that, I made an unforgivable gaffe which could have ruined our friendship. I was approached by a very pretty young woman in the lobby of our hotel. She was in her early twenties, with long, brownish hair, and she was accompanied by two young children. She said she was a great fan of Elvis's and asked if I'd ask him for his autograph for her and one of the children.

The request seemed harmless and she looked like a nice enough girl, so I said I'd do what I could. I persuaded Elvis to meet the girl and her little children the following afternoon and I went back downstairs and told her.

The next day Elvis and I and a few of the boys got into the service elevator on his floor. Up there, he always had at least two guards on duty to vet anyone trying to gain access to him. As we came out of the elevator, we saw the girl with her children, the three of them all looking very nice, though it did strike me as strange that she was wearing a trench coat in that part of the world.

She came forward and Elvis extended his hand to shake hers, flashing her that beautiful smile. All at once she opened her coat and there she was with nothing on, not even a tummy chain. We were, by this stage, in the hotel's main lobby. I don't think I've ever been so embarrassed in my life. People were staring - there was Elvis Presley, the most famous man in the world, confronted by a naked lady and the children's presence made it all the worse.

Elvis carried the whole thing off with his customary charm, as though she was beautifully dressed and they were chatting at a cocktail party. He even talked to the children. I tried to slip away, but his vice-like grip kept me with him.

"You stay right there," he said.

We made our way to the limo and I thought I was about to fall into the "cruel but necessary" category and disappear from his life, but instead he lectured me about being fooled by scheming women who posed as fans to get close to him. He said that not all of his fans had his best interests at heart: some meant real harm.

Elvis also said that he had to be very careful about the women he got involved with. He had really loved Ann-Margret, but one day she had announced that they were "going steady" and that he'd given her a bed and he had flipped and broken off their affair. It had been cruel but necessary.

Around this time, I attracted the attention of Colonel Tom Parker, the Dutch-born illegal immigrant and ex-fairground barker who posed as a Southern officer and a gentleman when he was neither. He was fat and brash and loud and he took an instant dislike to me because I was close to Elvis.

The Colonel had a credit on the film as "technical adviser" (whatever that meant) and, watching the way he interfered on the set - or tried to - reminded me of another control freak: my mother. I had told Elvis about some of the things my mother had done and he'd described her as "an Indian giver". When I said that the Colonel used the same tactics, he disagreed.

"That old man doesn't give me anything," he said. "He manages me and there's no one better in the business."

Elvis said he shared all his earnings on a fifty-fifty basis with the Colonel, but that he maintained complete control over all of the songs he recorded, as well as the artistes and musical arrangements; the Colonel never, ever, interfered with the recording side of things, except to set up the contracts.

He conceded, however, that his greatest disappointment was that he hadn't been given a chance to play more dramatic roles in his movies and that was entirely the Colonel's doing. He had proved that he *could* act in his early films for Hal Wallis and he had been offered the part of Tony in *West Side Story*, playing opposite his former girlfriend, Natalie Wood. He had turned it down under pressure from the Colonel, who had secured him a $1-million-a-picture deal with MGM to make "exploitation flicks". He was still loyal to him, though. "If it hadn't been for him," he said, "I could still be driving that truck."

Whenever he came on to the set, Colonel Parker created dissension and ill-feeling. He argued with everybody, mostly about inconsequential matters, just to show his power. Once, when Elvis was filming on the beach, the Colonel walked up to Marty Lacker and demanded that he give him $300 from the money that Marty was doling out to the boys for their week's work.

Marty refused to hand the money over and a shouting match developed between him and the Colonel. We had to stop shooting the scene while Elvis went over to sort things out. The Colonel walked off without his $300 and Elvis calmed Marty down. Marty said that Parker didn't need $300 anyway; he was just playing the big shot with Elvis's money to show he was in charge.

This episode was typical of the Colonel's attitude. On another occasion, we were about to shoot a scene and the Colonel was standing in the way. The assistant director pointed out to him that the cameras were ready to roll.

"Well, *she* ain't ready," Parker said, pointing his cane at me. "She hasn't got her make-up on."

In fact I was fully made up and completely prepared for the shoot. After that display of rudeness, I didn't even bother to say hello to him whenever I bumped into him at the hotel or on the set. I pretended he was invisible and he did the same to me.

"Watch out for that old man," Elvis said. "He's mean."

But Elvis needed someone like the Colonel to haggle with the money men on his behalf, just as much as he needed round-the-clock protection, and not only from scheming females.

One afternoon I was sitting on my hotel balcony (in the shade, of course) when I heard a radio show that introduced Elvis to Peter Noone, the lead singer of the English rock group, Herman and the Hermits. Elvis had mentioned something about it to me, but I hadn't had a chance to warn him that Noone was a cocky little brat and that he should be careful.

The show was going out live and it soon became apparent that Noone was trying to make a fool out of Elvis by conducting most of the interview in gobbledygook. I was horrified as I listened helplessly. I knew that if Elvis stumbled in any way, the press would never let him live it down. Somehow, Elvis carried on, never once giving Noone the satisfaction of asking what he was talking about.

Afterwards, Noone claimed that he had been speaking Lancastrian, but that, of course, is an accent, not a language. When I next saw Elvis, he was furious. "Are they all like that in England? You gotta warn me, baby."

In one of the scenes we shot in Hawaii, the sparks really flew between Elvis and me. Rick and Judy are arguing about his recklessness and Judy tells him that he is "bitter, arrogant and just plain selfish". Elvis gives back as good as he gets.

It was only one scene in the whole picture, but when we saw the rushes we realised that we had the potential to do much more serious stuff together if we had the right script.

Then we were back into the usual schmaltz: Judy changes her mind about Rick when he risks his license to rescue Danny and his daughter after their helicopter crashes on a rocky shore.

The *dénouement* comes when Rick invites Judy to a Polynesian feast and, when all of his girlfriends show up at the same place, his love life unravels in much the same fashion as Bernard's in *Boeing-Boeing*. Needless to say, Elvis breaks up with all of them and is about to kiss Judy for the first time when he is called away to perform his grand finale number, a singing, dancing, drum-beating extravaganza with dozens of Hawaiian extras.

We finished shooting in Hawaii and went back to Los Angeles to complete the studio work. I returned to my dressing room at Paramount and my suite at the Chateau Marmont, while Elvis moved into Jerry Lewis's old red-and-black dressing room and lived at a rented house in Perugia Way, Bel Air, with Priscilla and the Boys.

As a result of the Peter Noone "interview", Elvis was avoiding a meeting with the Beatles, who were in Los Angeles on their second American tour. The "Fab Four" repeatedly mentioned their desire to meet "The King of Rock 'n' Roll, Elvis Presley" nearly every time they were interviewed on TV and radio. Elvis liked the Beatles' music, although he would have had to have been superhuman not to have minded that they were outselling him in the charts. "Gimme info, baby," Elvis said and I told him what I knew about them.

I had met the Beatles and their manager, Brian Epstein, at the Ad Lib and I told Elvis that they were witty and very, very sharp. Elvis was worried. "It will be four against one," he said. I told him not to be silly; the Beatles really respected him, particularly John Lennon (Elvis's favourite of the group), who was always saying that Elvis was the biggest influence on his life. But the disastrous interview with Peter Noone had made Elvis cautious.

The Beatles were on a high. Earlier that month they had played Shea Stadium, home of the Mets baseball team in New York, to 55,000 fans - the largest rock-concert crowd in history - and in Los Angeles they were feted at Capitol Records by a host of Hollywood stars including Steve McQueen, Jane Fonda, James Stewart and Rock Hudson.

Trying to reassure Elvis, I said that success often brought a bit of big-headedness and it was nothing to worry about. I asked him if he had any discs - platinum, gold or silver - in Los Angeles. I knew that he had been awarded a vast number, but wondered if they were at Graceland or in the RCA offices. Elvis nodded and said: "I've got a couple of rooms full, baby."

"Well, why not meet the Beatles at your house and let them see them for themselves," I suggested. "That should even things up a bit." Elvis laughed and said he'd think about it and, with the Colonel and Brian Epstein both pushing for a meeting, he reluctantly agreed to meet the Beatles.

A couple of English reporters were travelling with the Beatles and they phoned me up to ask if they could meet Elvis and he was sweet enough to agree.

"Will it be good for you?"

"Sure, yes, I guess so."

Elvis finally met the Beatles at his home and they had a jam session together, with Elvis singing and playing piano and guitar. By all accounts, it was a tense evening and Elvis had no wish to repeat the experience. While he respected the Beatles as musicians, he considered that their political beliefs were "subversive" and a bad influence on young Americans.

Contrary to reports about Elvis's selfishness, he was always thinking about ways to help others, especially his true fans. I remember an English fan and her mother had been standing at the Music Gates at Graceland when the mother had a heart attack and died. This was broadcast on a local radio station, which would always be on in the background wherever we were. Elvis immediately had all of the arrangements made for the mother's body to be flown back to England and paid all of her daughter's expenses.

The Beatles apart, Elvis was also great with other performers who might have been considered his rivals. I was walking back from the commissary one day when I spotted Tom Jones looking nervously about him. I went up and introduced myself. Although he was a big star in Britain (and Elvis loved his strong Welsh voice), he hadn't yet broken into the US market.

Tom knew I was working on a movie with Elvis and asked me about it. I told him that Elvis made everybody feel at ease and offered to go and tell him that he was here. I could see that Tom was becoming increasingly nervous and my enthusiasm about Elvis wasn't helping matters.

"No, look, I think I'll come back tomorrow," he said.

"Sure, right," I began to reply, but he was already out of there.

The following day I saw Tom again and we went through the same ritual, but on the third day he showed up as usual and everything was fine. I introduced Tom to Elvis on the set at Stage 5 and they got along famously. Tom asked Elvis if he could have a photograph taken of the two of them together for the British press. Elvis agreed and, while the photographer snapped away, he astonished Tom by singing songs from Tom's first album.

"I was really dumbfounded," Tom said later. "I was thrilled that he even knew who I was. Our friendship started right then."

I received quite a few letters from fans myself, some from American troops serving in Vietnam. One day five soldiers who were home on leave came to my trailer. They were extremely polite, but their eyes seemed more dead than alive. They insisted on sitting where they could see the windows and the door. This was a war in which your girlfriend was likely to arrive for a date wired up to a bomb and kiss you, all of the time with her finger on the pin, waiting for the proper moment to create maximum carnage.

These men, the same age as me, had seen things that nobody should have to see. There had been talk after the death of President Kennedy that his assassination was a result of his decision to pull out of Vietnam. In fact, he had already started to put a withdrawal plan into motion when the arms dealers and the war-mongers stepped in. Kennedy's successor, Lyndon B. Johnson, was their man and he had recently committed another 50,000 American troops to Vietnam.

I was approached by one of Bob Hope's team to see if I would be interested in accompanying him on his next goodwill tour there. I said that I was willing to go, but would have to check with Hal Wallis first. I didn't think that this would be much of a problem as Ann-Margret and many other stars had already been to Vietnam. Hal reacted as if I'd asked to lead a sortie into the interior.

"Why have I put all of this time and money into you?" he asked. "Not to have some nutcase take pot-shots at you!"

There didn't seem to be much I could say to that, so I left it alone, but I always thought that the war should have been stopped long before it was.

If I was looking for trouble, there was plenty right just a short drive along Sunset Boulevard. Earlier that month, Johnson's Great Society had exploded into flames over the civil rights issue and the fires were raging over the Watts ghetto. From anywhere in the Hollywood Hills, you could see smoke, tinged pink by the sun, hanging over the city like a surreal light show. Elvis and Uncle Hal impressed upon me that I shouldn't go anywhere near the area, but I was determined to see it for myself.

Having finished work early one day, I set off in my blue Mustang and headed downtown. Almost as soon as I had entered the Watts district, I accidentally drove down a cul-de-sac. Walking towards me were three young black men, swinging bike chains.

I was frantically trying to turn my car around while, at the same time, shouting, "Excuse me. I'm British. I seem to have lost my way. Could you direct me to Sunset Boulevard."

Very Joyce Grenfell.

Luckily, they went for it and told me to get the hell out of there.

I said nothing to Elvis about that near miss. He would have called it "a definite slip in judgment".

Chapter 14

The Mean McQueen

"Macho does not prove mucho."

Zsa Zsa Gabor, *Hungarian actress*

"SUZANNA LEIGH!" I heard someone calling my name on the Paramount lot and looked around to see my fantasy, Steve McQueen, beckoning me. Even at a distance, his piercing blue eyes were like a magnet. He was sitting with his feet up on a hitching rail in front of his western-style trailer and I walked over to him.

"Like a drink?"

"I'll have some juice."

Inside the trailer, his "man", who was dressed all in white, including white gloves, produced some orange juice.

"Like a smoke?"

The servant offered me some cigarettes from a silver salver. I took one, lit it and noticed that it had an odd, musty taste. After a couple of puffs, I stubbed it out, thinking it must have been lying around for ages.

Steve and I talked about *Nevada Smith*, the film he was making and, when I was offered another cigarette, I lit up again without even thinking.

There were six-guns hanging from holsters on the walls of the trailer and Steve told me that, even though they were loaded with blanks, you had to be careful. Sammy Davis Jr had powder burns down one side of his leg from being too quick on the draw. To illustrate the point, Steve showed me how to draw a six-gun from a holster and I saw how easy it would be to cause a self-inflicted wound.

He was asking me if I liked motorbikes and if I'd like to go for a ride around the lot some time when, suddenly, everything he said seemed hilarious and I started to giggle uncontrollably. I got up to go and the room started to swim. I didn't smoke cigarettes often, so this happened for the first few puffs, but the effect never lasted for this long. I got back to the *Paradise* set, giggling about everything.

Fortunately, I bumped into Elvis, who laughed when he saw the state I was in.

"Oh, baby, you're stoned!"

"That was pot?"

"Who gave it to you?"

Through the giggling, I told him what had happened and he was angry with Steve for not asking me if I had smoked marijuana before.

"You can't work like this," he said.

He sent me back to my trailer and fixed it so that I didn't have to work that day. He also made sure that Hal didn't find out as he would have had Steve in front of Howard Koch for drugging one of his stars.

After that first encounter, I saw quite a bit of Steve. We rode around the lot on his Harley-Davidson and I took him on to the *Paradise* set and introduced him to Elvis. I was amazed at how few people Elvis had met in Hollywood - Tony Curtis, for instance, who lived virtually next door to him in Bel Air. I later read in Tony's autobiography that he did go on to the set and meet Elvis, but that he didn't think that he was all that he was cracked up to be. Of course, Steve thought he was great, but then he would, wouldn't he?

I had always dreamed about having Steve McQueen as a lover and it would have been easy to succumb to his sexual charisma. Although he was married, he played around with numerous young actresses and he made it plain that he would like to have sex with me. I wasn't into one-night stands, however, and the thought of an affair with a married man had lost all its appeal after my experiences with Richard Harris.

I was the only girl I knew who hadn't had sex with Warren Beatty and I managed to stay out of Steve's bed as well, but it took a lot of willpower and one thing that helped me a great deal was the knowledge that Elvis would surely find out.

Elvis must have sensed what was going on because he took a hand in proceedings when I accompanied him to the Paramount photographic studio, where he was doing some publicity stills. I was watching the photographer take pictures of Elvis dressed in a variety of outfits when Elvis invited me to do some shots with him, even though I wasn't dressed for the camera.

We had posed together for a couple of shots when Elvis suddenly turned me round, took me in his arms and kissed me on the lips.

The photographer snapped away and Elvis said: "This won't do your career any harm, baby."

When that picture appeared in the newspapers a couple of days later, the press office sent one of their reps down to my dressing room.

"The front office - (that is, Hal Wallis and Howard Koch) - want to know what's going on between you and Elvis."

"It's private."

He didn't like that.

"Look, this isn't just anybody we're talking about here. It's Elvis Presley and Elvis doesn't do things like that for fun."

"Honestly, we're just good friends."

He went away, disbelieving.

To avoid further rumours, I didn't go to Elvis's home in Bel Air, even when Priscilla was out of town, and we never went to restaurants or clubs together. Elvis told me that he wasn't very comfortable at parties or in public places and mostly stayed at home with the people who worked for him. He didn't need the A-list; he was in a list of his own.

Joe Esposito was Elvis's "main man", as it were, who sorted out the biggest problems. Joe was driving the "chariot", with Elvis and me in the back, when a female fan deliberately drove into us at some lights. It wasn't a serious crash, but serious enough for the drivers to exchange phone numbers and insurance details and I presume that this was the girl's plan.

Elvis asked Joe to "see to it" and Joe lent forward and took a small brown envelope from the glove compartment. He got out of the car, spoke to the girl and returned minus the envelope.

"It happens all the time," Elvis sighed.

He had paid the girl off on the spot rather than face the hassle of arguing the rights and wrongs of the case.

Elvis was thirty when I met him, but he had a maturity way beyond his years. He had been at the top of the music business for twelve years, making millions of dollars in the process, and, despite all the reports about his reckless spending on Cadillacs, motorbikes and jewellery, many people depended on him for their livelihood, and not just members of the Memphis Mafia or his father Vernon, his Aunt Delta, his Uncle Vester and numerous other family members in Memphis.

To his immediate circle, Elvis was like the chieftain of a Scottish clan and a Native American tribe rolled into one, an accurate comparison since Elvis's forebears on the Presley side came from Scotland and his grandmother on his mother's side was a Cherokee.

Added to that number, however, were literally hundreds of others who benefited financially from Elvis's talent. Paramount and MGM did not make movies starring Elvis Presley; they made Elvis Presley movies - he was the sole reason why they were ever filmed and why millions of people paid their money to see them.

These films, of course, provided work for actors, actresses, directors, photographers, script-writers, film crew, make-up artists and hairdressers, while songwriters, backing singers, musicians and technicians were hired for the soundtrack albums. As for the producers and distributors, not one of Elvis's thirty-one films ever made a loss - who else can claim such a record?

So Elvis shouldered many, many responsibilities and most of the boys - and there were as many as nine or ten on the payroll at one time - respected him for it.

Charlie Hodge was a really nice guy - you could just feel his love for Elvis and he never lost it, even when the going got tough. I also got on well with Marty Lacker because we seemed to laugh at a lot of the same things; he sometimes dropped into the Chateau Marmont for a Coke and a chat on his way home.

Marty told me that some of the boys took advantage of young girls who were desperate to meet Elvis. These girls would fling themselves at anyone in Elvis's group in the hope that, afterwards, they would be introduced to him. Many of the stories about Elvis's loose behaviour with young girls stemmed from members of his entourage taking advantage of girls who were little more than children and then shifting the blame on to Elvis.

Red West was the bodyguard I had the most to do with on *Paradise - Hawaiian Style* because he and Elvis worked out the fight scenes together on the set. I was watching one of these rehearsals with Red's cousin, Sonny West, when I said that I hadn't seen him around for a while: where had he been? It seemed that he'd been in a real fight and had lost a tooth, which "the boss had fixed for me".

He added: "Once I lost most of my front ones and the boss fixed those, too."

Elvis not only picked up the tab for medical and dental expenses for all those who worked for him, but also for their wives and children.

In my opinion, a lot of the problems that Elvis had with the boys emanated from the fact that Sonny, Red and several of the others were in an intellectual desert, while he was always out there, studying in the University of Life. For around twenty years, he had always been there for them and they could have made something of themselves from the resources he had placed at their disposal. In the end, all they could do was betray him by contributing to nasty books about him, purely for money.

Larry Geller, Elvis's hairdresser, was completely different from the others. Larry had been working at Jay Sebring's salon the previous year when he was summoned to Elvis's house to cut his hair and was invited to stay. Larry was Jewish, but he had a genuine interest in all spiritual matters and was well-versed in alternative religions.

Many people in California were either dabbling in the occult and observing pagan, even satanic, rites, or following Dr Timothy Leary and Ken Kesey on the LSD trail, or listening to the teachings of a mixed bunch of Indian gurus. Larry wasn't one of the crackpots, though, and he later became Elvis's friend and spiritual advisor until the Colonel burned his books and he quit in disgust, although he returned to work for Elvis in the Seventies.

But at this time Parker was more concerned about my influence over his billion-dollar star because, without Elvis, he would have no way of keeping the money rolling in for his one great love in life: gambling.

Paradise was Elvis's last picture under his contract with Hal Wallis and he decided that the only way for us to keep seeing each other was to do another picture together.

"I can't do another picture with you."

"Excuse me?"

"Everyone only does one."

"Well, you're gonna do two - how's that?"

Elvis went to see Hal Wallis and I was called up to his office. Hal was overjoyed because another Elvis picture was as good as money in the bank.

"Elvis has told me what he wants," he said. "We'll get good writers in and make this one really special. It will be specifically written for you."

This was the project that would turn into *Easy Come, Easy Go*. Elvis told me he wanted me to sing on the sound-track, but I said I had never had enough confidence to sing in public.

"Yes you can, baby. Just a few lessons will do it. You'll just be in the background. And there'll always be money coming in: all my records make money."

He didn't say this in a show-off sort of way; he was merely stating a fact.

Then the Colonel stepped in.

He heard about Elvis's plan to shoot a second movie with me and set out to sabotage it. There was a sort of hush when I walked on to the set one morning. Somewhat uneasy, I went over to Elvis's trailer, but the entrance was barred by one of the boys. I felt my face burning as I walked back to my trailer with as much dignity as I could muster. What could have happened?

Someone must have either felt sorry for me or wanted me to know what all of the fuss was about for myself; either way, there was a magazine, and a pretty lurid one at that, waiting for me on the mat. Inside the magazine I found a three-page article with the headline "Elvis & I, by Suzanna Leigh". It was illustrated with lots of pictures, but the bulk of the text consisted of quotes and phrases that Elvis had used to me, although anyone could have picked them up just from being around us.

I read this article, which I was supposed to have written, or even sold, and was devastated. Not only had I not sold a story about him, but I knew only too well how strongly he felt about betrayal of this type and that frightened me. I might never be able to get close enough to him to explain my side, and whoever had planted the story would, even now, be spreading more poison about me. It could only have been the Colonel - he had the motive and the malice and he was the only person capable of arranging such a thing.

I sat in my dressing room, staring at the wallpaper; so English and refined. I had been with Elvis for ten hours a day for months and the thought of losing him made me sicker by the minute. I wasn't needed on the set, except for a possible cover shot, and I didn't know whether to go home or stay put.

Sitting there, I realised just how much Elvis and his friendship meant to me and the fear of losing that friendship became too painful to bear. I changed into my denim skirt and the halter-necked top that he liked so much and strode out on to the set.

All eyes seemed to bore into me as though I'd turned up naked at a costume party. I saw the boys first: they were standing around Elvis's trailer, talking among themselves. I knew the way it would be : they would close ranks around him, his face would be like stone, I would be invisible to him and there would be no forgiveness.

Cruel but necessary.

My mind focused.

"Elvis," I said in my head, "I didn't do it - please believe me, please."

My heart was thumping loudly now because, behind me, I could hear Cuban heels, lots of them, marching towards me. The sound came closer, echoing on the concrete. Was he going to stop or merely pass me by? I tensed. As Elvis drew level, he pulled me to him without changing pace. He was dressed in black and his face bore a matching expression.

He stroked my cheek.

"I didn't do it, I didn't."

"I know, I heard you."

"You did?"

"Sure, you hear me sometimes, don't you? It's the same thing if you think about it."

He looked into my face, then through it into my very being.

"I knew you were innocent of all charges. I knew, even before I heard you. Don't say anything, just keep walking. I know who did it, baby, and I know why, but it ain't gonna change anything. It'll be hard on him, that's all."

He was referring to the Colonel.

Some of the darkness was beginning to fade from Elvis's face.

"I was frightened I'd lost you," I said.

Smiling, he slipped his hand up the back of my top and twanged my bra strap.

"Same thing, baby!"

We both laughed and the boys joined in, as they always did, when Elvis laughed. Our reconciliation had taken place outside Elvis's trailer, rather than in the privacy inside, and I knew he was making a stand in front of the Colonel. Even if the conniving old buzzard wasn't watching in person, his assistant Tom Diskin or one of his other spies would be there to report back to him.

Sure enough, as the days went by, the Colonel got madder and madder that his scheme had actually brought Elvis and me closer together.

It made him even more determined to get me out of Elvis's life once and for all.

Chapter 15

Exile on Sunset

"I survived because I was tougher than anybody else."

Bette Davis, *American actress*

IT was after lunch with Natalie Wood at the Bistro that I met Dr Mary Young, the clairvoyant everyone in Hollywood was talking about. She was regularly consulted by many stars in the hope of a glimpse into their futures. Some wouldn't even accept a film if she didn't approve. I was the only person I knew in Hollywood who had never been to a shrink or, at the very least, an astrologer. Nevertheless, my life was on the cusp.

Whenever I went out, everybody I met wanted to know about Elvis and I liked lunching with Natalie because the one thing we didn't need to talk about was Elvis. Natalie was seeing Dr Young after lunch and I asked if I could call by and meet her. After all, how often do you get the chance to meet a stargazer who lives on Saturn Street?

Natalie agreed and we pulled up outside a large, neat bungalow. The door was opened by a very sweet old lady with white hair.

Immediately something strange happened, or rather it was strange unless it was a massive put-up job, which I doubt, and even then it would have been brilliant. This little old lady smiled a greeting at Natalie, then, turning her eyes on me, clasped her hands in a joyful clap and exclaimed, "Oh, at last! Come in, please. I've been waiting for you for a long time."

To my amazement, I realised she was speaking to me.

"I don't think so," I said. "I'm just passing by."

Natalie was pushing me forward.

"Go on, Suzanna, take my place."

Then she whispered: "Go on! She never says that; it's not like her. I'll phone you later."

With that, she was gone.

Dr Young led me into a cluttered room and sat at a large writing desk. "You don't believe, do you?" she said, passing some sheets of tissue paper towards me.

"Can you just put your hands on these?"

I ran my hands over what appeared to be cooking parchment. She took the paper and felt it. I admitted to her that I didn't actually believe in any of this.

"Well, my dear," she said, "I'll just have to tell you the hard way."

With that, she told me that I had been sick with "shock asthma" when I was a little girl after finding my father's dead body and that I had suddenly recovered from this attack, all of which was true. According to her, my father had wanted to take me with him when he died, but he changed his mind (or had it changed for him) and that's why I was gasping for air one moment and breathing quite normally the next.

None of this talk about my father had ever been published in any newspaper and it was certainly not on my file in the Paramount publicity department. I was in floods of tears and, from that moment on, she had me hooked. I listened to every word she said, even though I didn't want to believe any of it.

She told me that my Hollywood days were drawing to an end and that I would soon leave America. She said I would have to leave behind a man who was very important to me - Elvis? - and that I would never see him again.

"Oh, but you don't understand," I burst out. "I've got a seven-year contract at Paramount and I'm going to make a new picture with Elvis."

"I can only tell you what I see, dear," she said quietly. "The thing to remember is that, no matter what happens, you will be looked after. Listen to the buzz in your head that signifies danger and you will be all right."

I left Saturn Street in a daze. I told Elvis about the meeting with Dr Young and her prediction. It was so final, so negative, that I didn't want to believe it. Elvis reassured me and I told him that I thought I loved him as much as I loved myself. "Same thing if you think about it, baby," he said. "We are as one."

He told me that if I ever wanted advice about something that I didn't want anyone else to know about, I should go into the bathroom and tell my reflection in the mirror and that the truth would come back.

"You can't lie to yourself when you're looking yourself in the eye," he said.

"Which eye?"

We both laughed.

Back in my trailer, I looked into the mirror for a long time, praying that what Dr Young had said wouldn't be true. I went to a little end-of-term party, as I called it, which was actually the end-of-picture party with the crew, and thanked everyone for being sweet and helpful. Elvis signed one of his movie posters "Happiness Always" for my sister-in-law, Sylvia, who was a member of his fan club in England.

I was still thinking about Dr Young's prediction when Elvis came to my trailer to say *au revoir*. He took my hands and kissed them, then looked deeply into my eyes, reading my thoughts. His face clouded as though he didn't want to believe what was going through my mind. I was about to say something when he suddenly took me in his arms and kissed me.

His only words were: "See you in February, baby!"

Outside, I heard the limo door slam and Elvis was gone.

An hour or so later I attended a press conference that Paramount had laid on about my future plans, then returned to my trailer to pick up some of the mementos that I had collected during my time with Elvis. These included several tapestries which I had sewn while waiting on the set, pictures of Elvis and posters of his movies, including the one he'd signed for my sister-in-law, and the sketch of a white gold bracelet, with "Paradise Lost" spelled out in sapphires, which he was going to give me when we started work again.

These precious souvenirs were all in a neat pile and I was going to take them to my suite at the Chateau Marmont for safe keeping. I had left the door of the trailer unlocked and, on entering, I saw that all of my Elvis things had been stolen. This spiteful act smacked of payback by the Colonel, the man who regarded Elvis as his personal possession.

With shooting on *Paradise* wrapped, I faced some tough decisions. Whether I stayed on at the Chateau Marmont or moved into a rented house, I needed my mother's permission. This was a strange time. I was attending my classes, but I was not working and the comparative inactivity didn't suit me at all. There were no lines to learn, no rehearsals, no Elvis.

I had to watch my step because there were a lot of unsavoury things going on. I had my hair done a couple of times by Jay Sebring, the archetypal mover and shaker who knew everybody in the piranha pool, but I avoided going out with his crowd: they were too fast for me. In the time I'd been away filming in Hawaii, the whole of Hollywood seemed to have embraced the drug culture.

The change was awesome: dinner parties in the homes of previously straight people were now all bangles and beads, and incense was burned to hide the smell of marijuana. So many people were stoned that I found it slightly frightening; not just young hippies, but producers and directors hanging out at the Bistro and Romanoff's.

Various people had offered me the use of their guest houses, so I hoped that when I rang my mother there wouldn't be too much of a problem because Hal had said the safest way of keeping my green card was for me to say in Hollywood. This would involve a period of about eight months or so without working if things got bad because Hal said there were rumours of all not being well with the Screen Actors Guild. He was having a bit of a problem with them, but nothing he couldn't handle.

It transpired that Charlton Heston, who was playing General Gordon in *Khartoum* in London, was in serious trouble because English Equity had objected to an American playing an Englishman on English soil. Their reasoning was that there must have been an English actor who could play the part just as well. The producers either had to move the principle cast to Ireland and recast the extras if they wanted to finish the film, or scrap it altogether. This was madness, treating actors as though they were local tradesmen.

I hoped that the Screen Actors Guild would not retaliate by using me to get back at English Equity. However, there were plenty of British actors working in Hollywood and nothing had appeared in the trade papers to point the finger at me, so there was only a vague possibility that I would be targeted.

That was the case until I heard that a group of American actresses had held a demonstration outside the guild's building on Sunset Boulevard, waving placards saying, "Me not Leigh".

The guild obviously could not afford to ignore a protest by its own members on its very own doorstep and, from that moment on, my name was thrown into the spotlight. Who was behind it? The only person outside of the front office to know that Elvis, for the first time ever, had requested a British actress to play the lead as an American in one of his films, was Colonel Tom Parker.

It seemed that I had no alternative other than to wait around in Hollywood without working, even though four film companies had tendered applications on the same day for me to work for them - all playing Americans.

I was an exile on Sunset, waiting in limbo for the powers-that-be to make the next move.

I rang my mother and told her that, in order to protect my career, it was vital that I stayed put in Hollywood and that I needed her authority to do so.

There was a disconcerting silence at the other end of the phone. After the pause came the storm: she said that if I stayed she would have to have my dogs put down.

"No, please don't do that!" I screamed.

She gave me no time to make up my mind - this woman did a lot of things, but making idle threats wasn't one of them.

I couldn't ask Aunt Sally to look after my dogs, either, because she lived in one of mother's flats. I was too ashamed to ask my friends: who would have believed that a rich woman like my mother would really have my dogs put down? To them, she appeared to be sweetness and generosity personified - only the previous Christmas she had given Ian's parents a Lalique salad bowl which had cost a fortune.

Uncle Hal had said that he would renegotiate my contract when I was twenty-one, but I couldn't tell him about the dogs because I knew his reply would be, "Let them go ... You're staying here."

I couldn't afford to fly the dogs over to California and, even if I could, I had nowhere to put them. Sobbing quietly, I thought about how much I loved my dogs, especially Monty. He had always been there for me to hug and cry with when I was lonely. Since I was nine, he had been my only true friend. I couldn't repay all of the love he'd given me by letting him die.

History is a strange story teller. Mary, Queen of Scots, lost her head because she allowed her heart to rule it. And now I was going to lose my Hollywood crown because of my love for my dogs. Grabbing my pillow and burying my face into it to muffle the noise, I screamed, "Roy, help me, please!"

Looking out of the window of the plane flying back to the UK, I thought that there must be a way; that I shouldn't keep looking on the negative side. I had *Barefoot In The Park* and *Anne Of The Thousand Days* lined up. Paramount would make me a big star. Elvis wanted me for his next film and they couldn't turn him down - nobody could, not even the Colonel.

I began to feel better.

Just in case something went wrong, I thanked God for letting me go to Hollywood at all.

Fate obviously decided that this was an apt prayer. By leaving Hollywood, I had taken Hal's trump card away from him and, as time went by, he never forgave me. But I knew that I would never have forgiven myself for Monty's death.

Yet again, perhaps, my mother did me a good turn by default. Less than three years later my friend Sharon Tate was murdered in Hollywood and I could so easily have been there that day.

And what was it that Natalie Wood said not long before she drowned? That she hated the water, but somehow always seemed to end up in it in her films.

So one gloomy evening in the English autumn, not the Californian fall, I found myself in a taxi driving along King's Road, Chelsea, marked "RETURN TO SENDER".

Part II:

...Address Unknown

Chapter 16:   Queen Bee

Chapter 17:   Her Majesty Requests...

Chapter 18:   Hammer Glamour!

Chapter 19:   The Caine Scrutiny

Chapter 20:   Natalia

Chapter 21:   Devil's Island

Chapter 22:   Polanski's Secret Shame

Chapter 23:   Nobs and Nobblers

Chapter 24:   Friends and Fiends

Chapter 25:   The Lichfield Break-up

Chapter 26:   Farewell, Dracula

Chapter 27:   Son of Flashman

Chapter 28:   Bullets in Beirut

Chapter 29:   The Day I Died

Chapter 30:   Elvis's Last Message

Chapter 16

Queen Bee

"In search of my mother's garden I found my own."

Alice Walker, *American writer*

MY experiences in America had liberated me from many of my old fears and insecurities. Beneath the Hollywood gloss, there were unmistakable signs of confidence. In London, I was a young Queen Bee.

Ian Heath wanted to get engaged, but I realised that I wouldn't make a very good *fiancée*. I didn't want to have to check with anyone if I was invited to a party; I wanted the freedom to make my own decisions. I was still a new face on the celebrity scene and I was in great demand.

Ian said we didn't have to break up; he'd fit in with the new arrangement as best he could. I pretended I wasn't going out with anyone, but I went to parties on my own - two or three in one evening wasn't unusual - and, if I fancied someone, I'd chat them up. Ian resolved the situation himself by dating other women, including Vicki Hodge.

In retrospect, part of me wishes I had married Ian, but that's the safe part. He would have protected me from a great deal of hardship, but, then again, you can't argue with fate.

As soon as I'd arrived back in London, I'd gone round to my mother's house to take presents for everyone. It was then that she told me I owed her a lot of money and I had better start to repay her. When I asked her what for, thinking of the dogs, she replied that it was for my school fees and keep while I was growing up, plus a fee for signing the Paramount contract on my behalf. I asked her to tell me the full amount, but instead she exploded about not going to Hollywood in Helen's place.

"Why didn't you send me an air fare?" she screamed.

"As you know, I didn't have the money."

"Well, there were plenty of old men you could have asked."

I was speechless; there was nothing I could say.

That day I started the long, painful process of paying her back for the money she'd spent on me as a child at £25 and £50 a time. In the beginning, she tried to offer me a typed receipt, but my expression of revulsion must have hit the spot because she never did that again.

Writing about this now is very upsetting. I struggled for years to make something out of our relationship, always hoping to make her pleased or proud, but it was never right. She always seemed to be in a position of power over me. I was ashamed, too; but who could I tell? Who would believe me? My aunt knew the truth and was so sad for me, but living as she did in one of my mother's flats she could do nothing, poor darling.

Despite all of this, I was still trying to get into my mother's good books and I did her a big favour. As Tony Curtis and Elvis were both with the William Morris Agency, I had joined them when I was in Hollywood. John Mather, the head of William Morris UK, had just moved from Rome to London and was busy house-hunting. I introduced him to my mother and he bought her old house, 79 Cadogan Place, where the three of us used to live before Eric got married and I moved out. Going back there for John's dinner parties, as I often did, had an odd feel to it.

My mother made a hefty profit out of that deal and, as she had disposed of The Cottage while I was in America, she promised to give me Eric's old house, 8 Belgrave Mews South, instead of paying me the commission to which I was entitled. In the interim, I rented a very smart first-floor flat, 7 Eaton Place.

London was wearing its "Swinging" mantle with more swank than ever. Actors, rock stars, models and designers were the elite of the new Permissive Society, but despite their visible fame this was really the age of the hairdresser. The crimper was the new courtier, his salon part disco, part boudoir, with gorgeous young men giving a new meaning to "wash and blow-dry". It was entirely apt that the spirit of the Sixties should be summed up in one word: "Hair".

Vidal Sassoon had several salons and the one I liked best was at the Grosvenor House Hotel on Park Lane. Some women had their hair done five times a week to keep up with the gossip and, like a scene from *Shampoo*, thought nothing of having sex with their favourite stylist. My hairdresser at Vidal's, Leslie Cavendish, also became my occasional lover.

After-hours, the hairdressers were to be found at Scotch of St James or one of the other hot spots for the "in" crowd, such as the Ad Lib, the Bag o' Nails, the Garrison and, shortly, Sibylla's. But it was the new Playboy

At last, I don't have to look at kidneys ever again. Tony Curtis was almost as relived as me I think.

What trick is Jerry Lewis about to pull this time behind my back?   "BOEING BOEING" - 1965

A selection from some of my favourite covers of that time.

Left: Skiing in St Moritz for the first time. - 1957/8
Right: Bibi and I went to a health farm after New Year. - 1966

Imogen safely in the sea in Kenya with me emerging from the famous pool. - 1970

Left: At my birthday party in 1975. Georgina and Anthony Andrews.
Right: Me with Jeremy Rudd-Price one of Tim's sweetest friends in Eaton Place. - 1977

These were from the Paramount Stills Studio where money was no problem.

Do you see the girl (Marianna Hill) that Elvis ordered the wig for is on the other side of Donner Butterworth (little girl). - 1966

Not the best of outfits for a shipwreck, but just another of my designs for "THE LOST CONTINENT" - 1967

HAMMER GLAMOUR!

Alan Warren took some lovely shots in the 70's - this was one.

Above: JUST MONKEY BUSINESS. Near the end of shooting Elvis took me outside "I want some shots of us, while you're in Europe." These are two from that reel.

Left: Taken just 10 days before he died - this is not a fat man - only he could keep on entertaining his fans he loved so much right up to the last minute. August - 1977

Club at 45 Park Lane that offered a whole new dimension in decadence behind its smoked-glass facade.

The Playboy's supremo was Victor Lownes, Hugh Hefner's urbane American partner, and he quickly became the party king of London. Champagne always flowed around Victor and his houses, first in Montpelier Square and then in Connaught Square, were packed with models, actors, visiting film stars such as Warren Beatty, Lee Marvin and Telly Savalas, and others who had won a ticket simply by looking gorgeous. Amphetamines, dope, cocaine, LSD, Mandrax and amyl nitrate proliferated among the swingers.

There was a rule at the Playboy Club that the Bunnies were strictly off-limits to members, but that rule didn't apply to the tall, slim, shaggy-haired, baggy-eyed boss or his friends, among them Roman Polanski. Victor and Polanski had met on the terrace of the Carlton Hotel in Cannes during the 1963 Film Festival when Victor, who had just been appointed head of Playboy International in Europe, was scouting the film world for useful talent. Polanski looked him up in London and Victor remembered him and greeted him affectionately.

While I had been away in Hollywood, Polanski seemed to have gone completely insane. He had finished making his second movie in Britain, *Cul-de-Sac*, starring Catherine Deneuve's sister Françoise Dorléac, and "celebrated" its completion by holding a little orgy in his apartment.

"He went on a twenty-four hour drink and LSD binge with a showgirl he picked up at a party after a West End show," John Parker wrote in his biography *Polanski*. "They took so much of the drug that they scared themselves half to death with the hallucinations and the girl passed out. Polanski became so worried that he managed to get her into his Mini and drove her to [Gene] Gutowski's house, where Judy put them to bed and cared for them until the effects of the drug had passed. The dancer left later that morning; he never saw her again."

Polanski treated vulnerable young women as sexual playthings, while, in his work, he stripped them of their dignity and exploited their bodies in furtherance of his "art". The source of his sexual hang-ups was, of course, his ex-wife Basia - as he later admitted himself: "I had a bad marriage, you know, years before, so I was feeling great because I was a success with women again and I just liked fucking around."

The party scene was so over the top that I was glad to go back to work. John Mather phoned to offer me *The Deadly Bees*, a thriller for Paramount, subject to a meeting with Max Rosenberg, the producer, and Milton Subotsky, an American writer-producer. The big inducement for me was that it would be my first starring role carrying a whole picture. It was also a drama rather than a comedy, with a genuine heavyweight, Frank Finlay, who had just played Iago to Lawrence Olivier's *Hamlet*, as my co-star.

The director was Freddie Francis, who had won an Oscar for his beautiful lighting camerawork on *Sons And Lovers* and he had also been cameraman on *Room At The Top* and *Saturday Night And Sunday Morning*. The prospect of working with another wonderful cameraman after Lucien Ballard was very exciting. Unfortunately, Freddie didn't have a very successful relationship with Milton Subotsky, who had written such classics as *Dr Who And The Daleks*, and he rewrote the script on the set every morning.

My character, pop singer Vicki Robbins, suffers a nervous breakdown while performing on *Top Of The Pops* with her group, The Birds, whose most well-known member was the guitarist Ronnie Wood, later of the Faces and the Rolling Stones. Vicki is advised by her manager to take a rest cure on a remote farm and, while she is there, weird things start to happen, the most weird of which is that swarms of bees stop making honey and start stinging the locals to death. From the size of dead bees found at the scene of one attack, it is obvious that a new strain of stinger is being bred for sinister purposes.

Michael Ripper (later one of the most famous faces at Hammer Films) plays both the inn-keeper and the policeman, while his wife, Catherine Finn, is the ill-fated Mrs Hargrove, one of the bees' victims. Guy Dolman is the good-looking Mr Hargrove, who becomes the chief suspect because he is always in the wrong place at the wrong time. The real villain, however, is Frank Finlay's friendly professor.

After a few weeks of filming, I felt that *The Deadly Bees* was turning into a tame imitation of Hitchcock's masterful *The Birds*, starring Tippi Hedren. However much I liked Freddie Francis, I knew this picture was losing it and, in the rushes, I was worried that the stuff with the bees just wasn't frightening enough. I also knew the saying, "If it's bad, blame the star. If it's good, where's the director?"

The dressing room next to mine at Shepperton Studios was occupied by two million huge Australian bees, which had been flown in because English bees were smaller and, at that time of year, apparently too sleepy to star in a movie.

"They're friendly," the beekeeper reassured me, "unless roused."

He gave me a few ground rules to obey: never wave smoke near them and never let them get anywhere near fire. Oh, and stay calm, because the smell of fear drives them crazy.

"Excuse me," I said. "Have you read the script?"

"No. Is there a problem?"

Miraculously, I was the only person not to get stung, even though most of the crew were wearing protective clothing and I had none. The bees would find their way in and you'd hear a muffled scream as a bee found its mark.

In one of the last scenes, I discover the professor's bee-mutating laboratory and obviously have to be exterminated. He sets a death-trap for me by setting fire to the farmhouse and sending in the bees to finish me off. I handled the bees well, considering I had only a slip on and there was thick smoke and raging fire everywhere and I had to beat them off with a towel while trying not to give off the scent of fear.

The next set-up was where I was at the top of the stairs and had to fight my way down through the flames, only this time I was fighting for my life for real. I had insisted on an escape route being built for me because Burt Lancaster had told me that the worst special effect to work with was fire because of its unpredictability. On his advice, I soaked all my clothes with water to the point that I was literally dripping wet.

As for the escape hatch, there was a lot of moaning from the front office about the extra expense and the time it would take to build. The special effects boys spent ages showing me how nothing could go wrong, but I dug my heels in because Hal Wallis had also told me how important safety was.

Thank God I did, because everything that could go wrong did go wrong, including the tap that worked the gas controlling the fire getting stuck, so they couldn't turn it off and it became a flame thrower.

At the beginning of the shot, Freddie Francis had warned me, there would be a lot of fire which had to be allowed to burn before we turned over, so I was not to worry. From my angle, I couldn't see if anything had gone wrong and, like a good soldier, I carried on. I was literally beaten back by the flames. The heat was intense and I could hear a lot of muffled shouting. I thanked God for the escape route, but even then one of the boys had to pull me through it.

By then, my clothes were bone-dry, the whole of my front was singed and a large part of the set was ablaze. They had hoped to do the scene in one take and that was all they got. If it hadn't been for prompt action by the fire brigade, Shepperton would have lost a stage that day.

In the end, *The Deadly Bees* held together quite well and pre-dated the killer bees craze of the mid-Seventies, which culminated in the 1978 all-star flop *The Swarm*, starring Michael Caine, Katharine Ross, Richard Widmark,

Henry Fonda and Olivia de Havilland to name only a few.

Although *The Deadly Bees* did little at the box-office the first time round, it was revived in the States in the Eighties and became a cult film, and a Johnathan Ross favourite of the genre.

Sally Shooter phoned me from William Morris and asked me to see Betty Box, a prolific film-maker and a pioneer among women producers, about a film she was producing, with her friend, Ralph Thomas, directing. The film was *Deadlier Than The Male*, which was going to be shot in Italy.

The cast had an international feel to it and was headed by Richard Johnson, whom I had met on the set of *The Amorous Adventures Of Moll Flanders*. Richard's leading lady in that picture was Kim Novak, whom he had later married, albeit briefly. Also starring with us would be two of the sexiest, most voluptuous women on film, the German actress Elke Sommer and Sylva Koscina from Yugoslavia.

Around that time, a magazine photographer had taken some wonderful photographs of me wearing a black wig and I convinced Betty that I would be better as a brunette in the film than as a blonde. It wasn't a good move: wearing a wig in that heat gave me a permanent headache.

The film was to be shot almost entirely on location in a small fishing village called Lerici. I was booked to fly to Rome from Heathrow and was given a rousing send-off by my friends in the press. Although it had been months since I had met Dr. Mary Young, the clairvoyant, I had been thinking a lot about what she had said. She had made me promise to act on my "buzzes" if and when I got them.

In the car on the way to the airport, I had some sort of psychic flash instructing me to not get on the plane. It was the first time this had happened and I felt compelled to act on my intuition. The events of the next few hours still leave me awestruck.

First, I refused to get on the plane. Sure, I'd go, but not on that one. The PR people for Rank/Universal were a bit upset with me, but, as I was not known to mess people around, they had to go along with it. Besides, I said I would give my best Fay Wray scream if they tried to carry me on board. They booked me a seat on the next flight and I took off about an hour after the first flight had departed.

The first inkling I had that anything was seriously wrong was when we began to circle the airport instead of starting our descent into Rome. I knew that something really awful had happened and that I would have been down there, too, if it hadn't been for Mary Young's warning.

I can't describe exactly how I felt at that moment, but grateful comes to mind. When we eventually landed, I saw that the airfield was littered with large pieces of debris and that the emergency services were in action all over the place. It seems that the plane had crashed on landing, with a large loss of life.

My name was still on the passenger list and several airline staff did a double take when I walked towards them in the terminal. Someone was already on the phone to London, talking about re-casting my role. I hope he won't mind me saying this, but the press guy on the film was a big boy. He had had the awful task of writing my obituary while I was circling overhead. He took one look at me and passed out cold on the concourse.

I swear the whole terminal shook.

Richard Johnson and I met up and decided to share a car down to the location. I was still a bit hyper over the plane crash, so I was relieved when we broke the journey for a little lunch and some sightseeing at the Leaning Tower of Pisa. Richard was very kind to me and, after we had checked into our suites at the Cristallo Hotel in Lerici, we had a romantic dinner in the old port.

Deadlier Than The Male was an updated version of one of the Bulldog Drummond books, with Richard playing Hugh Drummond, the archetypal British hero of an earlier, more innocent, age. In our story, he traces the murder of an oil company executive to the master criminal, Carl Petersen, who uses glamourous female assassins to carry out his dirty work. I play a reluctant baddie and, after lots of excitement involving fisticuffs and shootouts, I switch sides and end up in the arms of Bulldog Drummond.

There were no stunt doubles - at least not for the girls - and in one scene I have to throw a seventeen-stone tough guy, Milton Reid, over my shoulder. I was given lessons in judo and karate to do this scene and pictures of me tossing this huge brute through the air appeared in many British newspapers.

My secretary, Joanna, arrived from London and Richard nicknamed her "the Booby Hatch" because she spent most of the day running around in "only just" dresses. I was already feeling challenged on the figure front because, for weeks, I had been working with Elke and Sylva, who possessed two of the most stunning cleavages in the world.

One day there was an elegant dinner party scene in which all three of us were dressed to kill and there were breasts everywhere. Nigel Green was the chief baddie and fairly prickly he was, too. It had been a rather trying day because Nigel was having a problem, drying on almost every take. It went on and on and he was blaming everybody except himself.

I was sitting there trying not to feel intimidated by Elke and Sylva's overpowering *décolletage* when Ralph Thomas came over and asked me what was wrong. I told him that I felt a bit like a titless wonder compared with the other two girls.

He just laughed.

"Always remember, Suzanna, that you don't get diamonds brick-shaped."

And this was supposed to make me feel better?

I suppose it was inevitable that Richard and I should hit it off: we both fancied each others type; he loved blondes and I was a bit of a sucker for tall, dark and handsome. Moreover, he was divorced from Kim Novak, so there were no complications on that score.

After a suitable time had elapsed, we became lovers and the affair continued for a while back in London. Richard would like to have stayed in my life, but I wanted to get on with my career and becoming Mrs Johnson or, for that matter, Mrs Anybody, was not on the agenda.

I still missed Roy, but felt as though I was managing my life quite well with the help of my secretary and the people at William Morris. I had also become adept at handling bullies.

One of the parts I had been asked to consider was in *The Jokers*, a lively caper written by Dick Clement and Ian La Frenais in which two young brothers decide to steal the Crown Jewels and then replace them - don't ask! The only difficulty was that the director was Michael Winner, a man whose cockiness exceeded his ability as a film-maker.

The script had been sent to me in advance and, when Winner came round to my home to discuss it, he was so rude and offensive that our meeting ended abruptly when I whacked him around the face with his script. For once in his life, Winner was speechless - I doubt very much that anyone had ever treated him like that before.

The London premiere of *Boeing-Boeing* was held on May 25, 1966, and I hosted a pre-theatre party for my friends at the Dorchester. It was a wonderful night. As my escort, I invited the actor Maximillian Schell, who flew over from Germany especially to take me. He was a very sweet guy and, to make the night even sweeter, I was singled out for some nice reviews. Patrick Fleet wrote: "The girls are pretty enough. But it is not mere patriotism which picks Suzanna Leigh as the best. She gives a true comic performance."

I was on a promotional tour for *Boeing-Boeing* in England, Scotland and Wales when *Paradise - Hawaiian Style* opened nationally in America on July 6. When I returned to London, I busied myself renovating 8 Belgrave Mews South, which had finally become my home. I turned it into a doll's house, pretty, compact and suitable for entertaining. In the living room,

I had a bookshelf that opened into a bar and I tried to create a tented dining room upstairs, using coloured, metallic wallpaper and draped material, but never got it quite right.

For months, William Morris had been negotiating a part for me in *The Long Duel*, a Vivian Cox-Ken Annakin film set on the North-West Frontier in the Twenties. Trevor Howard was playing a British officer and I was to be an English girl caught up in a tricky romantic situation. The film was being shot on location in India and the money, around £30,000, was good. As I was being loaned out to another film company, I would split the fee fifty-fifty with Hal Wallis under the terms of our contract.

It was most important that I did this movie because it was a prestigious project and I had missed out on a number of excellent Hollywood parts simply by not being there. In August, however, I received a letter from Leonard Hirsham at William Morris in LA, saying that he had approached Hal Wallis with the final offer for *The Long Duel* and Hal had turned it down. Hal's reasoning was that if the film ran over, I would not be available to make *Easy Come, Easy Go*. Reluctantly, I had to let *The Long Duel* go - Charlotte Rampling got my part, her first big one.

To sweeten the pill, Hal said he would pay me a big bonus for *Easy Come, Easy Go*, in which I was to play a yacht-owning American heiress and Elvis a deep-sea diver. As for the Screen Actors Guild, he was confident that he could overcome their ban on me.

Hal told me: "I'm going to tell them that if they don't allow you to work here, I'll cut the budget in half. They won't be able to justify the loss of all those jobs on a Presley picture."

He sounded so sure that this would work that I assumed everything would be all right. I'd soon be back in Hollywood, properly organised, and this time for good.

Hal sent his ultimatum to the guild and the guild, after much hand-wringing, told him three weeks later that they were standing firm: I was still banned by the guild and, therefore, I could not get a work permit to enter America to do *Easy Come, Easy Go*. Paul Nathan broke the bad news to me in September. "I want you to know that we did everything possible to get Immigration to permit you to work here... and failed," he wrote. "Right up to the last minute, we kept resubmitting and getting further rejections. As you can imagine, it was a surprise because I never dreamed we wouldn't get clearance."

Elvis's friend Ty Hardin came to London and I invited him round.

"Elvis wants to know what's going on," he said. "Why aren't you in Hollywood?"

When I told him about the guild, he sympathised.

"Okay, I'll tell Elvis," he said.

I sent Elvis two little record players which fitted under the dashboard and played forty-fives as you drove along. He went ahead and filmed *Easy Come, Easy Go* in its cut-down version, with co-stars Dodie Marshall and Pat Priest.

Despite my problems with the guild, I was still under contract to Paramount Pictures and, when Robert Evans, the new head of film production, visited London, he invited me to lunch at the Connaught. Evans was the first of the new breed of Hollywood tycoon - a former actor and very slick. We got along well and he promised to keep me in mind when a suitable role came up.

It was agreed that I would transfer from Paramount America to Paramount UK, which would enable me to fly backwards and forwards across the Atlantic as required. I also retained my contract with Hal Wallis, but the momentum had been lost and nothing much happened on that front.

I saw Hal Wallis for the last time in 1969 in the Oliver Messel suite at the Dorchester, the scene of our very first meeting.

"This is very sad for me," he said.

"It's even sadder for me."

"Young lady, you just packed up and went and look what happened."

I apologised for leaving, but I still couldn't tell him about the dogs.

We agreed to dissolve our contract but, despite that unhappy ending, I wouldn't have missed my time with Elvis for anything. My Hollywood dream had come true and the King had found a soul mate.

As for Andreas Cornelius van Kujik, alias Colonel Thomas A. Parker: one day in Hawaii I had seen him on the beach, idly tossing coins into the sand - literally throwing money away. In the end, he threw away the millions that Elvis had made for him on slot machines and roulette wheels at the Las Vegas Hilton.

As Elvis would say, "What else can I tell you, baby?"

Chapter 17

Her Majesty Requests...

"I will make you shorter by the head."

Queen Elizabeth I

ONE of the rising stars at William Morris was David Niven Jr, alias Craperoo. I'd known his actor father for some time on the Chelsea circuit as a raconteur of rare wit and charm. David Jr had obviously inherited his father's "talking gene", as I had from my father, and we called each other "Craperoo" because we could talk the rest of the guests under the table at any dinner party without even trying.

David Jr was really sweet and had brilliant chat-up lines. One day I heard an incredible racket outside my home and, looking out of the window, saw him hovering overhead in a helicopter, bombarding the place with red roses.

Can you imagine someone doing that today? *"Airspace, you're in my airspace!"*

One evening we were going to Gordon White's place for drinks, then on to Robert Hanson's house for a party.

"Do you mind if we drop by the Dorchester on the way?" David asked. "I want to see Peter Sellers. He wants to tell me something."

I readily agreed because the only time I had met Peter Sellers I had laughed so much that I was in serious danger of dying. But at the Dorchester Peter looked as though he'd just buried his favourite cat.

"David, I'm thinking of getting married."

"Really, Peter, that's great news."

Pause - "Who to?"

"A girl I met in the hall, sitting in the hall in fact. I asked her in - she's Swedish, wants to be an actress."

131

I'm sure my mouth was hanging open in amazement and even the diplomatic David said, "Are you sure about this, Peter?"

Pause - Peter walked through to the bedroom.

"Yeah, I think so. She's very pretty."

"Oh, I'm sure she is. What's her name?"

Peter tossed a name at us from behind the door. David glanced at me and shrugged his shoulders.

"What was that?"

"Britt Ekland, I think."

David called out: "Look, Peter, we've got to run. I'll speak to you tomorrow, okay? Great news, good one!"

In the car, I said: "Do you think he's really going to marry that girl?"

"Oh, I don't know, Peter is Peter. I mean, he is who he is and sometimes even he doesn't know who he is."

I discovered that Peter suffered from manic depression, an ailment that afflicted some extremely funny men (and maybe women, too). Frankie Howerd and Tony Hancock were also sufferers.

One of the most talented and neurotic of the comedians was the young Woody Allen, who was making the James Bond spoof *Casino Royale* with Craperoo's father in the lead, as well as Deborah Kerr, Orson Welles and Peter Sellers.

I met Woody at the Royal Film Performance in March 1966. The film was *Born Free*, starring Virginia McKenna, her husband Bill Travers and a lioness called Elsa. Vivian Cox sent me an invitation and, as Her Majesty had a choice of three people for every slot, it was an honour to have been picked. It was the only time in the year that she could choose whom she met and I was even more delighted at the prospect of being presented to the Queen entirely on merit.

I consulted Alan Sievewright about my outfit because I wanted a dress to knock them out, but there were rules: white gloves and a long dress that didn't reveal too much flesh. My dress was quite spectacular, with a slit skirt and cut-out sides, which I covered up with a beautiful jacket with a high, jewel-encrusted polo neck and sable-trimmed cuffs. The collar seemed to be part of the dress, but, at the last moment, I whipped off the jacket to reveal the forbidden bits.

The film was being screened at the Odeon, Leicester Square, and everyone who was meeting the Queen was asked to attend a rehearsal. The women were shown how to curtsy and were then teamed up with one of the male stars who would introduce us as we walked down the staircase on to the stage. As there were more women than men, we all stood around, rather like at a school dance, hoping to be chosen. I couldn't believe it when Dirk Bogarde came forward and asked me to be his partner.

We also rehearsed the line-up, in which I was placed between Rachel Roberts and James Fox. Each person in the line-up was allotted a minute or so during which they either nodded or spoke as though the Queen was actually there.

We were all joking around when James Fox said to me: "Suzanna, do try to keep your curtsy as brief as possible. The Queen doesn't want to talk to you - it's me she's come to see."

I must have looked a little stunned because he added by way of explanation: "I was in *Those Magnificent Men In Their Flying Machines*."

I couldn't believe what I was hearing; maybe she wouldn't want to talk to me, but he really didn't need to say that.

Waiting back-stage on the big night was nerve-tingling and the more nervous among us threw up in a fire bucket. Deborah Kerr, who always looked cool and gorgeous, was standing directly in front of me. When her name was called, she suddenly turned around and said to me: "I can't go on!"

Turning her around and giving her a little push, I whispered: "Of course you can".

Then I heard Dirk saying, "And need I say more than 'Elvis Presley'? Of course, it's Suzanna Leigh!"

This was followed by a round of thunderous applause. I also felt a push from behind and began the long walk down the stairs towards him, with the Queen watching from the Royal Box. After the show, we lined up to meet her and, as arranged, I was between Rachel Roberts and James Fox.

When the Queen reached me in the line-up, she said: "Do tell me all about Elvis Presley - my son is a great fan of his. What we all want to know is whether he is going to come over here."

I told her that Elvis was wonderful and, if he ever toured outside of the States, I was sure he would choose England.

She asked me about *Boeing-Boeing*, which she said she was looking forward to seeing because she liked comedies. Then she asked if I was planning to make any more films in Hollywood and I said I hoped so.

By this time, I was having difficulty remembering to call her Ma'am after every sentence.

Finally, she said: "We are so proud of you representing us all in Hollywood."

I was so overwhelmed that I just curtsied and said a mumbled: "Thank you, Ma'am."

As for James Fox, Her Majesty had taken so long talking to me that she passed by him with just a handshake and a cursory smile before moving on to Raquel Welch and Woody Allen.

I met Woody again one Sunday night a couple of months later at a London TV studio when I was booked to appear on *The Eamonn Andrews Show* to promote *Deadlier Than The Male*.

I had been on a shoe-buying spree in Rome and was running late from the airport. With no time for a rehearsal, I ran on to the set still attaching my black wig to my head with a hair-pin.

Eamonn greeted me in his friendly Irish brogue and I did my spiel about the film without a hitch. Then Woody Allen appeared as the show's surprise guest and, as soon as the applause had died down, Eamonn introduced a magician who was going to perform some sort of levitation feat on both of us. I hadn't been warned about this and, judging by his expression, neither had Woody.

To make matters worse, the magician kept calling me "Janet Leigh", Tony Curtis's former wife, which drove Woody insane.

"*Suzanna* Leigh," he corrected.

I was still "Janet" when I was instructed to lie down on a rug on the studio floor.

"I can't," I said, "I'm wearing a wig!"

Eamonn was starting to lose his composure, so I held on to my wig to stop it falling off and lay down on the rug as instructed. The magician rolled me up in the rug and placed me between the backs of two chairs. I caught a glimpse of Woody's face at that point and he looked panic-stricken. The magician whipped the chairs away and - hey, presto - I was left suspended in space.

This is too much for Woody, who rightly figured that he would be next.

"That's it," he squeaked. "I've had enough of this."

Getting out of his chair, he ran off the set, out of the studio and disappeared into the night.

Fortunately, there was a commercial break at this point during which I was unrolled, so Eamonn still had one guest on camera when we came back on air. Woody's vanishing act, of course, that meant that the *Casino Royale* segment of the show had to be scrapped and Eamonn improvised by turning it into An Evening with Suzanna Leigh. He needed all his blarney to pull it off and I don't know which one of us was more relieved when the credits started to roll.

I was at John Mather's house one Saturday before our usual lunch at Alvaro's when he told me that the American actor Gene Barry would be starring in *Subterfuge*, a new thriller to be shot in England, and that there was a part I might be interested in.

The only thing I knew about Gene Barry was that he had made two successful TV series, *Burke's Law* and *Amos Burke, Secret Agent*. John arranged for me to meet Peter Graham Scott, who was directing *Subterfuge*, and Peter Snell, the co-producer.

The following day the script, written by David Whitaker, arrived at my home, with a note attached saying that the other female lead had just been cast: Joan Collins. I agreed to do the picture and was pleased when Richard Todd, Tom Adams and Michael Rennie were also signed. Filming was due to start the following Monday at Elstree Studios and the only location work would be night shooting on a beach in Hastings.

The story was about an American CIA agent, played by Gene Barry, who is on the trail of a gang of spies. Joan plays the wife of a double agent (Tom Adams) and I play a baddie who kidnaps her to extract money and CIA secrets.

I had met Peter Graham Scott when he was directing *The Avengers*. The female star, Honour Blackman, was leaving the series and there was a chance I would take her place. I had no intention of doing another long-running TV series after *Trois étoiles*, however, Diana Rigg stepped into the black leather jumpsuit. Leather was the look of the moment and Peter also dressed the two leading ladies in *Subterfuge* in leather: Joan in black and me in brown.

The first time I saw Joan she was in a leotard and doing a work-out scene in the film. She was slimmer and more petite than I had imagined she would be. She had been living in Los Angeles with her husband, Anthony Newley, and had just moved back to London. We got on really well from the outset and stayed friends after the film finished.

Joan and Gene didn't get on at all well, however, but then Gene had a talent for rubbing people up the wrong way. Over dinner one night the Vietnam war came up in conversation and, while Joan and I took the view that it was a terrible waste of life and should be stopped, Gene spewed out the sort of gung-ho, hard-line nonsense you would expect to hear from the CIA agent he was playing in *Subterfuge*.

He must have realised he'd gone too far because he came up to us later to make up with Joan.

"You know, Joan, if you ever want to tell an untruth to your husband, I'm your man."

Joan gave him a look that had to be seen to be believed: talk about turning a man to stone!

Gene also provided the best line of the movie, albeit unintentionally. He and the stunt man were working out some moves for a big fight scene when Gene suddenly shouted, "Mind the bridge-work, for God's sake, it cost me $3,000!"

Most actors have been known to say, "Mind the face", but "Mind the bridge-work" - oh *please*!

Most of the stuff I had to do in the film was with Joan and everything went well until one night near the end of filming. We were on the beach in Hastings and we'd already filmed the bit where I get shot in the stomach by a flare pistol. I had always wanted to die in a film ever since I had been a little girl and had practiced many endings, some taking an excruciatingly long time. But let me tell you there is only so much you can do in a death scene with flames jetting out of your guts without getting really scared.

It was getting light and we only had one more small shot to do, which was a lot of pushing and shoving between Joan and me. This was winter and it was so cold that I couldn't feel my feet.

Joan rushed at me and jumped on her mark; at least that's what she thought she'd jumped on. I felt something hot shoot through my foot, then nothing else. The take was good and we all headed for home. On the drive back to London, I noticed that one of my boots had split open.

Closer inspection showed that there was definitely something wrong and I decided to go straight to St. George's Hospital, where they had to cut the boot off my foot. It seems that Joan had broken my big toe and it was so cold I hadn't noticed.

Joan and Tony Newley lived in Park Street, but later when she was married to Ron Kass she lived at 30 South Street, next door to the house in which I had had my little skirmish with Otto Preminger. I met Joan's sister, the *Hollywood Wives* writer, Jackie Collins, and her husband, Oscar. Sunday evenings became a regular date at their flat in Stag Place, Victoria, where their upstairs neighbour was the Arab arms dealer, Adnan Khashoggi, and his then wife, Soraya.

There would be a group of us, which always included Roger Moore (a lucky actor, maybe, but one of the nicest and classiest), his then wife Luisa, Joan Collins and Johnny Gold, who co-owned Tramp with Jackie and Oscar.

There would also be visiting actors who were either making a movie in Britain or just passing through. We had to have an even number because, after supper, we'd play charades in very tight teams and there was no room for amateurs.

Stage actors saw themselves as the only real actors and always looked down on "Hollywood types", but I got a chance to even the score when I did Marc Brandel's *A Tale Of Two Wives*, a four-hander Play of the Month for the BBC. The other actors were Dinsdale Landen, Peter Jeffries and the very pretty and funny Amanda Barrie (Cleopatra in *Carry On, Cleo* and later Alma in Britain's longest running soap, *Coronation Street*).

In those days, TV plays were shot live and in one go. We were to rehearse for three weeks and then have our day in the studio. The rehearsals were a bit tricky for me because there were colour-coded strips of paper on the floor, which meant things. At least, they meant things to those who had been to drama school for the duration of the course and that included the rest of the cast.

I always seemed to be walking through a piece of paper that was either a wall or the stairs. The director was forever shouting, "No, not there, sweetie, you're standing in the middle of a bookcase", or "Oh God, will someone tell her she's on top of the wardrobe?"

This brought titters all round and provoked cracks about "film actors not knowing much". I took it well after initially going as red as a beetroot, but it was true.

As I found rehearsals more harrowing than being in front of the camera, which I loved, I came into my own when we went to the studio. I even knew a few of the crew and had worked with the cameraman before. I had been told that they never stopped the camera no matter what happened on stage: someone could die and it would keep rolling. The pressure was so great that actors who had been wonderful during rehearsals often threw up before the tape rolled.

So the tape started on *A Tale Of Two Wives* and all seemed to be going well until I had to do a scene involving a long-winded exchange with Peter Jeffries. Almost immediately, Peter seemed to go into a trance and then passed out on the set. They focussed the camera on me while Peter's unconscious body was being dragged away. Meanwhile, the floor manager was making frantic "keep going" gestures at me, which I did, even though I was talking to myself.

Now there is a limit to how long you can say your line first, then add, "Well, of course, what you should say is..." Finally, I just looked at the camera and said the "F" word so they would have to cut the tape.

Next time round, Peter Jeffries stayed on his feet for the entire performance, but it was definitely a case of hooray for Hollywood.

Chapter 18

Hammer Glamour!

*"When choosing between two evils, I always like
to try the one I've never tried before."*

Mae West, *American actress*

THE latter part of the Fifties had seen a renaissance of the old horror-film
genre through the vividly Technicolour productions of Hammer Films,
starring Christopher Lee and Peter Cushing. By the Sixties, David Niven,
Catherine Deneuve, Bette Davis, Joan Crawford and Deborah Kerr had all
dabbled in *l'écran fantastique*. At the onset of the Seventies, horror was
positively *de rigueur*, with Joan Collins, Michael Caine and Roger Moore
making memorable appearances.

My career was no longer being mapped out for me the way it had been
in Hollywood and the films I appeared in during this period were ones that
I chose personally from many offers. But I wanted a change of direction;
after all, everyone remembered Elizabeth Taylor as the high-class hooker in
Butterfield Eight, but who cared about the goodie-goodie roles so frequently
essayed by Sandra Dee?

I made my first foray into the perpetually misty world of Hammer
horror in 1967 when I was offered a part in *The Lost Continent*, a Hammer
production on a grander scale than most. Based on a Dennis Wheatley
novel, *Uncharted Seas*, the screen rights had cost the company a considerable
sum and the film was being bankrolled as part of a deal with Warner
Brothers-Seven Arts. Michael Carreras, son of Colonel (later Sir) James
Carreras, was producing the film, having already written it under the
pseudonym "Michael Nash" (his gardener's name).

Leslie Norman, father of eminent British film critic Barry Norman,
was directing, but he was sacked within days of principal photography

138

commencing for directing a racist remark at one of the film crew. This was unacceptable in the tight ship that Hammer ran and Michael Carreras stepped in for the rest of the shoot.

The picture had been sold to me on the basis of its strong cast, which included Eric Porter (the saturnine Soames in *The Forsyte Saga*), Nigel Stock, James Cossins, Jimmy Hanley and the German actress Hildegarde Knef. I was also attracted by the publicity blurb about the film's "great special effects". The beasties - a giant squid with twenty-foot tentacles, massive snail and scorpion crabs and man-eating clams - were to be created by the top people from Disney in Hollywood.

I was asked to design my own costumes and felt confident enough to do so. I felt I had really made it just prior to filming when I was driving down Oxford Street and noticed that all the mannequins in the windows of Peter Robinson (later Top Shop) looked just like me! Unlike my usual goodie-goodie roles, I went right off the deep end in *The Lost Continent* as Unity Webster, a nymphomaniac. In keeping with the character, I designed two seductive evening dresses and some other slinky gear.

In the film, Unity travels with her father, Webster (Nigel Stock), a doctor of dubious repute, in the tramp steamer *Carita*, headed from Freetown to Caracas under the command of Captain Lansen (Eric Porter). This is the *Carita*'s last voyage before being scrapped and Lansen has taken a huge gamble with the lives of all on board. The cargo - a richly rewarding one, but illegal - is a dangerous explosive, Phosphor B, which detonates on contact with water.

The other passengers are all disreputable characters who have paid large amounts to be taken on board: Eva Peters (Hildegard Knef), the discarded mistress of a deposed dictator, Harry Tyler (Tony Beckley), a drunken piano player, and Ricaldi (Benito Carruthers), a sleazy Latin gangster. The crew includes Jimmy Cossins as the upright chief engineer, Jimmy Hanley as the bibulous chief steward and Michael Ripper as a scar-faced seaman.

My evening dresses would have been fine at the captain's table in the *Queen Elizabeth*, but they were totally unsuited to shipboard life on this old rust-bucket. As much of the shooting at Elstree Studios was done in a huge water tank in which we simulated a shipwreck in the Atlantic with the help of wave-making machines and two aircraft-engines to create gale-force winds, I was wet and cold most of the time and my beautiful new dresses were soaked through.

Benito "Ben" Carruthers was Mr Cool personified. I had loved him in John Cassavetes's *Shadows*, emotive black-and-white stuff which could only be seen in art houses. In *The Lost Continent*, Unity sets out to seduce him on the ship's deck after her advances are rejected by Harry Tyler. As Ben kisses me, the tentacles of a giant squid reach over the side of the ship and grab me. Ben manages to free me with the help of a fire axe, but is dragged over the side himself.

Publicity stills from this scene decorated many of the film's reviews, but the really sizzling scene was between me and one of the crew members, Sparks (Donald Sumpter), in the bunk in my cabin. The whole of this scene was excised from the film at the behest of the censor and the cut created a serious dislocation in the film's continuity. Although this has now been reinstated for its release last year in the states.

The *Carita* springs a leak which threatens to ignite the Phosphor B in the holds. Led by the first officer, Hemmings (Neil McCallum), some of the crew mutiny and abandon ship into the teeth of a hurricane. The *Carita* is driven off course into a Sargasso sea of carnivorous weeds which surrounds the "*Lost Continent*", a land inhabited by monstrous creatures and a tribe descended from seventeenth century castaways.

To move across the carpet of seaweed and avoid the monsters, the locals float about with giant balloons strapped to their backs. One of the inhabitants is Sarah, played by Dana Gillespie, Britain's junior water-ski champion and later a successful blues singer.

Dana was a very well-endowed girl - we're talking *huge* here - and she spent much of the film with a pair of balloons strapped to her shoulders. The critics made much of this in their reviews, but what they missed was Dana's first take of her first scene. We were all positioned high up on the raised set when a shocked cry floated up from the studio floor. It was Ms Gillespie, complaining plaintively: "My balloons have burst!" Needless to say, we all feared the worst, but it was nothing that the studio technicians couldn't fix.

After making contact with the *Carita*, Dana heads off across the deadly weed with Tony Beckley, Jimmy Cossins and Jimmy Hanley in pursuit. Jimmy Hanley dies a ghastly death in the claws of a giant snail crab and the others are captured by the lost tribe and taken to an old Spanish galleon, the *Santa Anita*.

The lost tribe is ruled over by El Diablo (Darryl Read), a boy-king, who is under the influence of an evil Inquisitor (Eddie Powell). Jimmy Cossins, Tony Beckley and Dana Gillespie are sentenced to death in a pit of giant clams, but are rescued by Captain Lansen with the help of the Phosphor B.

For some reason, Hildegard Knef took a dislike to me and, as everyone neglected to tell me this, I had to find out the hard way. During one of our scenes together, Ms Knef had to take a swing at me and, obviously aiming for realism, she did it for real, belting me with such force that it knocked me silly. It wasn't very nice for me and it was inconvenient for Michael, because she left a huge mark across my face and I couldn't work for several hours.

Further down the cast list was the beautiful black starlet Sylvana Henriques, whom I knew pretty well from parties we'd both attended. During the film's cataclysmic finale, the old galleon explodes in true Hammer style. Always sticklers for realism, they used real phosphorus, a very nasty substance which, even when it has burned through to the eye, continues to burn unseen.

Predictably, they chose not to tell us that, so when the pyrotechnics got out of hand, Sylvana was very badly burned - the phosphorus ate right through the flesh on her back - but amid the panic that the scene required, her desperate screams went unheeded.

Sylvana recovered and apparently became one of the Marquis of Bath's numerous "wifelets" down at Longleat, his stately home in Wiltshire.

I made a wonderful friend in Tony Beckley and got some smashing reviews. *Time Out's* film directory now describes *The Lost Continent* as "a Gothic masterpiece", and although the film did well at the box office in Britain, it was out of step with trends in the States. When the film was re-released in 1999, a total of nine minutes were restored, including my bedtime romp with the crew member - God knows where they had kept it all those years!

One of Ben Carruthers's friends was the Rolling Stone Brian Jones, known to us as "Grandma Jones" because of the little velvet handbag he always carried with him. Brian and other members of Ben's clique had visited the *Lost Continent* set. Brian had a flat in Chelsea and I knew him, but not, apparently, as well as I thought.

One Saturday afternoon - March 16, 1968, to be precise - I was having lunch in Arethusa on the King's Road with Garth Wood, my very handsome and very rich young man of the moment. Garth was a perennial student who later became a psychiatrist and married Pat Booth, the best-selling novelist and former Vogue model.

I was eating a plate of juicy, king-sized Mediterranean prawns when Tommy Steele called out from the door: "What are you doing here, Suzanna? You're supposed to be in hospital."

Tommy beckoned me outside and pointed to an Evening News billboard, which stated unequivocally: SUZANNA LEIGH IN DRUG ALARM.

The story in the Evening News claimed that I'd been found naked and unconscious in Brian Jones's flat in Chesham Street. It seemed that I was fighting for my life a few miles down the road in St George's hospital.

This was news to me and I knew it wasn't good news. I left Garth at the restaurant, jumped into my silver MG-B GT and drove home. There were a lot of distressed people outside my door in Belgrave Mews and, after assuring them that I was perfectly all right, I rang the Evening News to tell them they had made a serious mistake. Instead of believing me, however, I was subjected to an interrogation about my private life to prove that I wasn't a hoaxer. Finally, the reporter had to accept that I was indeed Suzanna Leigh and that, far from lying comatose in hospital, I was wide awake and very angry.

The Sunday papers were already gearing up to do a big number and some had already written my obituary, so I called a press conference in my living room and fifty or so reporters and photographers turned up. It appeared that the police had received a call about a suspected drug overdose and, after breaking into Brian's flat, had jumped to the conclusion that the unconscious girl was me because there were loads of ten-by-eight photographs of me scattered all over the floor. They had booked the girl into St George's hospital under my name, even though she was dark-haired and anyone could see from the photographs that I was blonde. Some public-spirited citizen had then felt obliged to tip off the newspapers.

One thoughtful News of the World reporter even brought a copy of my obituary with him and read it out to me. I opened a few bottles of champagne and we toasted the fact that news of my death had been somewhat exaggerated.

When the press departed, I phoned Brian Jones to find out what the hell had happened. Brian had never been the most sanguine of people and recent events had turned him into a raging paranoiac. He had been arrested only a short time earlier on a drugs charge and was having a hard time handling his own problems, let alone mine. He told me what he knew, which wasn't much, although he confirmed that the girl in St George's hospital, a model called Linda Keith, didn't look anything like me.

I asked him why there were photographs of me all over his flat and he said she was a fan of mine. Sensing that I was upset with him, he started to freak out about it being a plot by the police to turn his friends against him. I ended up having to calm *him* down; he wasn't called Grandma Jones for nothing.

One of Brian's friends later explained that Brian collected my photographs because he had a secret crush on me. The stories in the

Evening News and the Evening Standard were almost identical and David Jacobs urged me to sue them both for defamation. The papers settled out of court and paid me damages, which I donated to David Jacobs's favourite charity, the Variety Club. They used the money to buy a Sunshine Bus for disadvantaged children.

Nevertheless, there were still a couple of unpleasant repercussions from that story: I lost a film part in Italy because the film company believed the old adage "there's no smoke without fire" and, more embarrassingly, a taxi driver threw me out of his cab for being "one of those junkie pop stars".

My next encounter with drugs was even more unpleasant. John Green and David Tree were a couple of opportunist photographers who hung out in a studio in Adam and Eve Mews, Kensington. These two dreamed up the idea of bringing out a coffee-table book with huge photographs and scant text on the most well-known girls in Swinging London. It was to be called *Birds of Britain*, a title that rightly provoked a reaction from the new breed of feminist.

In their studio, I posed for one of the photographers doing nothing more *risqué* than blowing bubbles and showing a bit of leg. Unknown to me, the other photographer was hidden overhead, shooting down through a false ceiling. From that angle, he got a far more revealing shot of me, which, of course, was the one they used in the book.

But it wasn't the book that was going to make them the real money. Green and Tree had targeted a few of us to do some even closer-to-the-bone photographs which they would sell to the soft-porn magazines that were popping up everywhere as part of the sexual revolution. Once again, they did not ask my permission to take these pictures. I had just turned down $20,000 from Playboy to do their centerfold and was hardly likely to do the same thing for nothing.

A few weeks after the initial shoot I got a call from one of these guys asking if I would do some fashion photographs for a magazine, posing in a variety of hats. I agreed and turned up at the studio. I can't remember much after drinking a vodka and tonic which the secretary handed to me in reception while I was waiting for John Green to set up. After that, everything had a dreamlike quality. I was there, but not really. There was a boa constrictor which was brought out of a hessian sack. Normally, I'm not too good with nine-foot-long reptiles, but this was all happening in a dream.

I woke up on my own bed, feeling groggy. I had heard of people blacking out after drinking too much, though I knew that I had had only one drink.

I phoned the studio.

"Yes, you got a bit tired with the lights, but the shoot went well."

I didn't know what to say because I was too embarrassed to admit I'd blacked out and had no recollection of getting home.

A few days later over lunch with Jeremy Lloyd, the sit-com writer, I suggested we should pop round to the studio and see the contact sheets. There was no sign of the photographers, but a female assistant dug out the contacts. At first, I couldn't believe my eyes. I was sitting in a chair, holding an enormous snake in my arms. The snake and I were looking at each other face-to-face only inches apart. It was also clear that neither of us was wearing any clothes. These days the photographs would be pretty tame stuff, but in 1967 they were dynamite.

Jeremy couldn't believe it and I adjourned to the loo, where I threw up. I took the contact sheets with me and gave them to David Jacobs, who promised to investigate. He had the photographs printed and blown up, then showed them to a Harley Street specialist. The doctor said he could tell from my eyes that I was completely drugged. I went round to see these two monsters and offered them £10,000 for the negatives.

I begged, I pleaded.

At first one of them just sat there saying nothing, then he started to laugh.

"All you girls are so worried about your careers," he said. "What about mine? This will *make* me. You have no idea how much I'll get for these and, what's more, I'll be able to call the shots from now on."

By then I was crying and desperate.

"I'll sue," I said.

"Oh please do," they said.

I drove home and then I sued.

I found out what "please do" meant when the papers ran headlines such as: SUZANNA LEIGH SUES OVER NUDE PHOTOGRAPHS. Everyone who hadn't bought a copy of King magazine proceeded to do so; there were four reprints to supply the demand.

The day the magazine came out I was on my way to work on *The Lost Continent* when I stopped at a gas station to fill up and there I was, splattered all over the place. I thought I was going to die. Going on the set wasn't easy. The cameraman had stuck one of the pages across the lens, as a joke I presume, but somehow I went on and laughed it off. I'll never forget that day - it seemed someone was reading that magazine wherever I went.

I dropped the court case because the damage had already been done and I wasn't going to give Green and Tree any more publicity. Nor was I the only actress they pulled that dirty trick on. As a result, there were a lot of angry boyfriends around Adam and Eve Mews and I understand that the photographers moved out after their tires were slashed several times and other strange little mishaps started occurring.

The whole sordid episode taught me to be less trusting and a bit more careful.

Chapter 19

The Caine Scrutiny

*"Experience is what really happens to you in the long run,
the truth that finally overtakes you."*

Catherine Anne Porter, *American writer*

ELIZABETH Harris spotted me in Vidal Sassoon's and was standing beside me before I could beat a retreat to the loo. "Ah, Suzanna!" she gushed. "I'm glad I bumped into you." Any fears I might have had that she had found out about me and her errant husband were dispelled when she added: "Can you come for dinner next week? It's just a small dinner for a few friends. Marlon Brando is coming with his new wife."

I'd always been a Brando fan - I'd seen *The Young Lions* eight times - and the chance to meet him was irresistible. I said I'd love to come. The Harrises lived in a crenellated fortress in Holland Park, a sort of urban Camelot.

One of the other guests was Patrick Walker, the Daily Mirror's astrologer, a lovable man whom I'd known for years. Richard, a Libran, held Patrick's astrological talents in high regard and often rang him to check with the Zodiac before making important decisions.

While we awaited the arrival of Marlon Brando and his wife, drinks were served in one corner of the baronial dining room. Richard paid so much attention to me that I was terrified Elizabeth would realise that we had been more than just friends in Hawaii.

Richard had got his big break in movies in another South Seas epic after being cast with Brando in the 1960 remake of *Mutiny On The Bounty* in Tahiti. "The whole picture was just a large dreadful nightmare for me," Richard was quoted as saying in the Saturday Evening Post, "and Brando was just a large dreadful nightmare for me."

But those fraught times had clearly been forgotten because, when Marlon walked into the room, the two men greeted each other with bear-hugs and it was plain to see that they adored one another.

Marlon was with his third wife, Tarita, who had been his Tahitian lover in *Bounty*. At least, I assume it was Tarita, mother of his tragic daughter Cheyenne, because she never spoke a word of English all night.

We sat down to dinner at a very long table, with Richard at one end and Elizabeth in the far distance at the other. I was placed on Richard's left, directly opposite Marlon. I was really looking forward to listening to Marlon speak in that famous method-acting mumble, but I had no such luck.

Whenever anyone said anything, Marlon would hold up his hand and translate the words into Tahitian for the benefit of his wife and the mouthful-of-marbles effect was completely lost in a foreign tongue.

Richard was no help. He spent most of the meal playing footsie with me under the table and, after he had consumed more drink, dived under the table on the pretext of picking up his napkin, but really to check out my ankles.

It was a relief when dinner was over and Elizabeth asked Patrick Walker if he would read our palms. When my turn came, Patrick led me into the next room and, after giving my palm a cursory glance, fixed me with one of his beatific smiles.

"Well, Suzanna!" he whispered. "What's all this about you and Richard then?"

You didn't have to be a clairvoyant to have spotted Richard's interest in me at the dinner table and the evening wasn't over yet. Richard decided we were all going to Annabel's for a nightcap and, when I got into my car, he jumped in beside me. Once again, I was worried that Elizabeth would put two and two together and realise that I hadn't been Frank Harper's girlfriend in Hawaii.

In Annabel's, Richard was drinking heavily again and, when he lurched towards the dance floor, I took the opportunity to slip away, thankful that things hadn't got any worse.

I saw Richard again a few months later at one of Victor Lownes's parties. Sprawled on the staircase, he appeared to have undergone a Brando-style transformation. There was a Native American headband around his long blonde hair and strands of beads were wound around his neck. He was wearing a short caftan with cotton trousers, a long, beaded waist-coat and moccasins, like a cross between Hiawatha and the Maharishi. He was obviously on some sort of spiritual quest, but hadn't quite decided which path to take.

Richard was chatting to Michael Caine, the boy from the East End whose role as the Cockney lothario in *Alfie* had made him the most popular, most desirable young actor in England. Michael and I had met many times at screenings and parties and we had also bumped into each other at Orly airport one day and I had bought him a drink while we awaited our respective flights. I had always found him attractive and thought, "Maybe..."

I looked around to see if his chum Terence Stamp was there; most nights, Michael and Terence seemed to be joined at the hip, but he was on his own for once. Richard gave me a big hug and took me to one side and told me how much our affair had meant to him and how he would never forget me.

Then, turning to Michael Caine, he asked: "Michael, have you met Suzanna Leigh? She knows the whole of *Under Milk Wood* by heart."

I smiled at Michael and received a wink and a sexy grin in return.

"Actually, it's Michael I've come over to see," I said. "Don't you owe me a drink?"

I think we both knew then that something was going to happen. I was in control of my feelings and this time I was going to go with it and enjoy what life had to offer. Why not? I was unattached, twenty-one years old and we fancied each other rotten.

We left the party early and I drove Michael to his flat in Grosvenor Square. His mother was there and we chatted for a while, had a glass of wine and picked at some food. When she went home Michael gave me a tour of the place, which was spacious and open-planned and overlooked the gardens. Like Harry Palmer in his spy film *The Ipcress File*, Michael loved cooking and the kitchen was the hub of his home.

Putting on some classical music he led me to his bedroom, which was dominated by a huge divan. He undressed us in time to the music, kissing me all the while. I slipped beneath the sheets, wondering in my naughty little mind how he would compare with Richard Harris.

"I'm going to make you climb the walls," he whispered.

Not long after that night, David Jacobs rang me in a more business-like mood than usual.

"Meet me at La Caprice for lunch today."

"I can't - I'm busy."

"I'll repeat that - meet me at La Caprice for lunch today."

Over the *aperitifs*, David gave me one of his professional courtroom scowls.

"It's fortuitous, my dear, that a certain lady came into my office this morning and asked me to represent her in her forthcoming divorce, naming you as correspondent."

My heart sank. I had kept my affairs very secret, even from David.

Elizabeth Harris had come to his office and said that she wanted to name me in her divorce from Richard. Thinking on his feet, David had said: "Ah, but surely, my dear, with his reputation, it would be better financially if you sued for physical and mental cruelty, rather than adultery?"

Looking at me, he said: "I presume that was the right thing to say under the circumstances? You weren't intending to be Mrs Harris, were you?"

If I had a halo, it would been down around my ankles.

"No," I whispered. "But it's true. We did have an affair. I was afraid Elizabeth would find out."

Apparently, Elizabeth had made some inquiries in Hawaii and, with the help of Richard's housekeeper, had established that I had spent several nights in his house at Diamond Head.

"We have to tidy this little mess up," said David. "Thank God Elizabeth came to me. I can deal with her. Can you deal with Richard? It will cost him a hell of a lot more, but he might listen to you. You've got till Monday."

This was Friday.

I phoned Richard at his basement flat in Chesham Place, Belgravia, and said I needed to see him urgently. He said there was a rugby match on the next day and he would be watching it on TV at home. Some of his friends would be there and Jim Webb, the American songwriter, was dropping in.

"You remember you said I had a good voice? Well, Jim has written some songs especially for me. I'd like you to meet him."

As arranged, I arrived shortly before the 3pm kick-off and Richard led me into the bedroom for some privacy. I told him that Elizabeth was planning to divorce him on the grounds of his adultery with me. It would be devastating for my career if I was named as "the other woman".

Would he do me a favour?

I outlined David Jacobs's plan that Elizabeth should sue him for physical and mental cruelty, warning him that it might be more expensive.

"More expensive?" he laughed. "She could take me to the bloody cleaners."

I reminded Richard in the nicest possible way that I had urged him to re-negotiate his contract on Hawaii with the Mirisch Brothers and that he had made a massive amount of money as a result.

"Very true."

There were screams of excitement coming from the other room

where the rugby had started and Richard jumped to his feet.

"Okay!" he said. "I'll do it!"

He dashed off to watch the match and I followed him. Some time later Jim Webb arrived and played some tracks from the album that Richard had just recorded. Richard asked me which song I thought would be best for him to release as a single. I told him that *MacArthur Park*, a song about the fate of a hash cake left out in the rain, was gorgeous.

"Oh Suzanna, don't be ridiculous," he said. "Do you realise how long that is? Six and a half minutes! No DJ is going to play a single that long."

"I still think you should do it."

I phoned David Jacobs on Monday morning to tell him that Richard had agreed to his plan and my name was duly omitted from the divorce proceedings in the case of Harris v. Harris.

Everyone was a winner, sort of:

Richard released *MacArthur Park* as a single and made a killing. It was also on his album, *A Tramp Shining*, one of the top-selling LPs of 1968.

And the next time I set eyes on Elizabeth Harris, she was listening to the sound of even sweeter music from Christopher Plummer.

So Richard Harris turned up trumps, but I cannot say the same about Michael Caine. Much as I liked him, I didn't trust him. His impoverished upbringing in the rough, and sometimes violent, East End had left a indelible mark on him.

One side of him was all softness and light and he could talk with child-like wonder about his newly acquired works of art, yet I felt it wouldn't take much to unleash the other, darker side which I felt sure was somewhere beneath the surface.

My suspicions proved correct over his treatment of Minda Feliciano, a small-boned, dark-haired, stunningly beautiful Filipino girl with whom I was very friendly. Minda and Michael had been engaged for almost three years and lived together, either in his flat at Grosvenor Square or his grand country house in Windsor called the Old Mill House.

When I asked her when they were getting married, she replied: "Michael and I will decide after I get pregnant. We are consulting a Harley Street specialist and he is showing us how, by watching changes of my temperature".

Late one night Minda turned up on my doorstep with just three suitcases and nowhere to go. She had received word that her father, the Minister of Public Works and Communications in the Philippines, was dangerously ill and not expected to live. Minda had been planning a visit when first she heard he was unwell but Michael refused to let her go and asked her to wait until he finished the picture he was shooting at the time. Minda was worried and insisted. Michael in a fury bluntly stated, "You do as you wish, but remember I didn't send you". Minda felt it was an ultimatum but was disbelieving.

Obviously, Minda had to go to see her father and when she returned to their Windsor house ten days later the housekeeper and her husband who Minda had engaged herself refused to let her in. Finally they took pity on her and gave her a room in the cottage away from the house. Even then when Michael heard of it, he sent his bodyguards to move her from the Mill House. Minda was completely distraught. She was very much in love with Michael and he had telephoned her in Manila every day telling her how much he missed her and how much he loved her. Suddenly, cutting her trip short, she flew back and found she was no longer welcome.

I calmed her down and said that she could stay with me; then I drove up to Windsor to see Michael to plead her case. I felt sure I could convince him to be reasonable, or, at the very least, to return the remainder of her possessions. The scenes that followed proved why he was the perfect choice to play the lead in *Get Carter*.

At first, Michael said he didn't want to let me in and I got the third-degree from his bodyguards.

Was he worried that I had a sawn-off shotgun under my mac?

I sat on the sofa, saying: "Michael, her father is dying. She has done nothing wrong. Why are you treating Minda like this? Where is she supposed to live now?"

In a scary, angry tone of voice, Michael responded to all my questions by hissing, "Just stay out of it, Suzanna - it's over and that's it."

All this time, two very unpleasant heavies were staring at me, while a huge Alsatian dog was allowed to growl and bark a few inches from my face. When I left Michael's house my knees were shaking so badly that I had to stop the car on the drive home and take deep breaths to calm down. Considering I didn't pose any sort of physical threat to Michael, the intimidating atmosphere of that evening staggers me even now.

A couple of days later there was still no response from Mr Caine, so Minda and I went over to Grosvenor Square. The porter smiled at Minda and said: "Good morning, Mrs. Caine." Many people referred to her in this manner, believing that she and Michael were already married. We went up in the elevator, expecting to collect her belongings and beat a hasty retreat.

We had not picked a good moment, however. Michael was at home with his mother and his brother, Stanley. The next scene will always remain with me.

Michael began yelling, "Get out!"

Minda was crying and pleading with him to talk to her and his mother was in a flap, trying to calm the situation down.

Suddenly, Michael yelled, "Stanley! Get her out of here!"

His big bruiser of a brother grabbed Minda and very roughly manhandled her out of the flat. Out on the landing and amid much screaming, Stanley hoisted Minda into the air and I realised he was going to fling her with a great deal of force into the mirrored wall of the open elevator.

I dashed into the elevator and cushioned the blow as Minda was hurled in. Stanley then reached in and pressed the close-door button.

The doorman's face was a picture when he saw the two elegant ladies who had swept in a few minutes earlier tumble into the foyer in a bruised and dishevelled heap. One heel was missing from my shoe and Minda's dress had been ripped.

The aftermath saw Minda going into a nursing home for a rest and, while she was there, Michael was rushing around London screaming, "She'll sue me for breach of promise."

Well, as they say, class shows through in the end and not only did Minda not sue, but only her closest friends ever knew of the situation. It was hard for her, but being a strong and resilient person she began to pick up the pieces. I found her a flat in Belgravia and Minda met the American singer Tony Bennett introduced to her by none other than Michael's closest friend, well known tailor of celebrities, Doug Hayward. Doug stuck by Minda no matter how hard Michael tried to dissuade his friend not to have anything to do with her. Tony Bennett and Minda shared a long relationship and have remained great friends.

I am happy to say that Minda today is a very wealthy and happily married lady - her husband is Norman Lonsdale who is a direct descendent of the Duke of Wellington and also one of Princess Margaret's former beaux. They own a 100 foot yacht called the "The Minda".

But such a delightful, kind-hearted person as Minda did not deserve to be treated in that shabby fashion.

Chapter 20

Natalia

"Avoiding danger is no safer in the long run than outright exposure. The fearful are caught as often as the bold."

Helen Keller, *blind, deaf and dumb American writer*

I WAS chosen as a member of a British film delegation which was being sent to Hungary in a bold attempt to thaw a few of the artistic icicles of the Cold War. I already knew about the repressive Hungarian regime from my school friend, Heide, but my political eyes had been opened on my travels and I wanted to see the situation for myself.

Not surprisingly, perhaps, my contribution to the official Hungarian-British cultural exchange agreement turned out to be a bit too political for the chaps at the Foreign Office.

The two other members of the delegation for British Film Week in Budapest were big shots of the film industry, Andrew Filson and Walter Shenson. We flew into Budapest on March 22, 1968, planning to show Hungarian audiences twelve films, including *Becket*, *Blow-Up*, *A Hard Day's Night*, *The Mouse That Roared* and *Thunderball*. On our first evening we were regally entertained at the British Embassy. A string quartet was playing under the chandeliers and I could see from the baroque splendour of the place why some of my mother's friends remembered it so fondly from pre-war days.

We had been instructed that we must stay with our official guides at all times, but I had to get the feel of the place and gave my guide the slip at my hotel, the Gellert, and went for a walk on my own.

I hadn't gone more than a few paces when a piece of paper was pushed into my pocket and, with a whispered "Don't read it now", a woman melted into the crowd.

I kept on walking, just as Claire Bloom had done in *The Spy Who Came In From the Cold*. Everything around me seemed so drab: gray cars, gray faces, gray clothes, and, worst of all, there were no smiles anywhere. The repression was so suffocating you could hardly breath.

I read the note in the hotel loo: "Would you like to know how actors and actresses really have to live in Hungary?"

The note suggested a time and a place, a Turkish bath-house which turned out to be within walking distance of the hotel. In the steam room, a woman of about my age sat down next me.

"My name is Natalia. Thank you for coming, Suzanna. I'm quite well-known, so I had a friend put that note in your pocket."

Natalia was very pretty, but terribly intense. She had approached me, she said, because she was a film star in her own right and wanted to explain the difference between her life and mine. She warned me not to be taken in by the state propaganda; the true position was that artists were penalised in Hungary. They had no freedom of expression and, despite the aims of our delegation, the regime would remain as oppressive as ever.

Natalia said that in order to pursue her film career she had to make pro-Communist radio broadcasts, appear on stage in approved productions and also work part-time in a factory. Her purpose in approaching me was that she wanted me to tell the rest of the world about the true state of affairs. I promised to do what I could, although at that moment I couldn't think of anything at all. Natalia disappeared into the steam.

The following day I was taken to visit a state-run film studio *cum* factory in the company of my guide and a couple of heavies who could only have been state security police. The actor/workers were assembled in front of a stage in a vast auditorium.

Surrounded by Marxist-Leninist dignitaries and the odd Stalinist commissar, I was led to a rostrum, where one of the officials started speaking into a microphone. An interpreter whispered in my ear that he was telling them that I was an English film star who had worked in Hollywood and that I was on a goodwill mission to their country.

When the *apparatchik* stepped away from the mike, I quickly moved forward and, smiling brightly, started speaking in English to the audience. I waved my arms and beamed at everybody, leading the nasty big men on the stage to believe I was thanking them.

Almost immediately, one of the actor/ workers started clapping slowly and others joined in until they were all clapping, very slowly and purposefully.

What I had told them was, "I know exactly what you're all going through. You have to work in factories as well as act. I will do whatever I can to let this be known in the Free World..."

The clapping was now very loud and everybody on the stage realised what was happening. One of the goons pulled the mike cord from its socket and two of them picked me up bodily and hustled me off the stage to a chorus of boos and jeers. I was manhandled into a car and driven by a round-about route to the Gellert Hotel.

On the way, they interrogated me.

"Who do you know in Budapest?"

"Who are your friends?"

"Tell us their names."

It was like one of the really bad scenes from *Subterfuge* and, thinking that indignation was the best line of defence, I demanded to be taken to the British Embassy. Instead, we arrived at the hotel and they escorted me up to my room. The place had been ransacked. Everything had been ripped to pieces and my money and jewellery were missing. They ordered me to sit down.

The door opened to admit a tall, nervous, thin man who spoke to them in Hungarian. They rattled something off to him and he appeased them and they left. The man introduced himself as a member of the British Embassy staff and asked me to pack my belongings.

"What about all this?" I said, indicating the chaos.

"Never mind about that. Do you love England; are you pro-British?"

"Of course I am. Why do you ask?"

"I have to be absolutely straight with you, Miss Leigh. You've upset the Hungarians no end with whatever you said to those actors. If you mention one word of what's gone on, you'll not only put your friends in jeopardy, but sabotage all our good work."

Would I give him my word that I would remain silent?

"I'll have to think about it."

"You haven't got time to think about it. They're waiting downstairs to take you to the airport. You're being deported."

Despite my protests about the missing money and jewels, he flung my belongings into my suitcase and escorted me out the door. I was driven straight to the airport and put on the first plane to London. They even put a man on the plane to check that I didn't speak to the press at Heathrow.

Back in Belgravia, I agonised for days about what to do. I couldn't claim insurance on my jewellery and other stolen belongings without disclosing what had happened in Budapest. Yet I had only to pick up the phone and the press would have come around immediately and the story would have been blasted all over the papers. Finally, I decided that the risk to Natalia was too great and I said nothing.

It was a tragic error of judgment.

A couple of years later at the Cannes Film Festival I was sitting on the terrace of the Carlton Hotel. There was a lot of table-hopping going on, with producers and such like milling about, shaking hands and slapping backs.

Two men came up to my table and one said in heavily accented English: "Suzanna, I was there when you spoke."

I looked blank.

"In Budapest. You made us feel that we were not alone."

The other man was introduced as "Natalia's brother".

"He doesn't speak English," said the first man. "But he says to tell you he is grateful to you.

"Tell him that Natalia is much braver than me."

"No, she said you were an inspiration. You gave us such strength. It was the first time anyone had spoken up for us."

"How is Natalia?"

"Natalia is dead," he said, looking at the brother. "She was shot trying to escape."

When I saw Roman Polanski at one of Victor Lownes's parties, I decided to raise the subject with him. After all, he was the most famous defector in the movie world and, whatever our differences, he would surely understand.

I started to tell him about Natalia and me standing up and doing my thing and being roughed up.

I didn't get any further.

To my amazement, Polanski drew away from me as though I had the plague.

"How stupid! Oh, my God, how stupid."

Far from championing the cause of artistic freedom behind the Iron Curtain, it was obvious that the only cause Polanski championed was his own. I didn't know at the time that he was reviled by members of the Polish underground who were fighting to bring an end to the Communist system.

But then, I still hadn't seen the worst side of Roman Polanski.

Chapter 21

Devil's Island

""The whole place is a glaring, gaudy nightmarish set."

Ethel Barrymore, *American actress*

WHILE I was holidaying in Malta, Sally Shooter from William Morris flew in to sell me on the idea of starring in *Dr Caribbean*, a four-picture deal about two doctors who set up their practice on a tropical island in the West Indies. It was an intriguing concept. I would play one of the doctors and have the leading female role in all four films: *Duty Paid*, *Blue Pigeon*, *Man With An Albatross* and *Private Gold*.

The other doctor would be played by Louis Velle, a well-known actor on the French stage who had also appeared in many films including *La Vie Sentimentale*, *Jean De La Lune* and, for television, *Les Amants Terribles*.

Filming would take place over a four-month period and each film would be shot in English by a French crew and distributed by the French company, Télécip, to TV stations around the world. The producer, Robert Velin, wanted to exploit the fact that *Trois étoiles* had made me a well-known figure on French TV, so much so that I was often recognised at Orly airport and waved through immigration.

I was definitely interested. Considering the low quality of films being shot in England in the late Sixties, it sounded like a high-class proposition. I had no boyfriend at the time and had lost all interest in the London scene, where the Playboy set was in full swing, so it suited me to leave town for an extended period.

I had already spent all of January and part of February, 1968, in Africa, where I had undertaken safaris in the Mara Mara game reserve in Kenya and the Serengeti national park in Tanzania. After roughing it in the African bush, I figured I could easily cope with the rigors of life on a tropical island.

Nor was I to travel alone. In Africa, I had had the services of Joe, a professional hunter, in the wild; in the West Indies, I would have a male assistant to act as secretary and general factotum.

I advertised in the Evening Standard for a "Man Friday to look after a film star on a desert island location" and chose Brian Larkin, a wiry, tanned young man, from the many applicants.

Brian was very enthusiastic about the job, regarding it as a personal challenge. This was just as well because I had underestimated the immensity of his task by several hundred per cent. To his credit, he maintained a sense of humour throughout the whole ghastly experience.

An added bonus was that I would have the company of well-known guest stars who would be flown to this tropical paradise for each film. One of them was the classical French actor, Jean Négroni, who had appeared in *Saint Just (La Mort De Danton)*, *Richard II* and *Les Batisseurs d'Empire*. There was also a strong American contingent, including Tippi Hedron (*The Birds* and *Marnie*, both for Alfred Hitchcock), Paul Massey (*War And Peace*, *Romeo And Juliet and Last Of The Brave*) and Jess Hahn (*Triple Cross* and *Topkapi*).

And the location itself?

Aerial reconnaissance in the Caribbean had pinpointed the perfect spot: an island shaped like a butterfly, with miles of unspoiled, white, sandy beaches, swaying palm trees and, unlike Malta, none of the corrupting influences of modern life, such as luxury hotels.

Guadeloupe was a French possession in the Lesser Antilles chain between Puerto Rica and Trinidad; put another way, it was a few hundred miles north of Isle du Diable, Devil's Island, the penal colony off the coast of French Guiana which it rapidly began to resemble.

Guadeloupe might have looked idyllic when it was photographed from the air, but in 1968 it was hell-on-earth and making a film there was not only foolhardy but downright dangerous. To start with, we were on the last plane out of Paris that May at the beginning of the rolling strikes which crippled France for eight months.

The trouble started when thirty thousand students were locked out of the Sorbonne and fought riot police with paving stones and Molotov cocktails. There were running battles along the Boulevard St Germain and, just before we flew out, I was walking across an intersection when a tank-like vehicle rumbled out of a side street and turned a water cannon on pedestrians. People were picked up and flung into the air like rag dolls by the force of the water jet. The jet just clipped my left-hand side, but it hit me with enough force to dislodge a small intestine in my abdomen, although I didn't realise this at the time.

When French workers joined the students in an all-out protest against De Gaulle's government, transport by air, rail and sea was severely disrupted. Guadeloupe was one of the most far-flung of all the French colonies, so it would be the last to get supplies when things did get moving again.

To make matters worse, my agents had failed to check up on exactly what facilities were available there. The island had virtually no sewerage or social amenities. I was to have two or three suites in the best hotel, which turned out to be the only hotel. It was called Hotel Les Alizes Moules and it was still under construction. Building work stopped the day after we arrived because they had run out of building materials and it never started again.

Nevertheless, Brian moved me into the half-built hotel and I studied the scripts. My character in the *Dr Caribbean* series was a hands-on doctor with a gun-slinging past which, judging by my accent, was somewhere in "Mid-Atlantic", that mythical place so beloved by film companies anxious to appeal to all nationalities.

My mode of transport is a four-wheel jeep and I become involved with drug smugglers and gun runners, as well as various rich and infamous types who turn up on big yachts. The stories were good and there was a strong cast of French and American supporting actors.

Our problems started almost immediately. Guadeloupe was not self-sufficient in anything other than bananas, mangoes, breadfruit, cane sugar and rum, and all other food supplies, including milk and meat, had to be imported from Martinique. Tinned food ran out within weeks and there was no flour to bake bread.

Luckily, our cameramen had brought his fishing tackle under the impression that he would do a little fishing when he wasn't working, but at dawn every morning he had to go fishing and we would wait for him to return with the daily catch.

Pointe-a-Pitre, the main settlement a few miles along the coast from the hotel, was a collection of wooden houses rather than a town. In French, its name meant Clown's Head, but as there was nothing even remotely funny about it and it smelled of old fish, the crew called it "Smelly Panties".

No one thought the emergency would go on as long as it did, but as time went by food shortages became chronic and the starving Caribislanders ate livestock, household pets and any wild animal that they could catch.

I rescued a three-foot-long iguana from two boys who had been throwing stones at it and were moving in for the kill. The iguana was badly cut and I carried him to the hotel and looked after him. I called him Anaclaito after the character played by Dirk Bogarde in *The Singer Not The Song*. He repaid me a thousand-fold by catching mosquitoes in my bedroom with his long tongue.

I also rescued a turtle from a flock of seagulls who were pecking him to death. Ruskin, as I called him, used to swim in the sea with me and always followed me back to shore and up the beach to the hotel. I set up a little sanctuary and added a wild black puppy which I found abandoned in the bush. The puppy had no manners at all and whatever he couldn't eat, he pulled to pieces.

Somebody should also have found out from the recce that there was no electricity on a regular basis in Guadeloupe and no cinema in which we could view the rushes, an absolute necessity as we were supposed to be shooting four films back-to-back. Back-to-back is a misleading term because it implies finishing one movie and then starting the next. In fact, what happened was that we shot bits of all four films completely out of sequence.

To make this work, the director would have to know exactly what he was doing and the crew would need maximum back-up from the parent studio in Paris. Everything went wrong: there was no way of checking the rushes and, owing to the strikes, back-up was virtually non-existent. If someone went sick, they were simply evacuated and not replaced.

The biggest drawback of all was that the French director in charge of *Dr Caribbean* was an incompetent called Getz. He might have been terrific at something, but it certainly wasn't anything to do with making movies. Getz was so lacking in technical skills that he wouldn't have made it to third assistant in Hollywood. His English was also very poor and, as most of the visiting stars spoke little or no French, there were frequent misunderstandings, which put everyone's nerves on edge. So making four films like this was like trying to bake a *soufflé* in a warm oven, but thank God this realisation came to us slowly.

Striding on to the set in a battered straw hat like a latter-day Gauguin, Getz, our director *manqué*, would shoot close-ups for all four films in one set-up, but then forget to do some of the accompanying master shots which were, of course, imperative. He would instruct us in French, "When we finish this take, we'll do a bit more in the same room", even though the next scene might be months hence in a completely different film. The result was that one movie overlapped with the next until everything was hopelessly muddled.

The tropical heat was exhausting. Brian tried to keep my spirits up and I did the same with everybody else, but after the sixth week I was starting to wilt. Whenever Getz asked me to do something, I would roll my eyes and say, "In this heat? With these mosquitoes? Oh, no!"

I was living on mangoes and vitamin pills and losing so much weight that, before filming each day, my dress had to be taken in by the wardrobe mistress. The sun was my main enemy because we were using big arc lights, run off our own generator, and the arc lights had to outshine the sun, otherwise I would be in shadow.

I would have to look at the sun with my eyes closed so that when Getz called "Action!" I could do the scene without blinking or frowning in the glare of 200-watt bulbs. Effectively, I was blinding myself. If we didn't get the shot we wanted in one take, I would have to go through my preparations all over again because my make-up would have been ruined by the sweat running down my face and my hair would have become a droopy, tangled mess.

There were eighty-odd people working on *Dr Caribbean* and most of them were adversely affected by the steamy, hothouse atmosphere. Mosquito bites and scratches turned septic, as did wounds inflicted by *oursin*, the spiky sea urchins that infested the rocky shore. Jess Hahn couldn't work for three days after walking into the sea in bare feet and stepping on a bed of *oursin*.

Ironically for a movie about two doctors, hygiene and basic health facilities were a major problem. There were no antibiotics and the island's sole doctor had a very rudimentary medical kit, which included a huge, stained hypodermic syringe of World War I vintage. Just about everybody turned to rum, both as an antiseptic and anaesthetic, with the result that there was a great deal of intoxication and a certain amount of friction among the worst of *les picoleurs*.

The clapper boy, who also played the guitar, was our entertainment officer and we'd join him in singing Bob Dylan songs to raise our spirits. Martinique had a radio station we could tune into and we heard the news of Bobby Kennedy's assassination at the Ambassador Hotel in Los Angeles, but it might as well have happened on another planet.

Making a film in a studio is a little bit like being in a commune with an extended family and, on location, you have to take the analogy one step further: the extended family goes on holiday. People make friends with each other immediately, or not, and sometimes there are romances.

The saving grace for me on *Dr Caribbean* was that the second unit director, Jean Pourtalé, was twenty-eight, quite good-looking and nice with it. He had been to the Sorbonne and spoke perfect English. He was also falling in love with me.

I had a small party at the hotel for my twenty-third birthday on July 26 and, that night, I took Jean upstairs and gave myself a birthday present.

I needed Jean's support because I was having quite a hard time of it. The intestine which had been dislodged by the water cannon was causing me a great deal of pain and I was developing colitis. In that condition, I was dreading one scene in which I had to work with explosives.

The script had me being chased by a couple of heavies as I was driving my jeep down a steep slope. I had to zigzag in the jeep so that the front wheels caught nine trip-wires which would trigger explosive charges one after the other. Apart from the physical pain I was in, I loathed working with fire or things that could go badly wrong, but I knew I had to do it.

The crew had been preparing this take for days and the two actors playing the heavies had been hanging around the hotel and the set, waiting until all was in readiness. I had become great friends with one of the actors, Matt Zinnerman, a Canadian; he was very funny and boy! did I need a little light relief.

This scene really had to be done in one take, not only because of the cost involved in setting up, but all the messing around. It was all going to be shot in a master shot, including me getting out of the jeep at the bottom of the hill and being held up by the heavies.

With the cameras rolling, I drove the jeep down the hill, hitting the trip-wires as planned and being showered with earth as the charges went off. Everything was going fine until I stopped at the bottom and felt what should have been a gun in my back and heard Matt's line, "Stick 'em up." But when I turned round, instead of a gun, he was holding two fingers together.

Matt had dropped his gun somewhere on the downhill dash and the scene had to be redone. What can you say to that? In the circumstances, I thought I remained relatively calm, but a few of the others were nearly up for murder that night.

Tippi Hedren, accompanied by her daughter, Melanie Griffith, arrived at the same time as Paul Massey to appear in one of the films, *Man With An Albatross*. Paul was a tall, complex, middle-aged American who drank imported whisky. I had little in common with him, but I hit it off immediately with Tippi. She was extremely talented and very beautiful, with the loveliest long eyelashes.

Tippi was also an animal lover and she adored my little sanctuary. Melanie was a delightful child who had the good fortune to inherit her mother's beauty, especially those long lashes, and it was great fun having her around.

Viviane Ventura, whom I knew well on the London circuit, also arrived to play a small part in one film. Viviane had expected to be in Guadeloupe for just a couple of weeks, but had to stay much longer and the primitive facilities did not suit her Chelsea lifestyle one bit. There was some consolation in the fact that she extracted a fat fee from the producers for the inconvenience.

Halfway through the shoot I became so weak and ill that I could hardly stand upright. I don't know why I had kept going for as long as I did: the show must go on, I suppose, although my loyalty to this particular show was now down to zero. I couldn't even get on the phone to my agent to tell him I needed to be evacuated. Brian had to locate an English island with a plane and I eventually got to Antigua by boat and then flew to London, where I spent ten wonderful days cocooned in the London Clinic on drips for colitis.

William Morris tried to renegotiate my contract for me, but, feeling revived, I flew back to Guadeloupe anyway, even though the doctors advised against it. I took the opportunity of being in London to pack my luggage for the return trip with a supply of hypodermics for B-12 shots, and loads of vitamins, antibiotics, antiseptic creams, tinned food from Fortnum & Mason, face cream, false eyelashes and shampoo.

The first thing I noticed when I got back to my hotel was that the puppy was missing. No one would admit to anything, but I'm sure he ended up in the stewpot - things were that desperate. Anaclaito and Ruskin were still in residence, but I was furious about the puppy's fate and hated the place even more.

One day I was photographed on the beach outside my hotel room for the English papers. I went to bed exhausted and, when I looked out of the bedroom window the following morning, I was astonished to see that the beach had vanished and the sea was swirling around the trunks of the mango trees and lapping at the side of the hotel. I had slept through a hurricane which had clipped the island and moved on.

There was a certain amount of hysteria among the local population and the storm had levelled many of our tropical locations. But anyone who thought this might have caused a rethink in our plans was disappointed; it made no difference at all. Frantic messages were coming over the radio from Martinique to see if we were all right, but to those attached to *Dr Caribbean* it was just a normal day on Devil's Island.

I had accumulated a huge amount of expenses in Guadeloupe francs and, with nowhere to spend it, took a boat to St. Kitts, one of the neighbouring islands. Feeling as though I was on parole from a long prison sentence, I bought some nice jewellery to cheer myself up.

Some of the illnesses were now very bad; we had to exist on a diet consisting almost entirely of mangoes, bread fruit, a little fish and, for those with stronger stomachs than mine, raw *oursin*. There was no bottled water and most of us suffered from dysentery in varying degrees from drinking the island's polluted tap-water.

I woke up one night with a raging thirst and went down to the kitchen to find a drink. I walked across the floor, searching the wall with my hand for the light switch There was a strong moonlight and, at first, I didn't think much of the fact that everything was black - the walls, the floor, *everything* - and that my feet made a sort of gravely, crunch, crunch, crunch sound on the floor.

I found the switch and light flooded the room. The place seemed to be moving and I realised that it was alive from floor to ceiling with the biggest, blackest cockroaches I had ever seen. They were as freaked to see me as I was them and clambered over each other in their rush to escape the light.

With that sort of pestilence about, it was a miracle there wasn't a fatal epidemic of some sort. Most of the crew had already been evacuated through sickness and we were down to a skeleton staff. The only survivors from the original cast and crew were the make-up man, the cameraman, director Getz, Jean Pourtalé and me.

One day someone said that this was the last scene. I thought I was hearing things, but it was true: we had run out of film. As no more film was available, there was nothing to do except abandon the shoot and, unbelievably, we were going home.

I took Ruskin in a boat to a turtle island and bade him a tearful farewell, then carried Anaclaito deep into the jungle in my jeep and drove off before he could follow me. I went by boat to Antigua, where I had my first real meal in months at the smartest hotel I could find, then flew to London.

As far as Jean was concerned, it was rather like some wines in the Sixties. Sancerre could never travel and location romances, on the whole, didn't travel well, either - they sort of go off on the flight back home. Jean returned to Paris and I went back into hospital in London.

I was down to five-and-a-half stone with the worst case of dysentery they had seen since the end of the war when our men were brought back from Japanese POW camps. I could relate to that: at times making those films had seemed like a form of warfare. Robert Velin, the producer, even wrote to William Morris, describing me as "a real soldier", which was closer to the truth than he might have imagined.

When I was well enough to leave hospital, I moved back into 8 Belgrave Mews South with Monty and Kimsham, and the first thing I did was to fire William Morris for their incompetence. Then I went back on to the party circuit and, when Jean visited me from Paris, I introduced him to some of my friends. I also had a lovely time going to Paris, where Jean had an apartment in Neuilly, overlooking the Bois de Boulogne.

We would spend evenings in Le Castel with his friend, Pacco Rabonne, the designer who was experimenting with metallic fabrics. Jean bought me some gorgeous clothes from Pacco's store and I was a metal girl for a while.

One night in Paris, just before I arrived on one of my visits, Jean developed a blinding headache in a restaurant and was rushed to hospital. He had suffered a brain haemorrhage, which left him with tunnel vision. Jean, however, refused to accept that he could not see properly and insisted on driving his Mini. We crashed at étoile (of all places) on the way to dinner with Pacco Rabonne, but made it to the restaurant nevertheless. Pacco noticed that my Chelsea boot was swollen and I found that a bone in my foot had been cracked in the crash.

The situation between Jean and me became increasingly tricky. What had been amusing and comforting on a desert island did not translate well to civilisation and his affliction only made matters worse. Jean was a Virgo and, while he had always been possessive, his illness had made him insanely jealous.

During a trip to London when he realised that I was cooling towards him, he said: "If I can't have you, no one will." He became violent towards me. Foolishly, I forgave him. Then Kimsham was run over and killed and I was so upset that I agreed to let Jean visit me again.

This time, he turned homicidal and I fled from my home in terror and sought help from my neighbour, the musician Alan Price. I rang Jean from Alan's house and warned him that if he was still there when I returned, I would call the police and have him arrested. Jean was gone when I got back home.

It was a sad end to our relationship and his illness was a tragic postscript to life on Devil's Island. As for the films we'd spent five months making there, as far as I know Getz is still in some cob-webbed cutting room in Paris, trying to edit those masterpieces together.

Ironically, I returned to an island - Malta again - for my next assignment, but this time it was first-class all the way. It seemed that both Hammer and their American distributor, Twentieth Century-Fox, were pleased with my turn in *The Lost Continent* because they offered me a leading role in one of the episodes of their first TV series, *Journey To The Unknown*.

Hammer brought in a new line producer for the series, Joan Harrison, who had been an assistant to Hitchcock and had produced his very successful TV foray, *Alfred Hitchcock Presents*. She was a rather formidable lady, but a sincere one and we got on well.

My co-star, Brandon de Wilde, had played the little boy in *Shane*, one of my favourite westerns, and I was very happy to act with him. We went on location in Malta for six weeks to shoot the pilot episode, entitled *One On A Desert Island*.

Alec Worthing, a wealthy young man, is shipwrecked on a desert island and, just as he starts to fear all is lost, the girl of his dreams walks out of the sea. I play the girl, Vickie, and, striving for maximum Aphrodite effect, strode from the waves at St Paul's Bay in a clinging aquamarine dress.

Alec and Vickie become lovers and set up home together, but he is alone when a navy party arrives to rescue him. Alec tells them that he murdered Vickie, but the rescuers are unable to find her body. They do, however, find the body of a parachuting pilot whom Alec has murdered in the belief that he would take Vickie away from him. The twist in the story is that Vickie never existed and that he killed the pilot over a figment of his imagination.

Despite the implausibility of the story, the *Journey To The Unknown* series was bought by the CBS network in America and ITV in Britain. Brandon de Wilde's career was cut tragically short. He was killed in a road accident while on tour with a play in the States.

Chapter 22

Polanski's Secret Shame

"In violence we forget who we are."

Mary McCarthy, *American writer*

MY friend Sharon Tate showed up with Roman Polanski at one of Gene and Judy Gutowski's Sunday brunch parties in Eaton Place and I just knew they'd slept together the night before. I grabbed her and took her into the bathroom.

"Well?"

"I know what you're thinking, Suzanna, but he's been so sweet to me. I think I really love him."

"Oh God," I groaned under my breath.

I had met Sharon when she came over to London from Los Angeles in 1966 and I knew from our very first meeting that she was a lovely girl. She had long blonde hair, the most stunning of figures and legs that went on forever. She also had a sweet personality and I don't think she ever said a nasty word about anyone until she met Roman Polanski.

Sharon was under a seven-year contract to Martin Ransohoff, an American producer known in our set as "Rancid". Ransohoff was acquainted with Victor Lownes and, through Victor, Sharon had met Polanski. He cast her in his *Dracula* spoof, *The Fearless Vampire Killers*, and they were lovers before the cameras started to roll.

Life with Roman and Victor was all very incestuous. So many girls were sleeping around that the Polanski Culture Club was like a rattlesnake farm, but Sharon wasn't one of the pushover types. She did, however, have a very peculiar taste in men and for some inexplicable reason took it as perfectly normal to be beaten up.

In Los Angeles, she had lived with a French actor who raped her and injured her so badly that she needed treatment at a hospital, but she refused to file charges against him. Her next lover was Jay Sebring, the kinky Hollywood hairdresser, who introduced her to drug parties, group sex and bondage games involving flagellation.

Sharon was so infatuated with Polanski that when she moved into his house in Eaton Mews she agreed to his bizarre demand that he should be allowed to have sex with other girls whenever he felt like it.

When shooting started on *The Fearless Vampire Killers*, she invited me on to the set to have lunch with her. This was the first - and last - time that I saw Polanski in action as a director.

Sharon was shooting the scene where she has just been bitten by a vampire. Wrapped in a towel, she is sitting in a bath-chair and, when the camera pulls back, there is an empty chair draped with a blood-stained towel. Sharon was her usual beautiful self, but her blonde hair had been coloured reddish - not an easy colour to carry, but somehow she managed it.

Polanski made me feel as though I was intruding, even though I had been invited on to the set. When the crew broke for lunch, he insisted on rehearsing Sharon over and over for the next scene. I was left hanging about for so long that I finally said, "I'd better go."

Sharon started to apologise and Polanski, just to let me know that I was getting in the way, cut in, "We're working here." Then he called for more cobwebs to be put in various corners of the set, as though that proved it.

Directors, of course, sometimes had to behave like this to get a film made; what really distressed me about Polanski was his apparent determination to show me that he had power over Sharon, even to the extent of denying her wish to have lunch with a friend.

Sharon and Polanski went to Hollywood in late 1967 and Polanski was grabbed by Robert Evans, who admired his dark talents, to direct his red-hot new property, *Rosemary's Baby*. Polanski's first priority, however, was to promote *The Fearless Vampire Killers* and he coerced Sharon into appearing naked in Playboy magazine in exchange for publicity.

Playboy published a set of sleazy pictures of Sharon, taken by Polanski himself, under the headline "The Tate Gallery" and, although the pictures created enormous interest in Sharon's body, they did very little for the movie itself.

To Polanski's fury, Marty Ransohoff had hacked twenty minutes out of it, renamed it *Pardon Me, Your Teeth Are In My Neck* and dubbed much of the dialogue in American accents. The stylised spoof that Polanski had carefully crafted had been reduced to a puerile Hollywood comedy and, predictably, it bombed.

I was in Africa in January 1968 and missed Roman and Sharon's wedding at Chelsea Register Office in the King's Road. Gene Gutowski was Roman's best man and Barbara Parkins, with whom Sharon had become friendly while making *Valley Of The Dolls* the previous year, was matron of honour. Barbara was also Victor Lownes' new girlfriend and Victor hosted a lavish reception at the Playboy Club for all the regulars from the film and rock worlds.

I was in the West Indies for much of 1968 on the abortive *Dr Caribbean* mission and lost track of Sharon for months on end. While I was in Paris in May waiting to fly to Guadeloupe, she was in the South of France, where Polanski had been invited to join the judging panel at the Cannes Film Festival. They checked into the Carlton Hotel and drove around in Polanski's fire-engine red Ferrari, which he had shipped over from LA especially for the occasion.

Almost immediately, his grandiose behaviour attracted critical comment from François Truffaut, who said bitterly: "All he could visualise was Roman Polanski turning up to show everyone what a great guy he was."

When the rolling strikes spread to the South of France in the second week of May, Truffaut and Jean-Luc Godard backed the workers, arguing that it was an inappropriate time to hold a festival celebrating the work of rich Hollywood movie stars. Polanski, however, told *Variety* that he had fled from Poland to escape the rigid controls of a state-run movie industry and accused the Left-wing French directors of "playing at being revolutionaries". Godard was so incensed that he told Polanski to fuck off back to Hollywood and, when the festival was cancelled, he did just that.

The following month, *Rosemary's Baby*, starring the youthful Mia Farrow, was unleashed upon a startled American public and created the furore that would ultimately cost Sharon her life. Based on a novel by Ira Levin, *Rosemary's Baby* is a Faustian tale with a twist in that Rosemary's actor husband (John Cassavetes) sells his wife to the Devil in exchange for fame. The deal is that the husband will get an acting part that he desperately wants if Rosemary will bear the Devil's child.

Rosemary knows nothing of these arrangements and has to be drugged so that she can be impregnated. Polanski's scenes of the Devil incarnate raping Rosemary as she drifts in and out of consciousness are among the most distasteful ever filmed.

Polanski had researched his execrable subject in his usual meticulous way, even hiring an avowed Satanist, Anton LaVey, to play the part of the Devil. However, this profane celebration of the triumph of evil over good broke the cardinal rule of Devil worship - secrecy - and that was enough to anger devotees of the more extreme sex-drugs-and-Satan cults that had sprung up on the West Coast.

One of those extremists was a song-writing psychopath named Charles Manson, who styled himself as "Son of Satan". To Manson and his followers - the so-called "Slaves of Satan" - *Rosemary's Baby* represented a betrayal.

Sharon discovered that she was pregnant while the Polanskis were visiting London that December and decided that her baby would be born in America. Returning to Los Angeles, they rented a ranch-style house in Cielo Drive on a rugged hillside off Benedict Canyon. It was here on March 23, 1969, that Sharon came face to face with Charles Manson when he called at the house.

Manson was looking for Terry Melcher, Doris Day's record-producing son, who had previously lived there with his girlfriend, Candice Bergen. Manson had sent Melcher some tapes of his songs and wanted them back. He was such an obvious oddball that some of Sharon's friends sent him packing, but not before he had learned that the house was now the residence of Roman Polanski, the director who had made *Rosemary's Baby*.

Sharon and Polanski were back in London that summer and I was pleased to see that she had sworn off the drugs that had always been an important part of her relationship with Polanski. In between parties, he was working on the script of his proposed new film, *The Day Of The Dolphin*, and, as he showed no signs of wanting to return to Los Angeles, Sharon was forced to leave without him if her baby was going to be born in America. As she was eight months pregnant, she was unable to fly across the Atlantic, so she sailed to New York alone in the QE2 towards the end of July and travelled overland to Los Angeles, while Polanski stayed behind in London to work on his script.

In fact, he partied the rest of July away with his pals Peter Sellers, Victor Lownes and another Bunny Club regular, Warren Beatty, who was spending time in London with his new girlfriend, Julie Christie.

When Sharon reached Los Angeles, she phoned Polanski constantly, asking when he was planning to join her and there were some heated exchanges about his apparent tardiness. He had a very good reason to be shifty, one that he couldn't tell his wife.

One Sunday soon after Sharon had left London, Polanski phoned me in Belgrave Mews South. We had never been outright enemies exactly, but he knew I wasn't going to sleep with him and I was surprised when he asked if I would have dinner with him that night.

I didn't respond immediately.

"Listen, Suzanna," he said. "I want you to do me a favour. When Sharon comes back with the baby, I want to do something good - make it different, the house."

"Oh, yes, sure."

I was into interior designing and always felt flattered when someone asked my advice about redecorating their home.

Polanski again suggested that we have dinner and I agreed. He picked me up at Belgrave Mews South and we went to the Rendezvous, a trendy restaurant in Fulham. We talked about Sharon and the baby and he was particularly charming, as he could be, rattling away in one of his odd monologues.

"You look beautiful tonight. Wad's that you're wearing? Fadtastic! I'll get one for Sharon. I went out with Peter Sellers the other night. Whacky guy, but funny - you know funny peculiar. Ha ha! You bin to Africa this year? You should take Sharon there some time - she'd love it."

After dinner, he said, "Ride, let's go to my place and you can tell me what you think."

We went to Polanski's house and I looked around the open-planned living room and offered some suggestions about colour schemes and so forth. Polanski wanted something done with the staircase. I left my handbag on the sofa while I went up the stairs to look down on the whole thing, then rejoined him downstairs. I asked him for a piece of paper to make a quick sketch. He said he would find some paper, but offered me a drink instead. I assured him I was fine and only wanted the paper. I sat down on the sofa and waited.

Suddenly, Polanski sprang at me from behind the sofa, catching me totally off guard. He was very strong and had two poppers of amyl nitrate under my nose in one hand, while he tried to rip off my clothes and pull down my pants with the other. It was all very aggressive. I pushed him away, but he came back again and suddenly I had this incredible strength and I fought him while trying not to breathe that awful smell of amyl nitrate.

Polanski was fairly violent in return: he'd sniff the amyl nitrate, then force it under my nose; the smell was very pungent, like dirty old socks, and I fought him off again. He punched me in the face and ripped my clothes, but I had never fought so hard: it was as though I was fighting for my life, not just for my body.

The attack lasted about a minute, although it seemed longer, and I don't know whether it was me hitting him or a combination of my blows and the amyl nitrate, but he suddenly passed out. On reflection, I'd learned a lot from my unarmed combat classes and I think I must have hit him very hard indeed. I ran to the front door, but it was locked.

Fearing that Polanski would wake up at any moment, I searched frantically for the keys and saw them lying on a desk. I grabbed the keys, all the while trying desperately not to breathe in too deeply because the smell of amyl nitrate was everywhere. My heart was pounding as I grabbed my bag, slid across the parquet floor and staggered out the door.

I was very disoriented, but I managed to reach my home. When I opened my bag, however, I discovered that my keys had gone. They couldn't have fallen out; Polanski must have taken them out of my bag while I was upstairs in his house. I could see that the window to my bathroom was slightly ajar, but there was no way I could climb up there. I couldn't go to a neighbour, either, because it was obvious that I had been involved in some kind of violent assault; my face and eye were swollen and throbbing and I was almost hysterical.

I wandered around the corner hoping for inspiration and the Irish Club came into view. I knocked on the door and it was opened by the night porter, a sweet man who immediately saw my predicament.

He took me in for a glass of brandy and patiently listened while I tried to explain (without mentioning names) what had happened. I don't think he recognised me, neither did the few other people who were drinking late in the bar. The whole thing was very fuzzy since I was still very wiped out on the amyl nitrate.

Three of the men volunteered to get a ladder and climb in through my bathroom window to let me in, which they did. Immediately I had a hot bath and took stock of the situation. My face was a bit of a mess and I was really badly shaken, but I hesitated about calling the police. Attempted rape was a lot more difficult to prove than rape itself and it would be my word against Polanski's.

The next morning, however, I went back to Polanski's house to confront him about the attack and to demand my keys back. I don't know what I expected him to say; I suppose, how sorry he was or something like. Far from being contrite, he was extremely rude to me when I knocked at the door.

Polanski was with his housekeeper and, I think, his secretary and clearly did not want to discuss the situation. When I asked for my keys, he called out that they were under the front-door mat, where I found them.

Somehow, he had confused the actions in his mind and it was as though I was the perpetrator of the crime. There's a word for that type of confusion: "situational" - it applies to somebody who is unable to comprehend the implications of their actions or see beyond their immediate situation. I suppose his immediate situation was that he had been violated by me: I had fought him and that was as far as he could see; he couldn't see *why* I had fought him.

Around August 8, Sharon rang me and invited me to come over to Los Angeles. She was bored, she said, and wanted company.

Would I like to be Godmother to her baby?

I'd love to.

We chatted.

Had I seen Roman?

I said I'd bumped into him and he was very busy.

Our friendship meant too much to me to tell her that her husband had used her as a pretext to invite me over to their house and had then tried to rape me.

Sharon told me that Polanski had promised her that he would be back in Los Angeles in time for a party she was planning for him on August 18 to celebrate his thirty-sixth birthday. Maybe I could come over now and stay on for the party?

I decided to go to Los Angeles and spend a few days with Sharon before Polanski got there, then make my excuses and leave. The last thing I wanted was a showdown with Polanski in front of his heavily pregnant wife.

"That's probably why the little rat is still in London," Sharon told a friend who called to see her at lunchtime on August 8. "He can't stand the sight of me fat and bloated."

True though that might have been, it was only part of the reason: the little rat's greatest fear was that I would tell Sharon what had happened between us.

The following night I was in my bedroom when Sharon's face appeared on the TV screen. The sound was turned down and when I turned it up I discovered that she had been murdered, stabbed to death in her home in Cielo Drive, Beverly Hills. Jay Sebring and three other people who had been at the house had also been murdered.

Frantically, I phoned Gene and Judy Gutowski and Victor Lownes, but everybody's phone was engaged. I learned later that Polanski was at home in Eaton Mews with Andy Braunsberg when he heard the news. He had collapsed with shock. Andy phoned Gene and Victor, who both dashed over to the house, and Warren Beatty had also turned up to lend his support.

I sent a big basket of roses to Sharon's funeral, but did not go to Los Angeles and nor did I attempt to contact Polanski. Victor accompanied him to America and stood by him during this terrible time when many people in Los Angeles were turning their backs on him.

It was some months before the Manson gang was arrested and it was two years before the horrendous story of what had happened that night was revealed; that Manson had sent four of his "apostles", the Slaves of Satan, to Polanski's house with orders to kill the inhabitants and leave a message - the word "PIG", which was scrawled in Sharon's blood on the living room wall.

Long before these facts were known, many people in the film community had decided that, even though Polanski had had nothing to do with the murders, he was still an undesirable character and should be avoided. Their judgment was more than vindicated by subsequent events.

I had lunch with Victor Lownes and he told me that Polanski had repaid his loyalty in typical dog-in-the-manger fashion. After Hugh Hefner had picked up the tab for Polanski's disastrous version of *Macbeth* in 1972, Polanski had slagged him off, saying that he couldn't stand the Playboy people and, moreover, that the food in the Playboy restaurants was awful! More importantly, he had been rude in front of Princess Anne when Victor introduced them and Victor had not really spoken to him since.

Victor told me he had sent back a solid gold phallus which Polanski had given him as a gift. He placed it in a box with a note saying, "In view of recent developments, I no longer care to have this life-sized portrait of you around the house. I'm sure you'll have no difficulty in finding a friend you can shove it up."

When I told Victor about the attack on me at Polanski's house, he said it made a lot of sense. "The man is a complete freak," he said.

In 1977, Polanski was accused of having sex with a thirteen-year-old girl after giving her champagne and drugs in the hot tub at Jack Nicholson's house on Mulholland Drive. Facing a jail sentence on charges of rape and sodomy, he jumped bail and fled to England before moving to France and staying there. At the time of writing, he is still banned from entering the United States.

It couldn't happen to a nicer guy.

Chapter 23

Nobs and Nobblers

"Love affairs are the only real education in life."

Marlene Dietrich, *German actress*

IAN Heath dropped in to see me in Belgrave Mews on the eve of his wedding and asked me to marry him. I knew he was marrying Vicki Hodge the following day, even though she was involved with John Bindon, a tough-guy "actor" from the Fulham end of Chelsea.

Ian told me that he was still in love with me and that he couldn't get married to anyone else without first asking me if I had changed my mind. If I would agree to marry him, he would tell Vicki it was over between them and marry me instead. His mother, he added, would be delighted.

I was completely taken by surprise and declined as gracefully as possible. I explained to Ian that it wasn't so much a question of turning him down, I just didn't want to get married to anyone.

So Ian and Vicki got married as planned. I didn't go to the ceremony, but I had been invited to the reception and went along as just another guest. It all felt very strange, knowing that I could have been the bride and this could have been my wedding. Not surprisingly, the marriage did not last long and Vicki was soon back with John Bindon.

Monty had reached the ripe old age of seventeen and was in a lot of pain so, very reluctantly, I had him put out of his misery. He had been such a great friend that I decided to replace him with another poodle, but a giant one this time. I consulted the Kennel Club, who recommended Vulcan Kennels and I drove out into the country and returned with Natasha, a gorgeous apricot giant poodle. I chose her from a litter of eight; or rather she chose me by leaving her mother's side and toddling over to me. It was love at first sight.

My hopes that 1969 might bring something positive in the way of work were lifted when I heard that ATV was making the first colour TV play to be screened in Britain. It was called *Plastic People* by James Saunders and I had to get a part in it. The ratings were sure to be huge and there was a part for a German au-pair girl that would suit me.

The TV people wanted me to read for them to see if I could do a German accent, but the script wasn't ready, so I picked up a copy of the London telephone directory and read it in my best *fraulein's* voice and got the part.

The star of *Plastic People* was Joan Plowright, a.k.a. Lady Olivier. Joan was a prestigious figure in the theatre world and also a creature of habit. She always wore exactly the same outfit for two days' running, then changed and wore the next outfit for two days before changing again.

We rehearsed for three weeks at a studio in North Kensington and, once more, there were little bits of coloured paper on the floor and I drove the director to distraction by walking through stairs and walls.

The highlight as far as the other actors were concerned was when Sir Laurence Olivier, as he then was, visited the rehearsal rooms and everyone lined up to be presented to him by Joan as though he was royalty. They were all grovelling and bowing and scraping, but I remembered how mean he had been to Vivien Leigh and made a discreet exit.

Joan plays Lisa, a wealthy, witty actress who rears her son (David Charkham) on heavy doses of liberalism. He is sent to a smart, free-thinking private school, but runs away to join a band of hippies and sample the delights of assorted au pairs. The generation gap between mother and son leads to an endless discussion about who are the real people and who are the phonies. All a bit esoteric for my liking.

We recorded *Plastic People* without mishap in one go at the studio and it received good reviews when it was shown on January 5, 1970. But the best thing about this show was that I met David Charkham, a former child actor who would become a great friend a year later and remain so indefinitely.

Maudie Spector, the casting director whom I'd known since Arts Educational, asked me to meet up with Geoffrey Reeve, who was directing *Puppet On A Chain*, a toughened-up Bond-style thriller. Geoffrey had fallen in love with the book of the same name, written by his great friend, Alistair MacLean. He had spent two years with MacLean, adapting the book for the screen.

I was to be the female lead, playing opposite a Swedish actor, Sven-Bertil Taube, whose father was the renowned tenor, Richard Tauber. Sven and I had lunch and he told me that, although he was well-known in

Scandinavia, this would be his first big film on the world stage.

The story line involved an intrepid American Interpol agent, played by Sven, hunting down a gang of heroin smugglers in Amsterdam, climaxing in an exciting boat chase along the canals.

The film was being shot entirely on location and I was always happy outside the confines of a studio. I also loved working with Geoffrey. It was winter and a freezing wind whipped off the canals, but things seemed to be going well. I was a baddie again, running up and down streets, ducking cranes on wharves and shooting at the goodies.

I got along well with most of the cast, particularly Patrick Allen, a Shakespearean actor who was a sweetheart, but I didn't spend much time with Victor's old girlfriend, Barbara Parkins, who seemed to be all hair and doe eyes.

Then it poured with rain when it shouldn't have, with only occasional sunny spells, and we started to slip behind schedule. I was on a daily rate, so it was getting expensive.

Alistair MacLean came over to cheer up Geoffrey and did some serious drinking, but couldn't do anything about the weather. The producer, Kurt Unger, also arrived and there were a lot of rows; weeks went by, followed by more meetings.

Then one night Geoffrey came into my hotel suite in a very distressed state and told me that Kurt had sacked him, the lighting cameraman and me. Poor Geoffrey, he was almost crying; he had spent so much time on his labour of love and couldn't bear to let it go.

The odd thing was that I was a major part of the movie and had shot more than half of my scenes, yet I wasn't replaced by another actress. Unger had made a serious miscalculation: he thought I had filmed fewer scenes than I had, so shooting round me turned out to be costly, especially as I was also mentioned in other scenes that I wasn't in. Even odder was the fact that, when the film was released, it still had my name on some of the credits.

Oh well, lose some, win some.

Back in London, I was fed up with what was on offer and, more to the point, acceptable on the social scene. I'd go to the opera with Victor Lownes, a secret culture buff, but I started to avoid the after-hours entertainment in Connaught Square. Nor was I attracted to the more staid dinner-party scene of Joan and Jackie Collins. They organised groups to go out to dinner and I accompanied one or two luminaries on these outings.

One of my escorts was Edgar Bronfman, an American whisky billionaire in his forties, who seemed keen to see more of me. But this was a no-comedy zone and I wanted to laugh. After Victor Lownes, the most brilliant party-giver in town was Lionel Bart, whose private life was the stuff of legend.

In the early Sixties, he was living next door to Francis Bacon in a great flat in Reece Mews, South Kensington. This place was the most louche rendezvous in town. Room led into room like a lure, or, in Lionel's words, it was a "Come into my parlor said the spider to the fly" kind of abode.

Lionel told me that Mick Jagger and his then girlfriend, Chrissie Shrimpton, and Keith Richards and Anita Pallenberg had moved in with him after he met their manager, Andrew Loog Oldham, in Cannes.

"I was walking along the Croisette with Pablo Picasso when this 16-year-old hustler approached us," he said. "He gave me some spiel about his parents leaving him behind and I gave him some money. As Picasso and I were sitting in a restaurant, Pablo said, 'Your new friend is doing rather well.'

"I looked out the window and saw that Andrew was pulling the same con on other tourists. I went over and told him I knew what he was doing. He gave me my money back, but we'd already exchanged addresses and I'd told him to look me up in London, which he did when he got a job managing the Rolling Stones."

It seems they all lived with Lionel until the place became too cramped for comfort, so he cleverly found the "Fun Palace", a former Tudor convent in Seymour Walk, off Fulham Road. It had a kind of history, that particular house - 3A Seymour Walk: it was next door to the house bought by Henry VIII for Jane Seymour. It had also been a studio for Aubrey Beardsley, but Lionel had removed the heavy Pre-Raphaelite stained glass windows to let in more light. It seems that in 1948 the place had belonged to an Irish film director, Brian Desmond Hurst. Lionel told me that Hurst used to greet visitors by saying, "Meet my butler." Standing there was Sean Connery, fresh out of the Royal Navy.

The main room was enormous, with a minstrel's gallery overlooking it like the helm of a ship. Lionel bought the candelabra which had been made for the set of *Becket*, exact replicas of those in Canterbury Cathedral, and the loo was in the form of a Gothic throne with a stone font.

But Lionel told me that he had grown tired of waking up to find his house full of strangers, eating the food, doing drugs and making love, and he put the Fun Palace on the market and looked around for quieter pastures. Lionel was great friends with Noel Coward and they were to be found at parties held by the elitist gay set. I was delighted when David Charkham invited me to join him and some of his friends at these parties.

David wasn't gay, but he knew Allan Warren, another former child actor, who had just moved into the home of the theatrical producer David Shaw in Kinnerton Street, Belgravia. There was a sea of pretty faces at these parties because David Shaw and his Australian business partner, Robert Stigwood, were casting the musical *Hair*, which was to be followed by *Jesus Christ Superstar*.

The rock world was represented by David Cassidy and Marc Bolan, TV by the terribly serious Russell Harty and sometimes the Royal Establishment by Lord Louis "Dickie" Mountbatten. The mix was positively magical for me. Noel Coward's pianist, Billy Milton, would strike a chord and the party would begin, even though it was only four o'clock in the afternoon.

You never knew who you were going to meet at these soirees, or what you were likely to hear.

So many well-known people were going in and out of Kinnerton Street for dinners, parties or afternoon tea that Allen decided to bring out a collection of celebrity recipes called *Nobs & Nosh*. Prince Philip, Mae West, Gloria Swanson and Roger Moore were all persuaded to contribute. I was pleased to be asked and served up my recipes for leek *vinaigrette* and roast lamb *à la Française*.

Allen held a *Nobs & Nosh* launch party and it was there that I finally met Gloria Swanson. She was very chic, well-groomed and heavily made-up and absolutely delighted when I told her that she was Hal Wallis's favourite actress and that he was always quoting her to me as an example of how an actress should behave.

Gloria said that she had adored life under contract to a studio and that she had always been well looked after. Gloria spotted "a dishy little guy" across the room and confided that she was looking for a new husband. Doing the diva bit, she sailed off to engage him in conversation.

Weekend parties were held at Robert Stigwood's country mansion, where Barry Gibb of the Bee Gees was one of his regular guests. David Charkham and I had started a floating affair and he decided that these parties were too grown-up for me. Stigwood had two dogs whom he adored, a beautiful but not-too-bright red setter and an ugly but extremely clever bulldog, and when David told him about Natasha, he offered her a part in *Superstar*.

As David also had a part in the show, we all trooped off to the Palace Theatre in August 1972 for rehearsals. Natasha had to play herself and trot on stage to add a surprise element to the over-the-top debauchery scene. She made such an imposing entrance that she completely upstaged an actor who was in the middle of belting out a song.

Clearly Natasha's performance posed a threat to someone and that someone decided that the only way to recapture the spotlight was to nobble my beautiful poodle. At the dress rehearsal just before the first night, this horrid person slipped some LSD on to one of her grapes and the poor darling freaked out.

I took her home from the theatre and, on the advice of the vet, gave her a tranquiliser to calm her down. I then walked her around St James's Park to keep her awake all night. She was jumping all over the place, hallucinating at shadows.

Oddly enough, the only discernible long-term effect of that LSD trip was that Natasha instantly became a non-meat-eating dog. She quietly retired from the business, deciding the price was too high and there were too many bitches there already.

Chapter 24

Friends and Fiends

"I've been through it all, baby, I'm Mother Courage."

Elizabeth Taylor, *American actress*

JOAN COLLINS was renowned on both sides of the Atlantic for her *hauteur*, yet her coolness masked a warm and caring heart. In early 1970, she invited me to stay with her in Los Angeles on my way home from the Acapulco Film Festival.

The festival was always held in February and the English guests that year were James Mason, Michael Caine, Lynn Redgrave, Rita Tushingham and me. Michael Caine was now accompanied by a very beautiful starlet, Camilla Sparv, whom I always thought took Nordic aloofness to the limit.

All we had to do as guest stars was to attend the gala first evening, a press conference and a couple of films and then it was two weeks of parties, dinners and more parties, some aboard fabulous yachts and one - the biggest thrill of all - at the actress Merle Oberon's wonderful house.

Joan's offer to put me up in her house in Los Angeles was particularly gracious because she was going through a dreadful time trying to sort out her divorce from Tony Newley. It was infinitely painful because they had two children to whom they were both devoted.

Joan let me borrow one of her cars and I shot around Hollywood, looking up some of my old friends. Driving past the Chateau Marmont and Paramount Studios gave me some powerful twinges of the "what ifs..." but I didn't have much time to reflect on anything.

One morning Joan called up to my bedroom that there was a phone call for me from England and it sounded important. I had given Joan's number to a couple of friends in case of an emergency. The caller was David Charkham, who said my mother had left a weird message for him to pick up any of his personal things that might be in my house.

I was having trouble getting my head around that when his next words completely knocked me sideways: "Your mother has sold your house."

"Sold my house? But that's impossible!"

"No - it's true. I've been round and the locks have been changed. I even peeped through the windows and everything looks different. The lights were on, so maybe someone has moved in already."

My heart sank.

After I had come back from working on *Puppet On A Chain* in Holland, my mother had started being really sweet to me. We had had some good times in those weeks. I took her out to the best restaurants and the theatre and bought her lots of goodies, including a gold-and-ruby bracelet from Dibdin, the jewellers in Sloane Street. The bracelet cost me quite a lot, but it was very old and beautiful and she promised she would always keep it. I was so pleased because it looked like we were bonding at last. But all this time she had been setting me up, just waiting for an opportunity to destroy me.

I booked a seat on the first available flight from Los Angeles to London. Ironically, I bumped into Samantha Eggar just as I was leaving Joan's house, but mercifully didn't have time to say more than a quick hello-and-goodbye. Joannie took me to the airport and I spent an agonising time on the flight to London puzzling over what could have happened.

Back in Belgrave Mews, I got the police to break into my house and, sure enough, somebody else's things were lying around and all my possessions - clothes, furniture, everything - had disappeared.

It was scary.

I went around to my mother's house in Cadogan Place. My Aunt answered the door and told me that some of my things were being kept downstairs, but she would be thrown out on to the street if she let me have them. She was crying and saying how sorry she was. I told her not to worry, that it wasn't her fault and that I would be fine.

Then I went up to see my mother in the manner of a supplicant seeking an audience with some distant ruler. On the way up to her apartment in the lift, I went over in my mind what could have happened in the three weeks that I had been away. I had never had the deeds to the house checked over by a lawyer because she had gone spare when I suggested doing so, saying: "What sort of daughter are you who can't trust her own mother?"

I didn't stay upstairs long, but long enough to thank God when I got out.

It seemed that as soon as I had left for Acapulco she had looked for, and found, a buyer for my house. He was told that he had a deal on condition that he could exchange contracts and move in within ten days, which he did - but that wasn't all. I had had a new kitchen installed and some other improvements done and had left some signed check forms with my mother to pay the builders. She could hardly contain her glee when I stood before her, stripped of all my worldly goods.

"You're finished," she said. "You'll be on the streets within six months. There's no money left in your bank account."

I knew this couldn't be right and said so, but she soon disabused me of that.

"It cost more than I thought and all the bills had to be paid before the new owner could move in," she said. "You haven't got a penny left."

I remonstrated with her, believing that it had been my house and that she could not sell it without my permission..

"You didn't think that, did you?" she scoffed. "Well, more fool you. Besides, I've got to think of the other people living around there. There have been complaints about the sort of people you've had in the house. People like you shouldn't be allowed to mix with decent folk."

Nowadays, I would have gone to a lawyer and appeared on Oprah Winfrey. Back then, I did nothing. The only lawyer I would have trusted with anything like that was David Jacobs, but he had died a year earlier. I was far too ashamed to tell anyone other than my dearest and closest friends.

I was effectively homeless - address unknown.

For the first few days I stayed with one of David's friends, the pop singer P.P. Arnold, her boyfriend and her two young children at their home in Pimlico. They were so sweet and didn't press me to talk. I was like a sleepwalker, unable to get my head around the whole thing.

One day I was walking aimlessly down the street when I was stopped by Gerry Marco, Joel Lerner's stepfather. He asked me what was wrong and I told him. From nowhere, he came up with the offer of a flat he owned in Shepherd Market, which he loaned to visiting friends or business partners. He said he wouldn't be needing it for a few months and would I like it?

Are you kidding?

Shepherd Market was the centre of Mayfair's red light district, but I moved in that afternoon and brought Natasha out of the kennels she had been in while I was away.

Things were looking up; all I needed now was some money.

Who could I turn to?

James Carreras, newly knighted, was a friend from the Variety Club - I had joined the Variety-at-Work committee which was committed to helping unwanted and handicapped children - so Hammer was my first port of call.

"Jimmy, I need a film *now!*"

This was Friday. I had read in the trade papers that he was ready to roll the following Monday with *Lust For A Vampire*, supposedly the sequel to Ingrid Pitt's *The Vampire Lovers*, which was raking in a fortune with its stylish blend of horror and eroticism.

"I don't have anything for you," Jimmy said. "I don't make your sort of movies."

I told him that this wasn't a career move, I just needed the money. After much arm-twisting, he offered me the role of the wholesome gym mistress, Janet Playfair.

Oh well, at least she wasn't called Vicky.

Jimmy removed the actress he had already cast in the role - not nice, I know, but I was desperate.

Terence Fisher, whom I had worked with on *Bomb In The High Street*, was slated to direct. Terry really cared about his films and had an air of great sincerity about him. One of his best friends had been Roy Montgomery and, like Roy, he loved his gin. Returning home from the pub one night soon after we started filming, Terry misguidedly played a game of chicken with a motorbike and had to spend several months in hospital.

With Terry out of action, Jimmy Sangster was drafted in to direct. The picture was actually made on Hammer's behalf by Fantale Films, an independent production company owned by Michael Style, Harry Fine (whom I had known since *The Pleasure Girls*) and Tudor Gates (who wrote *Barbarella*).

Tudor had written the part of Giles Barton, the dotty school master who becomes infatuated with a female vampire, especially for Peter Cushing, but Peter's wife was terribly ill and he pulled out to take care of her.

Ralph Bates, Jimmy Carreras's blue-eyed boy of the time, filled Peter's shoes admirably and everyone thought that he would do big things in horror films. Every morning he would appear all chipper and sprightly, but on his return from make-up he had become his character, complete with stoop and mad, staring eyes. After filming wrapped for the day, he would come bouncing out of make-up, exalting, "I'm back, I'm back!"

Barbara Jefford, a Shakespearean actress slumming it, was terribly stern as Countess Herritzen, the dowager vampire, while Michael Johnson was handsome but a bit vague as the disbelieving writer, Richard Lestrange.

Mike Raven (Count Karnstein, the chief vampire) was very much the man for horror films, knowing more about the occult than I had thought possible and always dressing in Gothic suits and capes. He had been cast due to his similarity to Christopher Lee and, in some shots, they actually edited in footage of Lee's eyes from a previous vampire epic.

Lust For A Vampire is set in 1830 when Countess Herritzen brings her niece, Mircalla (Yutte Stensgaard), to a finishing school for young ladies situated next to the ruins of Karnstein Castle, a former abode of the Undead in the mid-European province of Styria. As the school's gym mistress, one of my tasks is to wear a Grecian robe and lead the girls in some classical dancing in the school's grounds - actually the gardens of Hazelwood House, Abbots Langley.

It sounded simple enough, but the film held two surprises for me. The first came when I walked into the dormitory to tell the girls to hurry to bed. I marched on to the set confident that my reputation as "One-take Leigh" would see me through. What they had neglected to tell me was that some of the girls would be undressed and that two of them would be indulging in lesbian love play.

I froze.

They stopped the camera and called a lunch break. Over lunch, Jimmy Carreras explained that this was for the Swedish version, so unless I was planning to emigrate there, nobody would ever know that I had been in a scene with half of the supporting cast of the British Sex Film Catalogue.

Mircalla secretly feasts upon her voluptuous classmates, as well as various lasses from the local village, in an orgy of venomous fang-bites and hypnotic eyes. Then Giles Barton, who is researching the history of Karnstein Castle, discovers that Mircalla is an anagram for Carmilla and that she is a reincarnation of Carmilla Karnstein, a beautiful vampire who died in 1710. Barton, however, is besotted with Mircalla and, instead of exposing her, offers to serve as her slave. Mircalla quickly dispatches him with a love bite to the jugular.

Janet becomes suspicious of Mircalla and tells Richard Lestrange, who is teaching English literature at the school and with whom she is falling in love. Lestrange dismisses her suspicions and Janet realizes that he, too, has fallen for Mircalla's charms. Mircalla tries to dispose of Janet by seducing her with another deadly kiss, but Janet is saved by the crucifix around her neck.

In time-honoured fashion, the villagers discover that there is a nest of vampires in their midst and set fire to the castle. Mircalla dies with a burning stake through her heart and the vampires are wiped out until next time.

The second ghastly surprise about *Lust For A Vampire*, although it has its fans, was that Fine and Style had approached Jimmy Carreras with the idea of adding a pop song, written by another independent producer, Frank Godwin, and trilled by one-hit wonder Tracy. Without consulting Jimmy Sangster, Carreras decided that if the song cost him money it was out; if it could be covered within the budget it was in.

Selective cost-cutting saw it safely within the budget and Tracy warbled her way through a less-than-catchy number entitled *Strange Love*. The song had no place in the film, but the release (particularly in the States) was so low key that few people seemed to notice.

Variety commented that "the added allure of a bevy of beautiful girls, some gratuitous nudity, a glimpse of lesbianism and occasionally vivid blood and gore may bolster otherwise limited box-office potential".

Whatever the artistic merits of *Lust For A Vampire*, I am eternally grateful to Jimmy Carreras for helping me out of a tight spot.

No actor sets out to make a bad film, but I was the unfortunate victim of a director who seemed intent on doing just that. *Beware, My Brethren* or *The Fiend*, as it was known on release, was to be Tony Beckley's first big picture. He had graduated from a supporting role in *Lost Continent* to second lead in *Get Carter* and this film was going to make him a star. Tony asked me to be in it, playing a reporter called Paddy Lynch (oh dear!) I wanted to lynch him afterwards, but instead chose not to speak to him for six months.

Robert Hartford-Davis was directing and producing and his pedigree hardly inspired confidence; *Gonks Go Beat* and *Incense For The Damned* were as bad as their titles. I felt totally miscast as this dull, one-dimensional character, but I persevered for Tony's sake. The fact that Tony was rarely on the set, even though he was supposed to be the star, caused me a lot of concern and created friction between me and Hartford-Davis.

Hartford-Davis himself was almost as bad as the titles of his films - he certainly wasn't interested in the cinema as an art form and always had one eye on the purse strings. It's always difficult to wear the two hats of producer and director on the same film, but it was far worse in this case because I believe he was financing the film himself.

Patrick Magee, fresh out of Kubrick's *A Clockwork Orange*, was a Bible-bashing, Elmer Gantry-style preacher, a fitting role as Patrick seemed to be something of the crazy cleric in real life. The leading lady was Ann Todd and it was reassuring that I wasn't the only proper actress in the film. Ann had been in some great movies, including *The Snows of Kilimanjaro* and

THAT PHOTOGRAPH.
I had been keeping him company while he had some publicity photographs taken, when he swept me into his arms and kissed me. "Well that won't do your career any harm baby," Elvis said. The next day this was flashed all over the World. - 1965

Right: When he held you, you felt he was in total control. Whoever said he had no power in hollywood, can't have known him.

"THE DEADLY BEES"
With me as the star 2,000,000 Australian bees as my co stars.

Frank Finley showing off his bees, these little fellows had the dressing room next to mine.

*For the London Premiere of "BOEING BOEING".
I found myself without a date, so the Paramount boys
solved that little problem. Maximilian Schell flew in
from Germany to take me. - 1966*

*Left strip: Vicky (tricky Vicky) Hodge, Nigel
(polly) Pollitser, with her back to us. Pollys girlfriend
Erica Rafael.*

*Right strip: You can just see Maximillian in the last pic
on the right.*

Above: "SUBTERFUGE" Joan Collins and I on that beach at Hastings. 'Oh what a night'.

Right: With Gene Barry -on the table- Tom Adams and Marius Goring standing next to me. - 1967

Top & imediate left: THE ROYAL FILM PERFORMANCE 1966 James Fox's face speaks volumes. From left to right: James Fox, Me Rachel Roberts, Rex Harrison, Deborah Kerr and Dirk Bogard.

You can see from this below how flabbergarsted I am, also Rachel Roberts, who gave me a hug afterwards. - 1966

Far left: At the premiere of "ALFIE" and with its director Lewis Gilbert, - to whom I owe so much. - 1966

Top left: Checking out the sights in the harbour at Cannes. - 1967 Top right: This was taken by George Sidney - you can just see his pipe - of me with David (craperoo) Niven Jr and Liz Hooley in the Kings Road. - 1966

Below, why did I think I could get a tan on the beach at The Cannes Film Festival. - 1967

Top left & right: Hammer Studio shots. Top inset: The drama with Brian Jones was all over the newspapers.

Left: "THE LOST CONTINENT" 1967 Chatting with the crew while waiting for a new set up.

Below: Nigel Stock as my father getting a lot of stick from me.

Top: Michael and Minda in happier times. - 1969. Strip: Shots from the films in the West Indies. Above, having fun, ...not, with the director of "Doctor Carribean" in the West Indies.

On my beach the day before it disappeared in a massive storm in the West Indies. - 1968

Jean took some great photographs.

"LUST FOR A VAMPIRE".

Contact sheet of Yutte Stensguard trying her all to give me a bite. And stills on the lot at Bray Studios.

Above: Openings with friends; Alan Sievwright - now an opera impresario - at the opening of Barbra Streisand 'FUNNY GIRL'. Upper right: Jeremy Lloyd. Lower right: Peter Wyngarde and I looking all very 70's.

Rehearsals for The Variety Club Awards 1973. Left to right: Eric Morley of Miss World fame, Hughie Green, Michael Crawford, Liz Fraser. Me with a funky skirt on.

Klaus Kinski and doing the business with me "THE PLEASURE GIRLS"

On the set of THE FEARLESS VAMPIRE KILLERS Roman Polanski and Sharon Tate. She was one of the sweetest people, besides being absolutely stunning.

Tim the night he was called 'Mr Leigh' and never got over it. - 1974

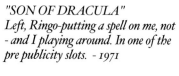

"SON OF DRACULA"
Left, Ringo-putting a spell on me, not - and I playing around. In one of the pre publicity slots. - 1971

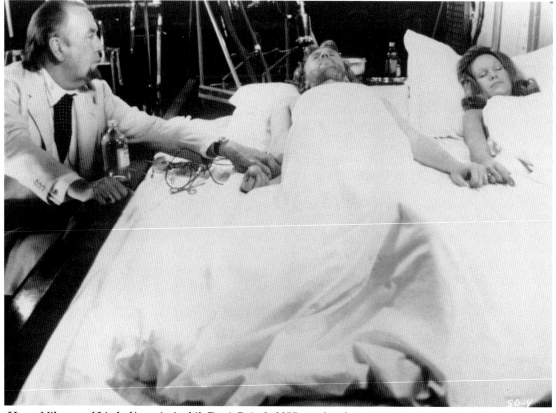

Harry Nilsson and I in bed 'corpsing' while Denis Price hold Harrys hand.

*Left: Beirut April 1975.
A short restbite from sniper fire, looking tired, urban warfare is mostly a nocturnal activity. Only hours later the big guns started that destroyed this city for ever.*

Back from Beruit, happy to in my garden in Rowan Road

Young Jimmy, one of the boys I used to visit a few times a year a active member of the Variety Club. - 1975

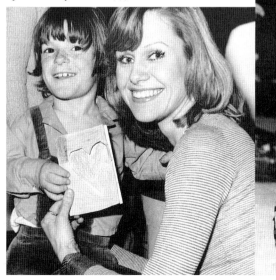

Things were looking good.

My Rolls Royce - who gave her life to save mine - or Butch Bertha as I called her. I was the first person to right off a Royce in the U.K. A record I would prefer not to have. - 1974

This was taken on the roof of the Savoy Hotel where I hosted a press party to announce being commissioned to write the 'new Bond' book. - I took Natasha - helping me get good press coverage.

Taste of Fear, but was perhaps better known as the former Mrs David Lean.

We got on really well and she told me about her legendary divorce settlement. She had asked for the marital home, but her husband suggested that she should take a 10 per cent cut of the gross of his next film instead. Thinking that the film wouldn't be anything special, Ann plumped for the house.

The film turned out to be *Bridge On The River Kwai*. Lean had said that she would regret her decision and, unsurprisingly, she did. Despite my friendship with Ann Todd, an air of impending doom hung over *The Fiend* and I started looking for a way out. Sadly, I couldn't find one.

Hartford-Davis was getting worse: he even made the actors feel guilty if they asked for another take. My agent, Barry Krost, was Tony's boyfriend and I was furious with Tony because he had somehow convinced me to appear in this mess in preference to *Get Carter*.

The Fiend is a horrible story about religious fervour, with Ann Todd, attired in steel-rimmed spectacles and shapeless cardigan, playing Birdy Wemys, a harmonium-pounding religious fanatic whose son, Kenny (Tony Beckley), a swimming instructor, combines piety with the nasty habit of strangling pretty girls under water. I discover his "secret room" and am about to become one of his victims, but I scream my way out of trouble in a blood-curdling finale when all hell breaks loose.

The critic for Films & Filming commented: "As the crusading reporter, Suzanne Leigh is pretty terrific. A true comedienne who looks good enough to eat, she must also be about the best screamer in the business since Fay Wray."

Once the merciful last day of filming was over, I had something else to worry about. I had done two low-budget horror films almost back-to-back.

Would I be typecast?

Fortunately not. Hartford-Davis failed miserably to secure a decent release for his picture and it finally went out as the support feature to *Tales From The Crypt* in the days of double bills. This latter film, starring Joan Collins, Peter Cushing and Ralph Richardson, made a phenomenal amount of money. *The Fiend* played at only a handful of cinemas and was quickly forgotten.

Things looked up when I had a call from the producers of a great new TV series, *The Persuaders*, saying they had had a discussion with the two stars, Roger Moore and Tony Curtis, and both had suggested me. *The Persuaders*, devised and produced by Robert S. Baker, was the most expensive TV series ever made and revolved around the partnership of two total opposites: Roger Moore as Lord Brett Sinclair, a to-the-manor-born English gentleman, and Tony Curtis as Danny Wilde, an American hustler from the wrong side of the tracks. The producers brought round the script of what was supposed to be the pilot episode, *Chain of Events*, which I read and agreed to do.

During rehearsals, however, I knew that there was going to be trouble. Roger and Tony were not only complete opposites on screen, but off it as well, and they took an instant dislike to one another. The series had originally been announced as *The Friendly Persuaders*, though this was quickly nixed when it was discovered that their relationship was about as friendly as snakebite.

Roger had an incredible ability for picking roles that complimented his suave style and Lord Brett Sinclair - Harrow, Oxford, Royal Ascot and all that - was right up his street. Having directed a few episodes of *The Saint*, he also knew his TV routine very well; in fact, he liked TV so much that he had made only two movies in the previous ten years.

Tony, on the other hand, was an uncompromising movie actor who was so serious about his career that he had actually paid for his own screen test to get the lead role in *The Boston Strangler*. He had never worked in television before and seemed totally flummoxed, even though the character of Danny Wilde, Bronx accent and all, was tailor-made for his talents.

To make matters worse, *Chain of Events* was directed by Peter Hunt, who had recently made the Bond movie *On Her Majesty's Secret Service*. Peter was not only a "name" director, but he got along very well with Roger Moore and they later worked together on *Gold*.

So Tony was far from happy - he was very much in Roger's domain, a far cry from where he had been as the centre of attention during his Hollywood years. To regain people's interest, he began ad-libbing and clowning for the crew. These antics annoyed Roger greatly and he made a number of cutting remarks about Tony. Tony, in turn, had nasty things to say about Roger.

In *Chain of Events*, written by Terry Nation, I play Emily Major, a British secret agent, who is searching for a black attaché case which is due to arrive from the Communist Bloc in the possession of a parachutist. Danny and Lord Brett are on a back-to-nature holiday in the drop area, with Danny roughing it in the wilds while Lord Brett lives in style in a tent equipped with all mod cons. Danny stumbles upon the parachutist who has been fatally injured in the jump and whose last act is to padlock the attaché case to Danny's wrist.

At the end of each day's filming, Roger and Tony strode off the set in opposite directions. If I spent time with one of them, it looked as though I was taking sides and that made the other resentful. When I had lunch with Roger, Tony didn't speak to me for the rest of the day. This was difficult because the majority of my scenes were with him.

My lot from British Intelligence are up against a gang of heavies, led by Peter Vaughan, who are also after the attaché case to sell to the highest bidder. So everybody is chasing the manacled Danny through forests and across fields until he and the attaché case take refuge in a nursing home. I apprehend him while he is taking a shower and then have to use my judo skills to defend him when the heavies show up.

Lord Brett, meanwhile, has discovered that the case, rather than containing Communist secrets, is actually a bomb which is primed to detonate when it is opened by British Intelligence. His Lordship gallantly disposes of the bomb and I wind up in a romantic clinch with Danny. In reality, I was avoiding both Roger and Tony by this time and sighed with relief when Peter Hunt wrapped the final scene.

A few weeks later Joan Collins was offered an episode of *The Persuaders*. She had heard rumours about friction on the set and rang me. She was good pals with Roger Moore, of course, but wanted to know for a more impartial source what Tony Curtis was like to work with. This was a difficult one for me because I didn't want to say that the only problems were those between Roger and Tony, so I told her that Tony was great fun and an excellent actor.

Reassured, Joan jetted off to make the episode, which was set in Monte Carlo. Tony was absolutely vile to her and she returned to London deeply offended.

Joannie didn't let me forget that one for quite a while.

Chapter 25

The Lichfield Break-up

"To have a good enemy, choose a friend; he knows where to strike."

Diane de Poitiers, *mistress of King Henri II of France*

PATRICK, Earl of Lichfield, was the Queen's first cousin and heir to Shugborough Hall, a very grand estate in Staffordshire. Patrick was an ex-Guards officer who had decided in the early Sixties to make his career in photography. David Bailey might be the Cockney cameraman who had worked his way up from the bottom, but Patrick Lichfield was the snapper who started at the top.

He was tall and slim, with a light-brown bouffant topping his aquiline features, an ascot raffishly tied around his neck and a signet ring on his little finger: the epitome of aristocratic chic. Privileged though he was, Patrick was anything but a *dilettante*: he took his work very seriously indeed and the results were highly professional.

We met on the circuit and he asked me to pose for him at his studio. The Daily Express published a photograph of him taking photographs of me, which was good publicity for both of us. We sort of drifted together early in 1971 - we went to the same parties and knew the same people; we were both unattached and it seemed like the sensible thing to do.

I was living in Shepherd Market and we'd go out to dinner then back to his studio to make love. Patrick was a ladies' man, but he stayed faithful to me and I was committed to him as well.

Joan Middleton, a freelance journalist friend, found out about the affair, but kept quiet about it. This was very sweet, because she could have made a lot of money out of the story; Patrick's sex life often made news. His main problem, though, had always been to pay off the crippling death duties that had accumulated from the estate of his father and grandfather. He had been forced to hand the house over to the National Trust, but retained a large section for himself. He was obsessed with getting his inheritance back and talked about it constantly.

It was in June 1971 that Patrick threw a house party at Shugborough. The house was full of treasures and the garden had the most amazing follies that the two previous earls had brought back from China and Tibet. There was only one rule: it didn't matter how much you misbehaved as long as you dressed for dinner and didn't do anything outrageous in front of the staff.

The guests that weekend included Brian Alexander, son of war hero Lord Alexander of Tunis, Dr T, a London physician, Willie Feilding, the artistic nephew of the Earl of Denbigh, and Aldine Honey, a South African model. The morning after we all arrived Patrick wanted us to try out his new toys - some small monkey bikes, which we were expected to ride round the estate.

I declined to take part, not wanting to put myself into any danger; as an actress, I didn't take unnecessary risks. But Patrick pointed out how small the bikes were and said I would be a spoil sport if I didn't join in.

The buzz in my head urged me not to get on that bike, but it was so small that I reasoned it couldn't possibly hurt me - after all, I'd been on bikes three times bigger with Elvis and Steve McQueen. As I was rebelling against my tried and tested intuition, I made a concession and pulled on a pair of high, double-leather boots and a thick pair of gloves.

I did not get further than the gravel drive which surrounded the house. When I reached a cattle grille, I crashed in a heap and the bike fell on to my left leg and right hand, and my big toe was stuck between the spokes of one wheel. The chain was still going and sawed through both layers of leather and grazed the skin before I could get the bike off me.

Patrick carried me into the house and Dr T was summoned. After checking my hand and leg, he said I had bruised the bone of my leg and would be all right; no need for hospitalisation. I was unconvinced, but Patrick said: "Whatever we might think of him as a doctor, he is one, so we had better take his word that you haven't done much to it."

That evening I was carried down to dinner in my smart dresses and jewels by Brian Alexander and joined in as best I could, but the pain was excruciating.

The following day I demanded that Patrick bring the car round and take me to Stafford Hospital. Dr T sat in the back, complaining that I was making a fuss about nothing. After I had been X-rayed, the doctor in charge asked why the "doctor" who had examined me hadn't noticed any broken bones. I had sixteen, two in my leg and fourteen in my hand. Missing one or two might be understandable, but to miss sixteen was inexcusable.

I was taken by ambulance to the station and travelled back to London, where I was admitted to the Harley Street Clinic. The only person who sent me a bunch of flowers or a note was Patrick's sister, Elizabeth, whom I really didn't know very well. I had been going out regularly with Patrick for several months, yet he came to the nursing home to see me just once - and that was a fleeting visit on his way to a dinner party at Buckingham Palace.

I did make a new friend out of the accident, however. One morning Suzy Kendall came round and was very sweet to me and, seeing the state I was in, she visited me almost every day. Things looked bad for my knee and nobody could come up with the name of an orthopedic surgeon who could fix it. Then I heard about Robert Young, who had performed miracles on injured people during the war; he had just retired to Malta.

I rang him and begged him to come back and treat me and he agreed. As time was of the essence, he flew back immediately, but it took him three goes to set my knee correctly and each time the plaster had to stay on for weeks. It was a frightening time, but Mr Young enabled me to walk again without a limp and I am eternally in his debt. I later met him in the street and thanked him again. "Don't thank me," he said. "Your phone call brought me out of retirement."

I couldn't work for a year.

Patrick Lichfield got Shugborough back after marrying Lady Leonora Grosvenor, daughter of the wealthiest man in Britain, the late Duke of Westminster. Brian Alexander was Patrick's best man and fainted in the middle of the service at Westminster Abbey.

I wasn't invited to the wedding, but I'm told there was a doctor in the house.

Chapter 26

Farewell, Dracula

"Don't compromise yourself - you're all you've got."

Janis Joplin, *American rock star*

IT was a phone call from Ringo Starr that hammered the final nail into my career as a horror-film actress. Ringo asked me if I would be interested in doing a movie he was producing, an indulgence on the part of a rich man who happened to be an enthusiastic movie buff: himself. The only trouble with this sort of approach is that, if you employ professionals, you should leave it to them; nobody had told him that.

Count Downe was a horror fantasy, with me playing the parts of all my favourite female film stars in the scenes I liked most from their movies. It sounded like fun and I was also allowed to take my own people on to the set. My little entourage was led by my hairdresser, Elaine Bowerbank. She was a great friend, good at her job and, most important, I could trust her. Just before a take, I'd say, "How do I look?" and she would tell me the truth. She would also sling me the odd line if I was struggling.

What really sounded good was a daily rate of £10,000 if they ran over. I needed that sort of money to get a new home; after all, I couldn't keep staying in the flat of my ex-boyfriend's stepfather indefinitely. I had turned down a few parts, so I was encouraged to hear that Freddie Francis was directing *Count Downe*; at least there would be some grown-ups on set.

Ringo asked me if I would go to his office in St James's Street to meet his friend Harry Nillson, the American singer-songwriter, who was to play *Count Downe*. Harry was 6ft 2in tall, blond and blue-eyed; good-looking, but only a passable actor. Ringo asked if I could do a read-through with Harry, to which I gladly agreed. We had been working for no more than half an hour, with both of them applauding every time I read a few lines and Ringo saying approvingly, "You can see she knows what she's doing," when everything suddenly collapsed into farce.

The door was flung open and in swept Marc Bolan and his wife June, wearing identical black-and-white outfits. Marc was the king of glam rock and he wanted to break into films playing someone other than himself, just as Harry Nillson was doing in *Count Downe*. Many rock stars were making the change from music to movies with varying degrees of success, such as Mick Jagger in "*Performance*" and Marianne Faithfull in *Girl On A Motorcyle*, (which I'd turned down on the strength of its abysmal script, even though Alain Delon was the male lead).

With the other glam rocker, David Bowie, about to hit the screen in *The Man Who Fell To Earth*, Marc Bolan desperately wanted a part in *Count Downe*. He set about persuading Ringo to cast him by jumping into his lap and feigning a "girl-with-big-producer" routine. The reading, of course, was completely forgotten.

Why wasn't I frightened stiff by scenes like that? Where was my sense of foreboding? Where was "the buzz"?

Marc Bolan didn't get a part, but there were already a lot of musicians in *Count Downe*, including Billy Preston, Peter Frampton - Peter's father was the Art teacher at the school that he and David Bowie went to - and my mad friend, Keith Moon, "Moon the Loon". When I discovered that they were all playing themselves, I thought there might be a slim chance that *Count Downe* could make it as a rock movie. Maybe it would emulate the success of *The Rocky Horror Show*, which was making a fortune as a stage play for its creator, Richard O'Brien, a friend of David Charkham's.

As soon as we started shooting, however, it became obvious to me that nobody knew what they were doing. So many drugs, mostly pot, were being passed around among the great many visitors to the set that you could get stoned without trying.

The most hazardous place was Harry Nillson's trailer, where the most stunning, long-legged, glamourous groupies, ladies of the night - call them what you will - were to be found. Three or four of them at a time would be flown in from LA or New York, arriving in big, flashy cars and, within minutes, would start rolling huge joints in amazing coloured papers.

These girls knew how to party big-time, but it was what they wore that had me rivetted: jeans or short denim skirts, with tops adorned by big diamond clips, and strings of pearls around their necks. The look was great; tarty but great. Nobody wore that kind of jewellery during the day: diamonds and pearls before six? The county set would have been apoplectic. It wasn't long before I was wearing diamond rings and clips on denim jackets and, within months, large, fake diamond accessories were being sold in the King's Road.

Meanwhile, the set of *Count Downe* had taken on an even more surreal quality. Everything - scenes, costumes, even story-lines - were done on a whim. It was as if Rome was burning and we were all out to lunch and, more worryingly, nobody seemed to care. What story there was concerned Dracula's son, *Count Downe*, who is a successful pop star. Sadly, he has a split personality, so when he's not singing, he's flashing his fangs.

Ringo played Merlin the Magician and I played Amber, whose role changed daily. Ringo had promised me that I could play my favourite female actresses, so I did cameos of Marlene Dietrich dancing in a cage and Rita Hayworth in *Gilda*. If Ringo liked the sound of a set-up, he'd say, "Why don't we do that?" and off we'd go again.

The only voice of sanity was that of Dennis Price, the only other paid-up member of Equity on the set. Dennis declared in his inimitable style that *Count Downe* was so far out of the mainstream that it "should be kept at home and only brought out in front of close friends, and then only after dark." I started referring to it as *"Downe-And-Let's-Hope-Never-Coming-Out"*, but with so many egos involved I was terrified that it would. My career, which I had been painstakingly building up over the years, was hanging on the most expensive home movie ever made.

Why didn't I just walk off the set? A contract is a contract and, besides, they would probably have demanded their money back. I had just found a pretty house in Brook Green, Hammersmith, and was moving in. When I had first heard that Dennis Price was to be in the film, it gave me heart. After all , he was a good, solid actor and I had loved him in so many English films, especially *Kind Hearts And Coronets*. But Dennis soon lost heart completely.

"My life has taken me through some bad times recently, my dear, and this is my Waterloo. It will be all right for you, Suzanna, you are young enough to be able to wait for ten years or so. But, for me, it's over."

"It won't even see the light of day. You're worrying too much."

I couldn't bring myself to tell him that I had been physically sick with worry the previous night. Dennis insisted that luck would not be on our side and, in funereal tones, declared: "I hear the death rattle of this whole sorry business."

Dennis was called away for a scene and left his white paper cup of steaming coffee behind. Feeling in need of a shot of caffeine, I picked up the cup and took a large gulp. The coffee barely masked the brandy.

Oh God, not him as well.

The biggest shock of all was to hear that, after a few days of extra shooting (for which I was paid mostly in crates of Dom Perignon), *Count Downe* was to be released in America as *Son of Dracula*. Ringo and Harry Nillson had collaborated on the score and Freddie Francis had somehow been able to find a beginning, a middle and an end among the miles of jumbled footage. I cried my eyes out that night.

We all knew the rules; if it's lousy, blame the stars.

Why, oh why did it ever have to come out?

I knew plenty of actors who had made bad films for lots of money and they had never been released. Three of those actors are in the top ten list, including two with Oscars, and yet they amassed their wealth from more than twenty-five movies which didn't come out in the Seventies.

Poor Dennis.

He died of cirrhosis of the liver in a Guernsey hospital, but at least he was spared the indignity of those reviews.

Chapter 27

Son of Flashman

"I prefer liberty to chains of diamonds."

Lady Mary Wortley Montagu, *English writer*

IT was almost at the end of filming *Son of Dracula* that I met "Son of Flashman", Tim Hue-Williams, a gorgeous 27-year-old with a bad-boy reputation with girls. He was standing on the terrace at Royal Ascot, holding a glass of champagne, languid, Byronic, the absolute embodiment of the upper-class bounder. I instantly fell in love.

I had gone to Royal Ascot with Joel Lerner and his girlfriend who had called at my house in Brook Green on the way. As I hadn't been out of my door for months, except to go to work, I hadn't washed my hair, but I found a hat that matched a blouse, pale apple green, long, beautiful and, most importantly, it hid my hair.

Joel's mother, Hannah Marco, a well-known racehorse owner, had her own box and it was filled with beautifully dressed people, eating salmon and strawberries and drinking champagne. Everyone was talking about the Ascot Gold Cup because the favourite, Rock Roi, who had been disqualified the previous year, was running again. Word in the boxes was that he was going to walk it this year and there were some big bets going down. "Never back a horse that walks, only those that run."

My daddy's words danced around my head.

Normally, I wouldn't have cared either way, but after spotting "Son of Flashman" on the terrace I had made some rapid inquiries to find out his name and had also ascertained that his aunt was Rock Roi's owner.

Furthermore, I had learned to my chagrin that his date that day was Lady Charlotte Curzon and that they were unofficially engaged. Tim had previously been engaged to her sister, Lady Mary Gaye, and he later told me that, after a weekend party, their father, Lord Howe, had said to him, "For God's sake, Tim, pick one of them - but leave me my wife!"

"Timmy Tom Tit" was the Marcos's nickname for him. He was a banker and stockbroker, although, like my father, he could have made a living from gambling. While Daddy spent days at the races, Tim spent nights at John Aspinall's Clermont Club in Berkeley Square, playing "chemmy" against the best of its members. As I had always loved a winner, I thought I had hit the jackpot.

I wanted Tim's complete and undivided attention, so I went down to the paddock to see his aunt's fantastic horse which would supposedly walk the race. Rock Roi looked very cool and classy, but, at the same time, disinterested. I looked around at his rivals and one of them caught my eye - Erimo Hawk, a magnificent beast that shot into the ring as though on speed, sweating profusely and jumping around. I decided that he would either win the race or drop dead on the spot. The odds of 50-1 made him a rank outsider, but I put £20 on him and rejoined the party.

During the race, I stayed at the back of the box, not daring to watch. Suddenly, there was a roar from the crowd as the names of the leaders came over the loudspeakers - Rock Roi and Erimo Hawk were neck and neck and they hit the line together in a photo finish. The air was alive with the sound of people frantically flicking through their form guides, trying to garner some knowledge about this unknown outsider.

I strolled out on to the terrace and smiled at Tim. He was looking a little tense. The minutes ticked by, while the crowd waited silently.

Then the announcement came through: "The winner of the 1972 Gold Cup is Erimo Hawk!"

A collective gasp expressed the feelings of the crowd.

I jumped up, exclaiming, "I've won! I've won!" and waving my ticket. The lack of response gave me the impression that I was the only one to have done so.

I studied Tim's face.

It had developed a slightly green tinge, but otherwise he seemed to be holding up quite well.

"How much did you have on it?" I asked him.

"Seven thousand."

He asked me why I'd backed Erimo Hawk.

"Because he had 'winner' stamped across his forehead!"

Tim said that I had clearly got the knack and that it was an art and I told him I'd inherited it from my father. I think it is safe to say that, by this time, I had his attention. I knew Tim could re-introduce me to the world I had been in with Patrick Lichfield and from which I had been unceremoniously dumped for having the bad taste to break my leg at a house party.

When I asked my girlfriend Bibi Blanger if she knew Tim, she told me not to touch him with a barge pole. She had been a debutante the same year as his ex-wife (he'd married at twenty and divorced at twenty-two), who'd become known as "Poor Badge" because he was so unfaithful to her.

Despite that, or maybe even because of it, I rushed straight in. There are times when love colours your vision and this was certainly one of them. It's amazing how a simple thing like a day at the races can completely change your life.

A few days after Royal Ascot we sat next to each other at Gerry Marco's birthday dinner at Les Ambassadeurs and things progressed from there. We had dinner after one of my Variety Club committee meetings and I took Natasha with me. Tim said later that he fell in love with her before he did with me, though I'd have said the same about him once I'd seen his cars. He had a blue Ferrari, a green Mercedes and a sky-blue Mini, which he claimed matched the colour of his eyes. This was the man who had eight copies of *You're So Vain* pushed through his letterbox.

Within a few weeks Tim had moved into my house at Brook Green, although he kept his flat in Eaton Place. He made me realise that I'd been working all my life and he spoiled me rotten, not letting me do any of the things I'd been doing, not only for myself, but for everyone else as well. He showered me with presents and, best of all, let me drive the Ferrari.

Tim laid down his attitude to our relationship: if we stayed together, we partied together and that meant mixing with his friends, Jeremy Palmer-Tomkinson, an Olympic skier who had doubled for James Bond in the ski scenes in *On Her Majesty's Secret Service*, and his girlfriend (and later wife) Claire Leveson, a former girlfriend of Prince Charles, Kevin Burke, George Drummond and Charlotte Curzon, who was intermittently engaged to another bounder, Rupert Deen.

I slipped into a lazy routine of eating, drinking and partying, interspersed with trips to health farms. These were the heady days of "psychedelia". Everybody's flats were painted all colours of the rainbow and they all seemed to be in Chelsea, Kensington or Belgravia. In geographic terms, Hammersmith was in "the country", but we spent most of our time on the King's Road, where we'd bump into so many of our friends that phone calls were superfluous.

My house at Brook Green was a pretty, leafy, two-story place at 26 Rowan Road. Upstairs, it had three bedrooms, with a terrace and a bathroom, and downstairs there was a drawing room, which led through French windows to a garden, a long galley of a kitchen and another bathroom. I turned two of the bedrooms into one spectacular bedroom with a walk-in dressing room, and the third bedroom became a study cum playroom with a roof terrace. The main bathroom was purple and white - very trendy colours - with lots of antique mirrors. In the living room, there were sofas all round, graduating from shot-silk yellow to beige and gold.

I bought the New Look from Barbara Hulanicki at Biba the day before it opened in Kensington High Street and I blacked out the windows of my Mini and installed speakers in the doors. Michael Fish and Ossie Clarke were the designers to go to for well-tailored but wonderfully flashy clothes. My most extravagant present for Tim was a full-length mink coat, which I had specially made by an East End furrier. My new hairdresser was Denny Godber, who owned Sweeneys, a trendy salon in Beauchamp Place, and my closest girlfriends were Imogen Hassall and Suzy Kendall.

Imogen, or "Imo", had been close to me since before I went to Hollywood. We had both made our film debuts in 1960; she in *The Bulldog Breed* and me in *Bomb In The High Street*. Although she was three years older than me, she had spent those years at RADA, whereas I had gone straight into films. In 1968, Roderick Mann, the show business writer, had described us as "two young actresses, both attractive; both, in champagne terms, *demi-sec*; both, professionally, caught up in the vortex of the Permissive Society."

Pretty accurate, really.

One of the other things that bound us together was that we had both worshiped our fathers. Imogen's father was the composer Christopher Hassall, who had worked closely with Ivor Novello and with her Godfather, Sir William Walton. But Christopher never got the credit that she felt he really deserved and, as a result, she and Sir William didn't see eye to eye.

The image that "Imo" presented to the press of a flighty, well-stacked brunette was very different from the girl I knew. Although she had lent a touch of glamour to films such as *When Dinosaurs Ruled The Earth* and *Carry On Loving*, she had proved her worth in less commercial projects such as *The Long Duel* and *The Virgin And The Gypsy*. However, she remained better known for her premiere appearances than for her acting. The image was, to a great extent, one that she projected herself and while such labels as "Countess Cleavage" were undeniably scathing, she always laughed them off.

Imogen had money from a trust fund set up by her father and was very successful at buying houses, doing them up and selling them and she lived well. I introduced her to the wonders of Africa and, over the years, we spent an annual four or six weeks there. It was a place where we'd found strength and power - that beautifully wild and simplistic lifestyle was like our spiritual oxygen. We'd spend a lot of time in the bush, completely removed from the outside world, and often helped Bishop John of Mombassa to build his church.

While we were staying at the Mombassa Beach Hotel on one holiday, we were asked to act as judges in the Miss Mombassa beauty contest, which was being held around the pool. I was running late and, while Imogen was waiting for me, she had been hitting the tequila sunrises in the bar.

Imogen was wearing a Zandra Rhodes butterfly dress and looked very beautiful as we set off around the pool towards the judging podium. Suddenly, some big arc lights were switched on and we were both temporarily blinded. I heard a little splash and, when I was able to focus again, there was Imogen, floating on the surface of the water like a little butterfly.

Suzy Kendall and I went into the property business by buying a house together in Corny Road, off Plumbing Station Road, Chiswick, which we planned to renovate and sell. We bought the house because when we called to inspect it there was a photograph of us in a newspaper on the floor.

We also collaborated in writing a TV comedy series, *Action - Take 2*, about two actresses who share a flat together. Whenever one of them entertains a producer at home, the other plays the maid to make sure there's no hanky-panky. Our series was never picked up, but when I saw *The Liver Birds* I realised how good it could have been.

In the spring of 1973 I finished a film script I had written called *Stash*, a spoof about a smooth guy called Simon London, who smuggles contraband in a catamaran. The cast was to be a galaxy of stars, with Simon Ward as Simon London and Omar Sharif as a drug baron. I also had Peter Cook, a good friend of mine, and Dudley Moore, who was married to Suzy Kendall, in mind. My secretary, Anne de Havilland, niece of Olivia de Havilland, sent copies to all of the actors for whom I had written parts. There was a craze for all-star entertainments at the time and it was all looking good.

Tim and I got engaged on March 30, 1973. He gave me a beautiful trilogy of sapphire and diamond rings from Collingwood. I gave the exclusive story of our engagement to the Daily Express and wore a two-tone satin brown-and-titian gold dress when we posed for photographs in the garden at Brook Green.

At the premier of *The Great Gatsby*, I wore half a million pounds worth of jewellery on loan from Collingwood and, although Tim and

I looked like the perfect movie couple, something happened that night that put him off the movie scene for good. As we were going up the stairs into the cinema, a group of photographers ran forward to snap me.

"One more, Miss Leigh."

"Mr Leigh, could you move over there?"

I tried to steer Tim away, but the damage had been done; he never forgot the slight of being called "Mr Leigh" and refused to attend any more shows with me. I developed such a reputation for turning things down that people stopped asking me. Once, however, I was having lunch in the White Elephant when a director came over and told me how rude I was not to have answered his letter. I said I had never received it. Not long afterwards, I found Tim binning an invitation that had been sent to me. I challenged him about it and was told that my duty was to him now, not to a load of nobodies.

It seemed as though Tim was offering me financial and emotional stability and, as he kept telling me that I was "the sunshine of his life", a song he played all the time, I believed him. In return, he asked that I should give up the life I had known and move into his world.

Although we were now inseparable, I always put off naming the wedding day because of "something". For one thing, we had decided not to get married until we had a baby. There was no immediate pressure - after all, it was the Seventies, the Me Decade, and we were part of the set that made its own rules.

As Elvis would have said, "You pay for everything", but then it was diamonds, beautiful clothes and champagne (a roomful of crates of 1964 Dom Perignon) that made me feel wanted and protected. Tim had bought a Rolls-Royce Silver Shadow and my absolute favourite gift from him was a Rolls-Royce Silver Cloud, which I nicknamed "Butch Bertha".

One day I was offered a film which was to be shot on location in Greece. I had been through a period of bad decision-making in terms of my career and, when Tim suggested we become a proper family and have a baby, it felt like the right thing to do. My only real concern was that I might become a mother similar to my own, but I felt that we were secure enough in our love to overcome this.

We made a big commitment: he gave up his business in France that took up so much of his time and I turned down the film I'd been offered. As a natural progression, I came off my agent's books, which meant that I was out of the business. This was a foolish and stupid decision and one that I still regret.

As part of the deal, Tim agreed to cut out whisky and brandy, but said that drinking wine with meals didn't count. Unfortunately, it didn't prevent him from developing a debilitating illness during a gastronomic trip to the South of France. We had allotted four days just to cover the thousand or so miles, breaking overnight in Paris. Bliss. Tim had rented a beautiful pink-and-white villa for the summer, which was situated next to Jacques Cousteau's lighthouse at Cap Ferrat and it came complete with its own jetty, swimming pool and jet riva boat. It also came with its own resident ghost.

The first time I felt the presence of the "Woman in White", as we called her, was before we had been there a week. I was walking down a corridor when a shadowy figure in a long, white Victorian dress swept past me, as though in a dreadful hurry, followed by the sound of doors closing. A coldness followed in her wake, chilling the whole corridor. The next day Tim had the very same experience.

We had invited Lionel Bart, who had just been declared bankrupt and was having a hard time, as a house guest and decided not to mention the apparition to him to see if he encountered her as well. I wasn't too pleased when he turned up in the dead of night with his own uninvited guest, Andrew Oldham, the Rolling Stones manager. Andrew was a very tricky guest. He would only eat food that had died "a happy death", a fact he chose not to mention until we were sitting down to boiled lobster.

The morning after their arrival Lionel wandered down to breakfast, saying, "Hey, babes, I thought you said that there was only us staying here at the moment, so who's that chick in white I passed in the hall?" Lionel was very cool about the whole thing when we told him we had a ghost for company.

Then the spooks got seriously scary. I was asleep when a hot breath on my face woke me up. I opened my eyes and, to my total horror, was confronted by an enormous black cat with huge yellow eyes. It was only inches from my face and I was so frightened that my only thought was that, if I was going to die, I didn't want to see it happen. I closed my eyes. The breath faded and, when I opened my eyes again, the cat had vanished. We were out of the house that morning and moved straight into a hotel, the Voile d'Or at St Jean Cap Ferrat.

When we got back to London, Tim had some tests and discovered that he had contracted hepatitis A. He was supposed to give up alcohol for six months, but he only cut down again. He said a few glasses of wine with food didn't count; besides, the doctors were talking about people who didn't drink good wine.

"I'd rather die than not drink Montrachet," I said.

"That's right, darling," Tim agreed, passing his glass across the table for me to fill.

Tim's illness meant that he slept for up to eighteen hours a day and I had to remain very quiet, but he seemed to recover and for the next few years we lived the high life again - eating out for lunch and dinner every day, going to parties and clubs, staying out all night; things that work had prevented me from doing in the past.

I was passionate about my work for the Variety Club, which did an immense amount to help children who had been put into homes from an early age. I was one of the pioneers who took them out of the homes into the real world. We would take 6,000 children to the circus at Christmas and that meant 6,000 goodie bags and 6,000 smiling faces.

We lived at Brook Green or in his first flat at 62 Eaton Place. We spent long weekends in the country with his friends, often going on a Thursday and not returning until the following Tuesday. Tim loved going shooting in Scotland, but, at my request, he put away his 12-bore shotgun.

The cocktail of pampering, weekly presents and constant shopping was overpowering, but marriage still wasn't something that either of us was easy with; Tim because of his failed marriage and me because I was terrified of messing it up.

Tim was a great raconteur and one of the stories he told me was that his great uncle was the Duke of Montrose, the exiled pretender to the Scottish throne. Tim's family was the Grahams and he had his own tartan. I loved the stories of the clans, but there was an unpleasant flip side to them. Once, we were walking down the street when we saw Margaret, Duchess of Argyll, coming towards us. The Campbells of Argyll were mortal enemies of the Grahams and Tim crossed the street and spat on the ground.

I couldn't believe he had done it, especially as I had dated Margaret's son, Brian Sweeny, and had attended some lovely parties at her Queen Anne house in Upper Brook Street.

Tim's circle lived by a set of unwritten rules which you broke at your peril. Secrecy was bred into them; it came with the family heirlooms. When anything scandalous occurred, they closed shields like the Praetorian Guard. This was never more pronounced than in the case of Lord "Lucky" Lucan, a friend of John Aspinall, Mark Birley, James Goldsmith and Dominic Elwes.

One night in November 1974 Lady Veronica Lucan staggered into a Belgravia pub close to our flat in Eaton Place after having been beaten around the head, she claimed, by her estranged husband. She was screaming, "He's murdered my nanny! My children, my children!" The nanny, Sandra Rivett, had been battered to death in the kitchen of the house in Lower Belgrave Street where Lady Lucan lived with her three children. Lord Lucan disappeared from his usual haunts that night and, while his car was found abandoned at Newhaven on the Kent coast the following morning, he has not been seen since. Not officially, anyway.

Lucky Lucan was a friend of Tim's, though they weren't terribly close. Only two nights previously, they had played backgammon, which Tim had won, and Lucan, a bad loser, had hurled the board across the room. The night of the murder our phone did not stop ringing and a meeting of Lucan's friends was arranged for the next morning, with Tim in attendance.

I never believed that Lucan had committed suicide, as that morning's papers proclaimed, and, although I wasn't privy to the meeting, I knew that they weren't mourning his death.

Eventually, the detectives investigating Sandra Rivett's murder and Lord Lucan's disappearance arrived at our flat. Tim had warned me that I wasn't to say anything if they did turn up, not that I knew anything. Tim was rather shaken as they all piled in, so he opted to sit quietly on the sofa, while I took over the interview. Throughout the conversation, I felt like I was acting in one of those British war movies, where the honest householder has to cover up for a spy.

The Lucky Lucan affair was handled by Tim's cliquey aristocratic circle, who had scant regard for the police and who considered Lucan to be one of their own, whether he was guilty or not. They had never held Veronica Lucan in much esteem; she hated going to the Clermont and sitting around the bar while her husband worked the tables.

It was my view that she should have thought about that before marrying a gambler. Many people think that Lucan is still playing cards in some little back-water town in South America, but, as Tim was never a main player in the affair, his fate remains a mystery to me.

I had failed to get *Stash* off the ground the previous year, but Desmond Briggs, a partner in the publishers Blond & Briggs, had read my script and I guess he liked it because he commissioned me to create a female James Bond. Her name was to be Connaught and the book would be called *Femme Sole*.

I needed time alone with my new project. Although I had written before, my work had always been on spec; this was the first time that anyone had paid me an advance and that put writing on a different level.

I became tough on myself and ultimately writer's block set in, though I didn't recognise it as such at the time. In fact, my self-esteem wasn't in the best of shapes, so I held a press party on the roof of the Dorchester Hotel in February 1975 to launch myself as a serious author. I took Natasha with me, which guaranteed that we made most of the papers.

The press coverage boosted my confidence sufficiently for me to finish the outline, but when I sat down to write the book I discovered that I couldn't write *and* party at the same time. I was searching for somewhere quiet to spend a few weeks when, in early spring 1975, I was invited to visit a girlfriend whom I had originally met at a health farm in England. She lived in Beirut, the Paris of the East.

It turned out to be the ideal place for a female James Bond.

Chapter 28

Bullets in Beirut

"Everything is so dangerous that nothing is very frightening."

Gertrude Stein, *American writer*

My heart has always gone out to the Jewish people who had to suffer the horror of the holocaust by the Nazis during World War II; Over the years every kind of persecution fills me with loathing that we have had to watch through the media. What happened to me that spring of 1975, I shall relate as it was.

I'll call her Nada. I suppose I knew that her sympathies lay with the Palestinians, it just never came up in conversation, when I accepted her invitation but Beirut was peaceful when I flew in and no one seemed to be expecting trouble. Here was a chance for me to finish the first draft of my book and to shop in some of the thousands of boutiques that Beirut had to offer. Whole streets specialised in one particular product or another, such as gold or diamonds or glassware or Paris fashions.

My shopping expeditions went according to plan, but after a few days at Nada's apartment in the city centre the constant noise of car-horns in the streets below was driving me crazy. It was impossible to concentrate on my writing with that racket going on all day and most of the night, so her family suggested I take their chalet in the mountains, where it would be much quieter. There was just one thing to remember: I should stay inside the chalet at four o'clock every afternoon because the Israeli Air Force did some low flying up there at that time of day and anything could happen 'just stay inside'.

This sounded too dramatic for words. I was not too up on Middle Eastern politics although I was vaguely aware that hundreds of thousands of Palestinians had moved into the Lebanon after being driven out of Jordan

207

by King Hussein in September 1970. An armed driver took me up to the chalet, which was set into the side of a mountain overlooking a valley.

The following day I ate lunch in the only restaurant in the village and was finishing off a glass of the local wine when my driver came in, pointing at his watch to indicate the time. Ah, I thought, the four o'clock thrill. I started to walk back to the chalet when suddenly everybody vanished and I was on my own.

The first thing I saw were two tiny black dots a long way off. Then they weren't dots anymore, but two massive jet fighters.

One fighter turned off, leaving the second plane with me; I glanced over my shoulder and, incredibly, it seemed to be able to hover, but in my panic I may have freeze-framed the moment in my mind. I was walking fast along a dirt track, with stones and rocks everywhere, when I heard a rat-a-tat-tat behind me and rock splinters flew in all directions, some of them hitting me in the left forearm and right buttock.

I jumped into the brush, trying to hide, and cut myself on brambles and a sharp piece of rock. Having got his kicks, the pilot veered off and disappeared down the valley. I reached the chalet and patched myself up with the help of a very well-equipped first-aid kit. This, I promise you, is what happened, if indeed the two jets were Isralies then I have to say that their pilots were a touch too zealous that day.

In the middle of the night I turned on the radio, expecting to hear some news about the Lebanon. Instead, it was all about the momentous events that were unfolding in Vietnam and I heard an eye-witness account of the fall of Da Nang as it was happening. The commentator was cut off in mid-sentence by Communist soldiers.

It seemed that the world had suddenly gone insane and this was confirmed when Nada phoned, saying there was some trouble in Beirut and I should stay where I was.

I stayed put in the chalet to give my wounds time to heal, but Nada phoned again a few days later to say that the trouble had got worse and it would be safer if we were all together in Beirut. I quickly packed, summoned the driver and we set off in the early evening. The drive down the winding mountain road was hazardous, with the driver fighting all the way against a tide of refugees who were fleeing Beirut in a never-ending stream of carts, car and trucks.

It was an awesome sight, watching smoke spiral into the night sky above the burning city and hearing the salvos of heavy guns echoing around the hills. The fashionable streets of Beirut had become dark and menacing and shells were exploding quite close to us while my driver tried to judge the safest route to take. He screeched to a halt and I dashed into Nada's block of flats.

After the initial relief of seeing that I was alive, Nada led me into the main drawing room. The room was full of people I hadn't seen before, men, women and children who were gathered in dignified little groups. There was a stillness in that room which spoke more eloquently of the danger than any words.

Then Nada's husband broke the silence.

"Suzanna, we are sorry that you are here with us at a time like this, although we hope the troubles will be over soon."

He shrugged his shoulders. He didn't know when that might be. Nada's brother, a rich and important man among the Palestinians, was speaking.

"You are my sister's guest and as such you are under my protection," he said. "You are one of us now - yes?"

"Yes, of course."

I wasn't quite sure what he meant, but I obviously couldn't say "No".

The men spoke to each other in Arabic.

"Tell me," I said, "what is it. What's going on?"

Now I was beginning to worry. Nada's brother came over and graciously took my hand, speaking as he led me to the bar.

"You know, something should never have to come up in life, but the troubles have made it necessary."

There were murmurings of agreement in the background.

"There is no easy way around this now," he continued. "We all have to arm ourselves. Do you know how to use one of these?"

With that, he pressed a button and what had been a cocktail cabinet turned on itself and became an armoury. Taking an automatic weapon off the shelf, he offered it to me. It was a Kalashnikov.

"Oh yes, I do," I said. "It's called the Widow-maker."

This was the only type of gun that I knew anything about because of the time I had spent on safari in Africa with Joe the white hunter and some of his mercenary pals.

The stillness in the room was accentuated by the sporadic rat-a-tat-tat of machine gun fire coming from somewhere in the city. I went to bed, but hardly slept. The furniture in my room had been rearranged so that I would not have to go near the windows. All night long there was the rat-a-tat-tat of gunfire, but in the morning the car horns were silent.

I tuned into the BBC World Service to hear about the siege. There was not a word. All my friends laughed at my naivete when I complained.

They said that nobody in the West was interested in the fate of the Palestinians. I said little, having learned my lesson from the fighter jets. It was some more days before a radio program was given over to the story.

By then, we had got into some sort of routine, staying out of sight and gathering information from a Paris Match correspondent who would come to the flat after dark to eat with us and tell us which part of the city was being fought over that day.

It seemed there were three million Palestinian refugees living in camps in the Lebanon and the Phalangists, members of the Christian Centrist Party, were intent on driving them out, as well as destroying their Moslem allies. With women and children being killed in the crossfire, it all seemed so brutally cynical.

On about the fourth night, with buildings around us under fire from light anti-aircraft guns, the St George's Hotel was badly hit. I had my own scare a few minutes later when a gunman climbed over somebody else's balcony on to mine. He stood still for a while, his eyes catching mine in the mirror.

He simply nodded and moved on.

That night, there was a lot of talk about the British Ambassador's wife, who insisted on going out every day to get fresh bread and water. The Arabs thought she was mad, but I was proud of her (and told her so when I later met her in London). The following night, however, a friend came over to tell us that she had been shot in the ankle by a sniper who had also killed many soldiers and civilians. The sniper was on a roof and only showed himself for a moment to shoot. "Everybody has tried to kill him," he said, "but he's too clever".

I told them about something I'd seen in a film and they were so desperate to get rid of that sniper that they made a phone call. Some young men arrived at the flat the next afternoon and drove me to the street where the sniper was operating.

The plan was very simple. One of them attracted the sniper's attention by taking a random shot at the roof, then ducking out of sight. That was the signal for me to let out my Fay Wray scream, which ricocheted off the buildings and echoed all around the rooftop.

The sniper had obviously never heard anything like it before and raised his head above the parapet to see what had happened. The gunmen had the rooftop in their sights and opened fire.

They did not miss. The Ambassador's wife had been vindicated.

The events in Beirut had a profound effect on the way I viewed the world. The luck of being born in one country or another could so easily alter the freedoms that we took for granted in the West.

With the situation growing worse, Nada's family decided that I should be evacuated. We made two trips to the airport, driving through the ruined streets, with me on the floor of the car and guns at the ready.

The airport was open only for brief intervals and if you happened to be there when a plane was taking off, then you jumped on. The first two attempts failed, but it was third time lucky and I scrambled aboard a plane just before take-off and flew to London.

I was never more grateful to get home.

Chapter 29

The Day I Died

"Get my swan costume ready."

Last words of Anna Pavlova, *Russian dancer*

TONY Beckley, Lionel Bart, Diamond Lil (an outrageous character whose real name was Clive McKay-Kemp) and Ben Carruthers were among the friends who trooped down to Brook Green on July 26, 1975, for my thirtieth birthday party.

Anthony Andrews, the star of *Brideshead Revisited* on TV, was there with his wife, Georgina Simpson, heiress to the department store, Simpson's of Piccadilly. Jane Asher brought a fantastic birthday cake in the shape of a poodle and Ned Sherrin organised the charades.

The garden was looking lovely and the apple tree was festooned with fairy lights. Allan Warren was gazing up at them when an apple fell down and broke his nose.

It had been that sort of year.

A few weeks later I was the victim of a burglary in which I lost most of my jewels and things that I'd collected over the years. The papers proclaimed their value to be £50,000 and that wasn't far short of the figure. The insurance company, who had been charging me an enormous premium for years, pointed out that, in the small print (so small as to be invisible to the human eye), there was a clause stating that my jewels weren't covered unless they were kept in a bank vault, so I was entitled to absolutely nothing.

I had moved back to Brook Green in May, although I was still seeing Tim several times a week. I had be unable to write anything in Beirut and we had decided to have some space from each other while I finished Femme Sole. With the book taking up most of my time, Tim said that things weren't the way he wanted them to be. He started having affairs, one with a South American contestant for the Miss World crown whom he met through a friend of ours. But I was feeling great again because I had something of my own to work on, instead of always listening to Tim's "City talk".

When I had first met Tim, I asked him what he did, other than writing me poetry (a side of him that I loved). He told me about all of these companies that he had - "Great," I thought, although it seemed a bit odd for a man who had won the Winston Churchill Award for Poetry at Harrow.

What I didn't know then was that all he did was strip companies of their assets (which always sounded like a form of rape to me) and that he never made anything other than money. Tim had been a good cricketer at Harrow and had been approached to play for Kent and was a brilliant squash and rackets player. It seemed such a waste.

1975 had already been a difficult year for me, but it's always dangerous to assume that things won't get worse if you don't take care. A friend of mine, Robert Naggar, a stockbroker whom I'd known forever, asked me out to dinner on December 5. We went in Butch Bertha, my Rolls-Royce, with me at the wheel. On the way to the restaurant we popped into a cocktail party hosted by the actress Julie Foster, who had starred in *Half A Sixpence* directed by George Sidney with Tommy Steele, and after dinner we dropped into Tramp, where I danced with some of my old chums. Tim was in there with the South American girl and we greeted each other like old friends.

When it was time to go, the rain was dreadful.

It had been chucking it down all of the previous night and most of the day and there was no sign of it easing off. By the time we left Tramp around 1.45am on December 6, I felt that I really shouldn't be driving. Initially, we tried to get a taxi, but the doorman said the rain would ensure a long wait. On top of that it would have meant my having to collect the car the next day. Despite a warning buzz in my head, I decided that if I drove really slowly we would be all right.

I wasn't exactly dressed for driving. My dress was very tight-to mid-calf, midnight blue and heavily beaded. My shoes were strapped and very high. I had seat belts in my Rolls-Royce, but I knew only one person who used them. Most of the people I knew foolishly considered them to be an infringement of their liberty, as well as being uncomfortable and restrictive to wear.

I planned to drop Robert off at his house in Ovington Mews, Chelsea. I drove slowly, very slowly, and made it as far as Robert's tiny street without mishap. The problem arose when I pushed my foot on to the brake to stop.

My thin shoe was soaking wet and, as it made contact with the pedal, it slipped off and jammed between the brake and the accelerator. I tried to wrench it out, but the result was that I pushed even harder on the accelerator. The strap stayed put when I twisted my foot, frantically trying to free it.

We were moving fast now.

The car seemed to rear up. A wall loomed in front and I had nowhere else to go. I glanced at the speedometer - 53 miles per hour. My mind raced - nobody survived a collision at that speed.

Robert must have come to the same conclusion as me and not been able to handle it: he passed out. I knew that I couldn't afford such a luxury - somebody had to be awake to switch off the engine after the impact. Steve McQueen once told me that more people die after a crash from the engine catching fire.

Then we hit the wall.

I don't remember that moment, but I do the next - the rear-view mirror connected with the bridge of my little nose, but at least it stopped me going head-first through the windscreen. As I pulled my head back, a small fountain of blood began.

But I was alive.

Switching off the engine, I looked for Robert. He was on the floor, moaning. More to the point, he wasn't bleeding, which I took to be much worse. It was only then that I noticed the steering wheel. Normally so huge, it had been buckled to half its size.

"Shit, that must've hurt something," I thought.

We needed help.

I saw some movement at a few of the curtains in the surrounding houses. I waited, but nobody came out to help. In fact, nobody did anything. By now, I was frightened for Robert. Opening the door, I fell out on to the wet street. It was then that I realised what had taken the beating from the steering wheel. My right leg appeared to be about two feet shorter than my left.

I crawled like a snake across the cobbled street towards the little houses and tried to bang on a door. At that early hour on a Sunday morning, the noise in that quaint mews would have woken the dead. Sadly, not even the living responded. The inhabitants of these houses had obviously decided to stay out of sight and not to get involved.

Time was ticking by. The little stream of blood had turned my white fox jacket into a nasty mess straight out of a Hammer film. I needed help and the local residents clearly weren't going to provide it.

I screamed the Fay Wray special.

Soon, somebody was running towards us. Thank God - a policeman. As he approached me, I could hear him calling for help on his radio.

Robert walked away from the smashed Roller with only a frozen shoulder as a keepsake. I was pretty lucky, too, I believe, being one of the first accident victims to benefit from a trauma paramedical team who arrived in an ambulance. They offered me oxygen. At that point, I felt no pain - not the best of signs. I had learned that in Beirut - after a raid, a man walked down the street, asking people if they were all right, all the time carrying his own arm in his hand.

According to hospital records I wasn't admitted to the casualty department at St. Stephen's Hospital in the Fulham Road until 3.50am. The accident department was fully staffed and working normally despite a doctors' strike. This was the mid-Seventies and someone was always on strike, but the doctors were working that night - thank God - and they were very sweet. They kept me out of sight of the police, who were outside the door, talking about breathalising me. I'd already given Tim as my next of kin and, when the hospital phoned him, he turned up with my own doctor.

Things were going to proceed at a faster pace now. The objective was to stop the bleeding from my nose before I ran out of blood and to work on my right hip.

"By the way, Miss Leigh, we won't be able to use an anaesthetic," said one of the doctors said. "Mixing it with alcohol would be lethal."

"Shall we go?" somebody asked politely.

I was pushed on a trolley into an operating theatre. It was 10.30am by the clock and music was blaring from a radio. It seemed incongruous to hear the same sounds that I'd been listening to in Tramp earlier on. The lights were on full. The doctors were busy tidying up my nose. Suddenly, one of them barked, "She's gone, she's gone - give me that quickly!"

He grabbed a hypodermic.

Filling it with adrenaline, he jammed it straight through my dress and into my heart. Meanwhile, amid the chaos, I had come out of my body and found myself in a corner of the room, observing the frantic scene. I was detached from the action: a bystander with a vague interest in events, though I was too happy where I was to give much thought to anything else.

Surrounded by the most brilliant translucent white light, I was at peace. There was no pain at all. One of the doctors shouted at the nurse closest to my corner, "Cut this bloody dress off!"

I could see that they were having trouble.

"What's the point?" muttered the nurse. "She's dead anyway."

Although she had said it under her breath, I heard every word.

"That's not very nice!" I said, but she couldn't hear me.

I felt that she should have been joining in with the others, who were busy thumping the body on the table and generally doing what doctors do when they're trying to revive a clinically dead body.

Then, all at once, the moment was broken.

The music stopped and I recognised the voice of Kenny Everett coming over the airwaves.

"Oh shit," he said, "one of my best friends, Suzanna Leigh, has just died in a car crash!"

It was those few words from Kenny that brought me back. All at once, I was in my body again and I sat bolt upright.

"No, I'm not!" I said to no one in particular.

Looking at the nurse at the end of the bed, I added: "And it wasn't very nice of you to say that it didn't matter about cutting off my dress just because I was dead!"

Going a lighter shade of gray, she staggered out of the theatre. What I learned was that, when we die, there is definitely somewhere else, a higher place, not merely nothing as some people suggest. I know I died, even if it was only for a few minutes. I had been watching the clock and it was now nearly eleven.

The next day one of the doctors told me that he had seen these things before at the point of death. It seemed that I had lost five pints of blood - "That's more than an armful," I said, thinking of Tony Hancock's line in *The Blood Donor*. I was informed of just how lucky I had been and, to this day, I remain an avid anti-drink-driver. I can only thank my Guardian Angel for seeing me through.

The doctor said that, in the crash, there had been three concurrent accidents as far as I was concerned: first, the car hitting the wall; second, my nose making contact with the mirror, shattering the cheekbones as well, and third, my hip buckling the steering wheel.

When the pain finally did kick in, it was cosmic. My mind was consumed with images of dead and dying soldiers lying alone in muddy fields in Vietnam, waiting to be picked up.

The pain was driving me crazy and I was screaming for help. At last, the doctor showed up.

"I need to tell you something really important."

"Give me a drug," I hissed through clenched teeth. "I am lying on broken glass with a red hot bar burning into me where my leg should be."

"I will," the doctor said, "but I need you to be coherent because

I want you to make an informed decision."

The doctor told me that I had sustained a smashed hip; in a way, it was so bad that it was to my advantage because the impact had not torn the skin and the break remained inside; with youth on my side, the prospects of it gelling together were good, with little risk of scarring. He explained that it would be necessary to put my leg in traction for six weeks.

"Six weeks in this sort of pain?" I exclaimed.

He said that they would give me shots, but not many and only when I really needed them. He continued: "If you leave here you will be taken to a private nursing home, where they will pump you with drugs every four hours whether you need them or not, which could prove difficult later. They will also put a pin through your leg to suspend weights and keep you in for months in order to justify their fat fees."

I replied: "I don't think you understand; I don't care what they do, or how much it costs. If they can stop this pain, it sounds just fine to me."

The trouble was that I had gone a little too long with the pain to make any rational decision.

In retrospect, I now know that he was giving me a true account of what would happen, but at the time I couldn't think ahead of the pain; I had lost all reason. I spent the night in the Harley Street Clinic.

During this period, my two greatest friends were Jane Asher and her boyfriend, the cartoonist Gerald Scarfe. Apart from Tim, they were probably the first to get to me. I remember them being around the bed (or trolley) on the actual night of the accident and one or both of them came to see me in the clinic nearly every day. This special friendship was such a blessing. We had met at the Cork Film Festival some years earlier and had often gone around together.

Unlike Patrick Lichfield, Tim was constantly at my side, often spending up to ten hours a day at the clinic. Every day he would bring cards, candles, lacy pillows, cuddly toys, smoked salmon and champagne. Friends and fans were fantastic - one even sent me the flowers from her wedding reception at the Dorchester.

At Christmas, Tim and our friend, the Honourable Philip Harvey, converted my suite into a magical place. They brought a refrigerator, a video recorder and a huge Christmas tree with sparkling lights. So many people turned up to see me that there was standing room only. Several reporters, disguised as doctors in white coats, smuggled themselves into my room, but I spotted them and they were quietly escorted from the premises.

My hip had been set in two operations - one at St Stephen's and one at the clinic - and now I auditioned various plastic surgeons to rebuild the bridge of my nose. After showing them a blown-up photograph of my face before the accident, I asked them if they could restore it the way it had been. All said that they could. I then asked them what they did in the way of hobbies, not a question that they were expecting. Most said gardening or golfing. I hired Freddie Nicol when he said he was a sculptor in his spare time; that was what I wanted - a sculptor rather than someone who pruned rose bushes or hacked a ball around a golf-course.

Freddie did a superb job and, in one go, my nose was back to normal. After the bandages came off, I held a small press conference in my room and my photograph appeared in most newspapers, showing everyone that, despite the dire medical bulletins of the previous month, I was making a complete recovery.

When I left the clinic, I moved into Jane's dining room, which she had turned into a bedroom. I couldn't climb stairs, so it was preferable to Brook Green or the first-floor flat at Eaton Place. As time went by, Jane and Gerald became a couple and, when they had their lovely daughter, Katie, Jane sweetly asked me if I would be her Godmother.

I moved back into Eaton Place with Tim some time during 1976. He said he wanted me back and there would be no more girls. The South American beauty queen came round to the flat to see him and, while he hid in the dining room, I had to tell her it was over.

Tim decided that I should become properly domesticated and I learned to cook "designer" meals for us and generally run the home. Diamond Lil had fallen on hard times and I paid him £10 a week and all the vodka he could drink to take Natasha for walks.

But it was a tricky time all round.

The stock market was reeling and a lot of people in the City were in dire straits. Tim was in his office in Throgmorton Avenue when a colleague plunged past his window. Tim needed to raise some cash himself and, as I wasn't using the house in Brook Green, he suggested that I should sell it. I replied that perhaps he could sell his Rolls-Royce instead, but he said he needed it to maintain his image.

I was appalled at the prospect of not having a home again, but Desmond Briggs was demanding that I repay his advance because I had been unable to finish the book, so I also needed some ready cash.

In that case, said Tim, I should sell the house and pay off our debts - we owed £1,500 to Wheeler's - and give him some of the money. In exchange, he would assign the remainder of his lease on the Eaton Place flat to me and open an account in my name at his stockbroking firm, Foster & Braithewaite.

That is what we did and it proved to be a catastrophic decision on my part.

Tim gave me the impression that the stress related to my accident had made him ill again. His recurring hepatitis didn't help matters and nor did the long hours he spent asleep. He also suffered from migraine headaches which required him to lie in a darkened room in total silence. Unfortunately, the family upstairs were extremely unruly and the noise coming through the ceiling from their wooden floors was hard to take.

One Monday evening Tim and I were sitting around in silk caftans. It had been a bad weekend for noise and we were fed up. I heard the head of the family going past our front door, so I went out to talk to him about it. He dismissed me with a remark about an "Indian squaw" and carried on down the stairs.

Tim shot off the sofa and charged after him. There were raised voices and our neighbour hit Tim in the face and he went down. Then the two of them were rolling about and not holding back. I suppose the next thing pushed me over the top because the neighbour grabbed a huge chunk of Tim's hair and was pulling it out. Tim spent a lot of money every year at Philip Kingsley's trichology salon and retaliated by punching the neighbour in the eye.

I rushed into the flat and, taking Tim's 12-bore out of its case, broke it open to check that it was unloaded. I stood at the top of the stairs, the gun low-slung, and said to the neighbour, "Leave him alone."

I looked the part - mad and mean.

I stood there pointing the gun while they both gaped at me. Then Tim disentangled himself and came upstairs.

After that, Tim became even more reclusive, so much so that the few friends he would tolerate around us called him "Howard Hughes", which he took as a compliment. But inside the flat he took his problems out on me. Life closed in on me and I was losing myself on a daily basis.

Tim had changed over the years from a charming, generous lover into a bully and a jailer. Princess Diana once said that it was easy to dismantle a personality by isolation and that is what was happening to me. Tim cut me off from the world and, having lost my career and my home, I seemed powerless to prevent it.

It took the most tragic of events to bring me back to life..

Chapter 30

Elvis's Last Message

"Better by far that you should forget and smile,
than you should remember and be sad."

Christina Rossetti, *Italian poet*

AROUND eight o'clock on the night of August 16, 1977, I went to bed at Eaton Place and fell asleep almost immediately. I woke up in a large room, more a space, really, of the most brilliant, luminous white - in fact, the white I had seen once before when I died after my car crash.

Standing before me was Elvis, also in white. This was the young, slim, tall, gorgeous Elvis that I knew when I first met him.

He smiled at me.

"There's something I have to tell you, baby."

His eyes seemed to sparkle.

"I've been sick, baby, but I'm in no pain now."

"Have you been ill? - I'm so sorry."

I went to move towards him, but he held his hand up.

"It's been in my colon, but it's over now. I feel fine now. Tell them all I love them."

"Tell who, Elvis?"

"You'll know when the time comes. I have to go now."

He moved backwards, so I called: "Elvis, I love you."

"I love you, too, baby, always have, always will."

He melted into the whiteness and disappeared.

The phone was ringing. Picking it up after that dream was the cruelest awakening.

"Suzanna Leigh? Miss Leigh, this is CBS News - you're live to New York. Could you give us your reaction to the death of Elvis Presley?"

The drum began beating inside my head - loud, precise, deafening. There was the same rush of blood that I had experienced when I found my father dead; then, as now, a terrible jolt of pain as though I had been shot and was flying through the air in slow motion. My mind was frantic, but silent.

"Hello, Miss Leigh, could you comment, please?"

"No - no I couldn't," I whispered.

Then numbness.

I suppose, like most of his fans, I thought that Elvis would never die and I simply wasn't prepared for the after-shock. The King was dead at forty-two, the same age as my father had been when he died.

The media were already camping outside my front door and more pressmen were trying to get through on the phone. I was about the only the person in England who had worked with Elvis, so everyone wanted to interview me.

I agreed to do one TV show and, on the way to the studio, I counted back the hours to the time of my dream. The time difference between Memphis and London meant that Elvis had left us around the same time as he had appeared to me. But what did he mean about telling them? I didn't know what that meant, but I didn't have to wait long to find out.

The president of the British fan club, Todd Slaughter, myself and other fans were about the only people on the TV show, but after a short while they brought in another big British name on the phone from the States: Tom Jones.

Great, I thought, wonderful - another person to sing Elvis's praises. But Elvis hadn't been dead for more than a few hours when the Judases came out.

Tom Jones: "Elvis had a big problem with drugs and I'm not surprised if he did die of a drug overdose."

I lost it. TV or not, how dare Tom Jones say that about Elvis! It was then that I knew what Elvis had meant by "telling them". He meant his loyal fans.

"Tom, it's Suzanna Leigh. Do you remember me? I introduced you to Elvis. Firstly, it's not true that he died of a drug overdose. Elvis died because of a colon problem. Anyway, how could you be so disloyal, even if drugs had been the case."

How could someone who owed so much to Elvis betray him like that?"

"Mr Jones, Mr Jones - hello, hello. Er, I think we have a disconnection."

I knew then how things were going to be. More than anyone, Tom

Jones owed Elvis a huge debt, not only of friendship but also for the success of his Las Vegas show.

"I learned from Elvis to move while I was on stage," he admitted in an interview. "He just did what felt natural. I did the same thing. Yeah, I really got the whole idea from watching Elvis."

When I heard that a well-known British actress was going to sell a story about the "secret love affair" she had supposedly had with Elvis, I gave an interview to the News of the World, saying how wonderful Elvis had been and how we had been friends, not lovers.

"I think the reason we became such good mates was that I was the only leading lady who didn't want anything out of him," I said. "All the others were out to trap him. They all wanted to be Mrs Presley. He knew I didn't care a damn."

Of course, I couldn't say that I had been with him on the night of his death, so I said we had spoken on the phone. "He told me he was in terrible pain and couldn't breathe properly," I said. "What a terrible tragedy his death is. It's like a part of my life being torn out."

Many people were now openly claiming that Elvis had died of a drug overdose and I was almost alone in the world in maintaining that it had been a colon problem that had triggered a cardiac arrhythmia.

I stuck to my guns and, ten years later, I was a guest on the *Terry Wogan Show* with Elvis's stepbrother, David Stanley, when the subject of Elvis's death was raised. David said that it had now been proved that Elvis died of a "busted colon".

Since then, there has been further confirmation from the medical profession. In 1994, Dr Kevin S. Merigan, an American clinical pharmacologist and toxicologist, studied the toxicology report on Elvis and concluded: "It couldn't have been an overdose. None of the drugs [found in Elvis's system] are associated with arrhythmia or causing the heart to fail."

Dr Merigan and Dr Dan Brookoff, associate director of medical education at Methodist Hospital, Memphis, were interviewed for the book *ELVIS: In the words of those who knew him best*. Dr Brookoff told the authors, Rose Clayton and Dick Heard: "The drug overdose theory just doesn't fit at all... Elvis had colitis - they found at his autopsy what they call megacolon [an enlarged colon]."

Dr Merigan again: "However you look at it, divine intervention, the Lord, or the forces of nature, it was just his time; and it wasn't a result of drugs."

I made my first visit to Graceland in 1998.

Through the Music Gates, I walked under the shade of the oak and elm trees towards the four Corinthian columns of that famous portico. Elvis, of course, had gone one step further and, instead of having a pair of peacocks in the grounds, I was told that he had bought a whole flock and, with all the people coming and going from Graceland, they had made such a terrible racket that he had given them to Memphis Zoo.

The biggest surprise, however, was waiting for me inside Graceland itself. Through the front door, I turned right into the blue-and-white drawing room and took in its Sun King clock over the mantelpiece, its vast mirrored wall, its thick, lily-white carpet and long, white sofa and, suddenly, my eyes fixed on two beautiful figures set against a glittering backdrop at the end of the room.

I moved closer.

Oh my God! Elvis had put a life-sized peacock, with tail plumage fully extended, in a stained-glass panel on either side of the entrance to the Music Room.

This is where Elvis had lain during his funeral service, his body flanked by two of these magnificent birds who, some believed, symbolised eternal life.

I wanted to burst out crying, but I had to laugh because, at that very moment, the memory of that deep, rich, wonderful voice was so vivid that it seemed to fill the room.

"Just covering all angles, baby."

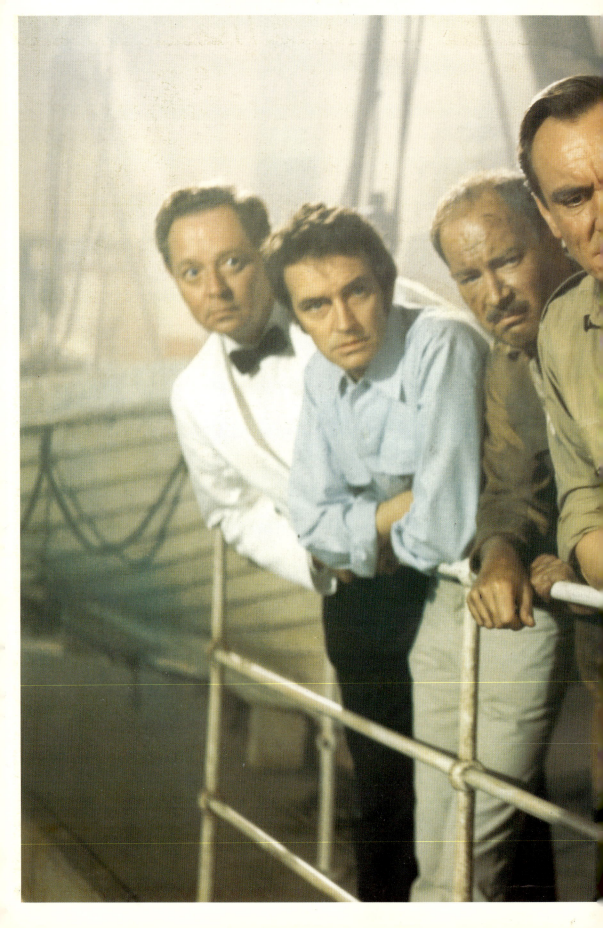